MW00478535

CRIMINAL
INTELLIGENCE ANALYSIS

Edited by

Paul P. Andrews, Jr. and Marilyn B. Peterson

All rights reserved. No part of this book may be reproduced or transmitted in any form or by means, electronic or mechanical, including photocopying, recording or by any information storage and retrieval system without the written permission from the publisher, except for the inclusion of brief quotations in a review.

Copyright ⓒ 1990, Jack Morris

Library of Congress Catalog Card Number
Pending

International Standard Book Number
0-912479-07-8

PALMER ENTERPRISES
P.O. Box 1714, Loomis, California, 95650

The publisher dedicates this book to the memory of

LIEUTENANT JOSEPH PETROSINO, NYPD

America's first criminal intelligence commander
who was murdered in the Plaza Marina, Palermo, Sicily
by unknown assassins
near the turn of the century
while gathering intelligence about members of the
Black Hand Society

CRIMINAL INTELLIGENCE ANALYSIS

CONTENTS

BIOGRAPHIES

Paul P. Andrews, Jr. *(Collection and Analysis Plans)*
Special Agent/Analyst for the NJ State Commission of Investigation; former principal Intelligence Analyst with NJSP Intelligence Bureau; M.S., Criminal Justice, Eastern Kentucky University; Military Intelligence Officer (USAR).

Charles C. Frost *(Intelligence Report Writing)*
Associate Professor of Justice Systems, Northeast Missouri State University. Former Senior Management Analyst and Training Advisor, Drug Enforcement Administration. Authored Criminal Intelligence Reports. Ph.D, International Finance, Fletcher School of Law and Diplomacy.

Robert Kelly *(The Development of Inferences)*
Professor, Brooklyn College. Edited, authored, and contributed articles, chapters and books on criminal justice topics and organized crime. Ph.D in Sociology, City University of New York.

Elizabeth Reuss-Ianni *(Network Analysis)*
Director of Research, Institute for Social Analysis, New York. Co-author of numerous books and articles with F.A.J. Ianni. M.A., Urban Anthropology, New York University.

Francis A. J. Ianni *(Network Analysis)*
Professor, Columbia University, Author of numerous criminal justice articles and books including The Black Mafia and A family Business: Kinship and Social Control in Organized Crime. Fullbright Scholar, Ph.D in Sociology and Anthropology, Pennsylvania State University.

Frederick T. Martens *(The Intelligence Function)*
Executive Director, Pennsylvania Crime Commission, former Assistant to Deputy Superintendent, New Jersey State Police, former supervisor, New Jersey State Police Intelligence Bureau Analytical Unit. Author or co-author of various books and articles on law enforcement intelligence and organized crime.

Marilyn B. Peterson *(Telephone Record Analysis, From Analysis to Synthesis)*
Practitioner, lecturer, consultant. Management Specialist, Division of Criminal Justice, NJ Department of Law and Public Safety. Former manager for multi-state regional information sharing system. Numerous awards and publications.

Roger W. Shuy *(Tape Recorded Conversations)*
Head, Sociolinguistics Program and Professor of Linguistics, Georgetown University. Member of several linguistics editorial boards. Recipient of numerous study grants. Authored, edited, and contributed to over 100 publications on sociolinguistics. Ph.D., English and Linguistics, Case Western Reserve University.

FORWARD

The 1980's were a period of tremendous growth in the United States for the field of law enforcement intelligence analysis. Computer technology, data on crime groups available, and analytical techniques were all significantly expanded and made attainable to even the smaller departments during the decade. Concurrently, the recognition of non-traditional organized crime groups (such as the outlaw motorcycle gangs, the Jamaican posses, the Colombian drug cartels and others), the diversification of traditional organized crime (aka La Cosa Nostra) into the corporate world and the expanded complexity of crime (money laundering, containerized smuggling, etc.) made the use of intelligence and analysis a necessity. And while the authors represent American experience and concerns, we have been assured by colleagues in Canada, Australia and the Far East that their countries have experienced similar changes.

The impetus for this volume was two fold. First, we wanted to have material on the primary methods of analysis available to the burgeoning community of analysts and intelligence officers in the law enforcement field. Secondly, we wanted to create a text so that the fundamentals of analysis could be taught in college and university criminal justice programs.

This text was envisioned in the mid-1980's as a larger volume which would be a manual for practitioners. Its final evolution resulted from practicality of time and resources to an eight chapter book which combines the most basic methodologies of analysis -- toll analysis and link charting -- and more complex forms of analysis, such as conversation analysis and strategic analysis.

The choices in content were not meant to imply any greater importance to these types of analysis nor were they meant to slight any methodologies not covered here. The methods included are those upon which there was something more to say than had already been stated and in which we had qualified writers. Given our choice, this text would be the first in a series of such volumes, the rest of which would cover the areas missing here.

The chapters are intended as a representation of current analytical thought and , although written over a five-year period, are no less timely for their span.

"The Intelligence Function," by Frederick T. Martens, documents "the failure of law enforcement to integrate the intelligence process with the operation of investigative units" and calls for the integration of economic, linguist, sociological models and operations research among others.

In "From Analysis to Synthesis: Exploring the Context of Law Enforcement Analysis," Marilyn B. Peterson gives a global view of the analytical methods appropriate to the data to be used.

"Collection and Analysis Plans" by Paul P. Andrews, Jr., takes a look at the managerial elements that profoundly impact on the intelligence process and an ensuing product. In addition to areas being discussed, presented are collection and analytical plans suitable for tactical and strategic intelligence production.

In "Network Analysis" Francis A. J. Ianni and Elizabeth Reuss-Ianni bring a sociological perspective to law enforcement analysis, showing network models that assist the analyst in not only graphically depicting relationships among conspirators but also in how to interpret those relationships.

"Telephone Record Analysis," a second chapter by Marilyn B. Peterson, discusses the technique of both manual and computerized telephone record analysis, including a sample analytical report.

In "The Analysis of Tape Recorded Converations, " Roger W. Shuy provides an incisive look at conversation analysis which details the key elements of conversation and potential variations in its interpretation.

"The Development of Inferences in the Assessment of Intelligence Data," by Robert J. Kelly, explores the logic of drawing conclusions and shows the need for sound arguments and valid reasoning by giving several examples of syllogisms and related materials.

In "Intelligence Report Writing," Charles C. Frost completes the book with an overview of the final product -- the intelligence report -- and includes several formats of those reports as examples.

The volume, then, progresses from a rationale for using analysis, through overview methods of tactical and strategic analysis, to four specialized methods of analysis, to the conclusion of the process, drawing hypotheses and writing the report.

As with any work of this nature, the road to publication is not a short one. Each contributor was asked to write a chapter on speculation. For this, they deserve our deepest thanks, particularly for staying with the project over the ensuing years.

Other acknowledgments necessary are to Charles H. Rogovin, Professor of Law at Temple University and to Superintendent Justin J. Dintino, of the New Jersey State Police. These two individuals, as experts, as mentors, and as demanding taskmasters, are more at the genesis of this work and our work in the field than any other individuals.

Special thanks also go to Jack Morris, of Palmer Enterprises, our publisher, who is an expert in his own right, and to Barbara Kupiec who donated time and energy typing various chapter drafts.

Paul P. Andrews, Jr.
Marilyn B. Peterson
March 26, 1990

CRIMINAL INTELLIGENCE ANALYSIS

Edited by

Paul P. Andrews, Jr. and Marilyn B. Peterson

Chapter One

The Intelligence Function

Frederick T. Martens *

Introduction

Slightly more than twenty years have passed since the Commission on Law Enforcement and Administration of Justice (hereafter, President's Crime Commission), devoted an entire volume to the report of its Task Force on Organized Crime (hereafter, T.F.R.). That report contained an analysis of organized crime and law enforcement's response to it. In that work, academics, prosecutors, and one former New York City police detective made possible a far-reaching and visionary understanding of why law enforcement was ineffective in its approach to organized crime. One outgrowth of the President's Crime Commission's work was the creation of the Law Enforcement Assistance Administration (LEAA) -- a resource organization for local and state law enforcement and criminal justice agencies. Police departments throughout the country availed themselves of funds allocated for organized crime control, and intelligence units proliferated. This infusion of moneys sparked the interest of progressive law enforcement executives determined to initiate new approaches and strategies in the "war against organized crime."

Considerable time has elapsed since the demise of LEAA, and law enforcement again finds itself struggling to understand what is a rapidly-changing organized crime subculture. Many intelligence programs have been abandoned and nearly all that remain have failed to realize their potential. New ethnic groups are encroaching on or taking over the business and territorial domains of the Mafia, and law enforcement again finds itself ill-prepared to address the new technologies, cultural mores, and values these new groups bring to the illicit marketplace. Containing organized crime -- including the elimination of monopoly control that has been achieved in certain criminal markets -- will require the operation of sophisticated intelligence programs. To that end law enforcement executives must not only provide adequate physical and financial resources, but perhaps of greater importance, intellectual rigor and managerial commitment. Only if this combination occurs will there be rationally designed and effectively implemented new policies in the organized crime field.

The Intelligence Process

In their classic text, Basic Elements of Intelligence, Godfrey and Harris (1971) provide a comprehensive description of the intelligence process and explain how, if effectively imple-

---

* Special note should be made of the most valuable editorial contributions made by Professor Charles H. Rogovin of the Temple University School of Law.

mented it can be used in the containment of organized crime. The process, as they point out, is not only physical but perhaps more importantly, an intellectual exercise -- a phase that essentially defines the essence of the process. By describing intelligence activity as an "intellectual" endeavor, Godfrey and Harris have, in effect, removed the intelligence process from the realm of traditional police activity, and added yet another dimension to the investigative process; a dimension that encourages proactive as opposed to reactive responses. Since a common understanding of the intelligence process is critical to the discussion of what follows, it is useful to briefly discuss the components of the process.

The intelligence process involves five steps or phases, the end product of which is the transformation of raw data into what is commonly called finished intelligence. First, among these steps is the collection of raw information. It is this collection activity that initiates the process; turning what is the often merely reactive response to organized crime into one that is proactive. By clearly delineating the data that must be acquired to explore a particular question or issue, an intelligence officer or agent is provided with a "road map" for the collection of data. This "collection plan", which is usually the combined work product of management personnel, intelligence officers, and analysts assigned to a project, provides a rational and pre-planned design for collecting raw data.

The intelligence officer(s) is provided with a hypothesis -- some definition of what it is that is sought to be proved, disproved, or explored. For example, one may wish to know the role of loansharking in the control of illegal gambling. A hypothesis might be developed that postulates that the control of illegal gambling is effected by the lending of moneys to bookmakers who are unable to cover their action" (Goldstock, 1977). This hypothesis suggests that the more insolvent a bookmaker is, the more likely he is to patronize the services of a loanshark. Thus, an enforcement policy that creates financial insolvency among bookmakers may unintentionally organize the gambling market by forcing insolvent bookmakers to patronize loansharks. This then becomes the working hypothesis -- a statement that eventually guides the intelligence officer in the collection of data.

Data collection should be a focused and well-defined activity. The collection effort channels the intelligence officers' energies and resources toward a specific goal rather than permitting or encouraging the random collection of what is often irrelevant and nonessential information. By creating this working hypothesis, intelligence officers take a proactive posture, seeking an answer to an issue that will ultimately impact on enforcement policy. Thus, rather than merely wait for inquiries from operational units, the intelligence unit is anticipating and ultimately directing the strategies to be employed.

As information is collected from a variety of sources, including informants, electronic surveillances, investigative journalists, concerned citizens, other police officers, and persons arrested for bookmaking and other offenses, that data is evaluated as to its validity. In evaluating it the collator -- the person who receives the data -- will assess how a particular piece of information corresponds with other data, whether there is conflicting data that contradicts what has been found by another intelligence officer(s), and assess the origin of the data (e.g., whether the source of information has been reliable in the past). In many respects this evaluation process is crucial in the subsequent steps that must be taken to refine the data into a finished product. Indeed, it is the responsibility of the collator to act as a "quality control officer" ensuring that the information collected by the intelligence officer is not only consistent with the mission of the intelligence unit, but is also valid and reliable. This requires the collator to evaluate the data against what exists within the system, and when conflicting information is found, inquire of the submitting officer(s). The intelligence officer(s) is then tasked with making further inquiry of the source(s) in order to clarify and/or validate the data.

Following initial evaluation, the data is then organized, perhaps around specific categories (e.g. crime "families" or networks, criminal specialties such as "loansharking," narcotics, gambling, etc.; *modus operandi*; or geographic territories). Through this categorization of data, patterns and trends may become more obvious. Indeed, as seemingly discrete and unrelated data is collected by intelligence officers in the field, and placed in one of the enumerated categories, it is not unusual to find a "pattern" emerge that, for example, may *suggest* that a criminal network is acquiring a greater share in loansharking activities in a particular locale. The "pattern" may be sufficient to stimulate a more intensive data collection effort directed at a specific criminal network or criminal activity that may raise a new set of questions that deserve further investigation.

Once the data is organized, the analytical component within the intelligence unit is tasked to interpret the data, in terms of either an immediate enforcement response (e.g., tactical intelligence) or a long-term reorganization strategy (e.g., strategic intelligence). The analyst(s) tend to operate from the perspective of specific disciplines (e.g., applying sociological, economic concepts) in interpreting data. Once the data has been analyzed, it is then packaged into what is referred to as an "intelligence assessment," a detailed written report that includes graphs, charts, and diagrams. It is then transmitted to an operational unit for enforcement action, or to the agency chief for use in redirecting enforcement priorities. Unfortunately, the analytical phase of the intelligence process is the least understood and utilized. When an analytical component does exist (frequently in name only), it often does little analysis and is more related to routine clerical tasks.

While the above process description is addressed primarily to what may be termed "strategic" intelligence, it should not be perceived as distinct from "tactical" intelligence. The data used to address a strategic intelligence issue emanates from sources that are primarily tactical in nature: criminal informants, electronic surveillances, arrested bookmakers, etc. Thus the tactical and strategic aspects of the intelligence process are not distinct, but rather, interrelated and interdependent (Dintino, 1983, p. 114).

Essentially, then, the intelligence process is no different from basic research: define the problem, collect the data, assess the data, collate or organize that data, analyze the data, and disseminate the data to the appropriate persons. Yet, despite the logic of this management tool, the role of intelligence in the "war against organized crime" has been and continues to be ambiguous, sporadic, and inconsistent. While public pronouncements and law enforcement rhetoric have championed the need for and the utility of intelligence, few law enforcement agencies have effectively engaged this process in their efforts to contain organized crime. Its value for the containment of illicit markets and/or the criminal organizations that control these markets has never been fully understood. As a result, there is unfortunately much support to be found for the oft-repeated charge that intelligence is seldom more than an accumulation of often irrelevant data that serves only marginally-useful purposes. Obviously, merely collecting names of persons involved in criminal activity does not suffice as intelligence. The process of intelligence -- involving a continuing series of questions and answers -- must take relevant data and *interpret* it so that it has some meaningful value. Assembling networks through a technique known as "link analysis" serves to define what may have heretofore been unknown networks. Or, taking data that relate to the concept of a criminal monopoly" and developing an enforcement strategy that divests this monopoly, is the essence of what the intelligence process is all about.

The irony is that more than twenty years have passed since the Organized Crime Task Force of the President's Crime Commission (1967) correctly noted the need for intelligence in the "war against organized crime." It declared, "Police departments in every major city should have a special intelligence unit solely to ferret out organized criminal activity . . . Relevant disciplines, such as economics, political science, sociology and operations research (must) begin to study organized crime intensively" (p. 15). Harris and Godfrey (1971), in their classic text on police criminal intelligence, argued that law enforcement agencies, through intelligence, can "detect and anticipate criminal trends" that will put law enforcement in the position of initiating long term action, rather than merely reacting to criminal behavior. Again, in 1967, the National Advisory Committee on Criminal Justice Standards and Goals, stated:

> The unique characteristic of the criminal intelligence function, then, is that, when properly carried out, it can effectively pinpoint and predict organized criminal activities so that they can be prevented or neutralized. Through intelligence, law enforcement agencies can gauge the magnitude, scope and potential threat of organized crime elements in their jurisdictions. This knowledge helps them plan the most effective countermeasures against organized crime (p. 122).

Notwithstanding this well-intentioned advice, a 1977 Government Accounting Office report on the Federal Strike Force program, found that "existing data collection was directed more toward evidence gathering than toward intelligence information . . . data analysis is extremely limited . . . and analysts assigned to the strike forces are not intelligence analysts but are merely computer input specialists" (G.A.O., P. 32). Similarly, a government-financed study in 1978 found that the "state of the intelligence art within most (law enforcement agencies) is essentially reflective of the pedestrian quality of intelligence work . . . Put simply, intelligence activities continue essentially as a collection effort, with little effective analytical work achieved." (Blakey, et al, p. 13).

This dismal evaluation of the state of the art certainly pinpoints the problems encountered in implementing the intelligence concept -- a concept that remains alien to most law enforcement agencies. Indeed, what we find is a "war against organized crime" that lacks a defined direction; a campaign where progress is assessed by the use of inappropriate measures of effectiveness. The reasons for this can be found in both the nature of the police environment and the contradictions in the intelligence process.

The Law Enforcement Milieu

Perhaps the primary reason for the failure of law enforcement to integrate the intelligence process with the operations of investigation unit is the lack of commitment to the fundamentals of organized crime research. By "research," reference is to a process that differs substantially from conventional investigation. In fact, the case-by-case approach to investigating organized crime frequently undermines the intelligence process. To maximize the value of the intelligence process there must be a commitment beyond "making cases". Understanding the criminal environment requires the collection of critical information -- the methods of territorial allocation, financial flows and the economics of markets, allegiances and loyalties among participants in criminal networks, and the cultural mores that govern these interpersonal relationships -- necessitate an acknowledgment that information gathered can be used not only for "making cases," but also for policy development. For example, random arrests of bookmakers or narcotics traffickers, while certainly necessary, is not synonymous with containing organized crime. In fact, experience and research suggest that such an enforcement policy may in fact organize rather than disorganize criminal markets (Rottenberg, pp. 165.166). Thus, if we are to appreciate and measure the value of enforcement efforts on disorganizing illicit markets, intelligence units must concentrate less on developing evidence for criminal prosecutions and focus more on the types of data that bring clarity and understanding to the scope and dimensions of the problem. This, of course, has the effect of reducing support from enforcement personnel, since investigators and prosecutors are in the business of "making cases," irrespective of their impact on the market.

Within this context, we find that when intelligence is perceived as a "research" effort, as opposed to an enforcement adjunct, it is generally afforded low status and receives little recognition from law enforcement administrators. The political milieu within which law enforcement administrators operate is such that symbolic arrests often dictate priorities and "truth" is grounded in mythology. Police, it is believed both within and outside the institution, are in the business of making arrests; activities that detract from this goal are generally afforded low priority. Unfortunately, goals and objectives are often confused. Illustratively, a goal of enforcement may be the containment of organized crime; an objective in terms of that end may be an arrest, if necessary, to effect this containment. Succinctly stated, however, to many persons in law enforcement whatever does not result in an immediate arrest is seen as nonproductive and of only marginal utility. When an organized crime unit's effectiveness is measured solely by the volume of arrests, without assessment of the quality or impact of these arrests, there are few incentives for the selective and judicious allocation of intelligence resources. The intelligence function is thus invariably among the first victims of this prevailing enforcement reality.

In order to position the intelligence process as a credible candidate in the contest for allocation of resources, it is imperative that collection of information tasks be well defined and clearly focused. A poorly-designed collection effort does not only jeopardize the intelligence process, it is also a waste of valuable resources. Unfortunately and far too often, we find that the collection of information is isolated from the analytical function. Indeed, as noted above, the collection of information is often a random, non-focused activity that bears little relationship to the requirements of subsequent data analysis. To establish a well-defined collection effort, the analytical function must guide the data collection. In a well-ordered scheme, this is usually accomplished by developing a working hypothesis and then an appropriate collection plan that serves as the vehicle to focus the collection of information. This allows for the collection of data that is both goal oriented and clearly relevant to the criminal activity/network being examined.

To a large extent, the random ad-hoc nature of data collection is an outgrowth of the traditional investigation process found in law enforcement agencies. In this investigative process a crime occurs, it is reported to the police, and an investigation is initiated. In essence, investigation is usually a reaction to an external stimulus. Seldom do we find intelligence units undertaking detailed assessments of criminal markets or organizations and transmitting these assessments to operational units for investigative action. Rather, the intelligence process is subservient to the investigative process. In effect, the "tail is wagging the dog;" investigations guide the intelligence process. For sound policy to emerge, it is essential that the intelligence process be used as a mechanism to develop well-reasoned assessments, which are ultimately transformed into investigative plans implemented by operational units.

To some extent this problem can be attributed to the lack of training of both police administrators and intelligence officers. Police executives are seriously deficient in the ability to use intelligence products in their decision-making. At the same time, intelligence officers frequently lack the necessary skills to discriminate between what is relevant or irrelevant information. Conditioned to think in terms of collecting "evidence," collecting "information" that will describe the reciprocal relationships between operatives in a criminal organization, or equally important, the financial flows of revenues in a criminal market, is often an alien concept that few intelligence officers understand. Thus, what is often labeled "intelligence" is nothing more than a collection of evidential facts that tells little about a criminal market or organization.

For example, we find that most intelligence officers place great value on collecting the names of persons involved in criminal activity. This collection activity is aimed at relating a specific person to a specific crime, determining the stature of the individual in the context of a criminal network, or relating what are seemingly unrelated or innocuous data (e.g., the cost of narcotics, its purity) tells us something valuable about the nature of the market and those networks that seek monopoly control. It serves little useful purpose, however, merely to catalogue names in the indices of files, without understanding the *relationship* such persons have to others, and to any *pattern* of criminal activity that a network is seeking to encourage or implement. The essence of a collection process must be directed toward understanding organization -- both market and network. Lacking this fundamental quality, data collected serves as nothing more than the basis of an index system on "suspected offenders" -- a nebulous category, especially in a democratic society. The collection or information should be perceived as a unique specialty. It requires that intelligence officers be fully cognizant of the information needed to assess a particular criminal market and/or the organizations that control or operate within these markets.

There is available to intelligence officers a broad array of informational sources that offer a variety of data. For example, the data extracted from an electronic surveillance, while certainly useful in a criminal prosecution, can often tell a great deal about the allegiances, loyalties, and reciprocal relationships that exist within a criminal network. For enforcement purposes this data can be used to focus on those persons most vulnerable to "turning" -- becoming witnesses against their colleagues. Moreover, it can also suggest enforcement activities that could cause conflict within or bring pressure upon competing organized crime networks or factions.

Other sources of information, such as scholarly studies and intelligence assessments from other agencies, criminal and noncriminal informants, and of course, those offenders arrested and convicted, offer intelligence officers a smorgasbord of informational sources. Of course the quality of this data, as well as the motives of the sources (e.g., informants, offenders, reporters, academicians), must be constantly and critically evaluated.

Given the foregoing assessment of the past and current utilization of the intelligence process in law enforcement, it is important to understand why it is that intelligence as a function has not achieved the influence necessary in the effort to contain organized crime. It cannot be attributed solely to apathy, ignorance, or indifference on the part of law enforcement executives. Rather, there are a number of structural dilemmas in the intelligence process that complicate the problem.

Notwithstanding the more obvious reasons (Dintino, 1983, pp. 18.21) the intelligence process in and of itself has a number of inherent contradictions that has affected its usefulness in the "war against organized crime." To the extent that intelligence is to serve as a management tool, its product must be both relevant and timely. This mandate is perhaps the most important factor in ensuring that intelligence is useful. "Timing is everything," as the phrase goes, and this is most appropriate when we speak of intelligence. It is most important that the intelligence product be consistent with the policy agenda of the moment. If it is not, more than likely the product will be ignored. For example, it would have been inappropriate to argue in the mid-1970's that narcotic enforcement efforts should be directed toward the "little guy," the street-level retailers, for the mood of the times placed more value on "wholesalers." Today, there is a growing body of literature that supports a return to street level enforcement (Moore, 1977; Rand, 1984; Kleiman, 1984). Thus, we find that unless the intelligence product is relevant to the policy concerns of the times, it will usually receive little official recognition.

This of course suggests an inherent contradiction in the process. Is intelligence solely to be used to support the administrator's perception of contemporary organized crime control policy, or should it be more daring and challenge existing policy and practices? Without doubt, intelligence must be bold, critical, and visionary. Yet when it is, it risks its credibility, for few law enforcement executives are willing to take positions that are untried, untested, or politically precarious. Such reluctance is certainly not unexpected or unnatural. It merely represents the reality of the political world. Clearly, if an intelligence unit supervisor seeks to pursue a course of action, argues for a change in policy, or represents a questioning of existing practices in favor of those that are innovative, which challenges conventional wisdom, he must be prepared for the political consequences. Given this inherent contradiction, it is little wonder that most police executives will opt for the status quo, continuing a policy or practice that is of questionable or marginal utility. Illustrative of this point is the existing policy toward gambling.

Historically, most law enforcement officials have contended that illegal gambling was the "lifeblood of organized crime" (T.F.R., 1967, p. 2). The two, gambling and organized crime were (and are) regarded as inseparable. In 1982, Reuter and Rubenstein challenged this belief with the first empirically-based study of gambling in New York (Reuter, 1982). Unfortunately, their study has been ignored or cavalierly dismissed by many in law enforcement as a piece of academic discourse that failed to uncover the subtle but pervasive influences that allow "organized crime" to control policy in New York City. This is not to suggest, of course, that an intelligence officer or analyst should accept carte blanche the findings of others who may not have access to the "real world of organized crime," nor should policy toward gambling be changed merely on the basis of one study. Rather, what is suggested is that an intelligence unit administrator must have the courage to challenge the conventional wisdom. If and when it is found erroneous, he must possess the political courage and acumen to seek a change in existing policy. This, unfortunately, presents still another problem for the intelligence unit commander and, one that represents still another contradiction in the process.

If intelligence is used to successfully challenge and then change an outdated policy or belief, we must recognize that subsequent events may fail to confirm the wisdom or validity of the new approach. For example, if the findings of the Reuter/Rubenstein study were to be accepted, and law enforcement executives decided that enforcement of gambling laws in New York City has little to do with undermining the financial base of organized crime, how can they be certain (a political imperative) that a policy of non-enforcement would continue this market condition, when it may have been this enforcement posture that "deregulated" the market in the first place? The answer is, of course, they cannot. The fact of the matter is, intelligence as a management tool must be sensitive to and understand the difference between intelligence and its use in making policy.

Notwithstanding the symbolic reasons for continuing gambling enforcement, there still remains a real obstacle to changing a policy when the ideal market conditions are attained -- in this case, an open, competitive gambling market. In short, to withdraw resources from a particular problem once the goal has been achieved presupposes that the condition will not reappear once those resources are withdrawn. Yet there is little incentive to continue a policy that has achieved its goal, for then the question arises: are resources being allocated wisely, efficiently, and effectively? Furthermore, if through the commitment of resources to a particular problem, the market structure is altered and organized crime is *prevented* from gaining entree or control, it could be argued quite persuasively that the commitment of such resources was unnecessary for the problem never manifested itself. Thus, if an enforcement policy is successful at initially *preventing* entree into an illegal market, more than likely the warning, if repeated, will be ignored because the initial experience indicated it did not occur as predicted. Anderson (1979) makes this very point, when she states, "it is questionable whether the current level of resources devoted to fighting organized crime is warranted . . .," given her findings about the Benguerra family (p. 141). It may very well be that the commitment of federal resources was responsible for the apparent decline of this family, although we will never have a conclusive answer to this question. Moreover, we cannot know what might have been the situation had these Federal resources not been applied.

It is quite clear that successfully integrating the intelligence process within an organized crime containment or control program requires police executives who are sensitive to these contradictions, and understand the environment in which intelligence must operate if it is to be an effective management tool. For an intelligence unit to attain its maximum level of effectiveness and efficiency, it must seek to minimize the bureaucratic, operation, and authoritarian constraints that are prevalent in other phases of policing. Absent this, the intelligence unit will be hard-pressed to achieve its real purpose -- the acquisition of knowledge that is accurate, timely, and relevant to the goals of the agency.

State of Research

The nature of the intelligence function (e.g., its covert and unobtrusive character) has limited the ability of researchers to investigate it. Indeed, most of what can be found on intelligence activities is confined to the military and foreign policy sectors and what does exist on the subject of domestic intelligence tends to address subversive intelligence activities commonly referred to as "Red Squads." While a number of researchers have referred to the need for law enforcement agencies to engage in a more rigorous study of organized crime and illicit criminal markets, the fact of the matter is, few have heeded these suggestions. In what is perhaps the only study ever undertaken of domestic organized crime intelligence units, the authors (Blakey, et al 1978) concluded, "if an organized crime control unit is to develop an appreciation of the problem it faces . . . it must establish some systematic method of regularizing the now largely unsystematic approach to gathering, indexing, analyzing and disseminating intelligence related to organized crime units" (p.33). Edelhertz (1981) in his study of Arizona's response to the threat of organized crime found a similar situation, arguing for a more effective intelligence system that would "orient to users of intelligence to actively convey their needs to intelligence units . . . (and) intelligence personnel must explore ways to deliver their "product" in a form which will be useful . . ."

Despite the paucity of research into the nature and functions of units, there are a number of useful guides to what could be accomplished by them. Ianni, skilled in anthropological research techniques, was able to bring a new insight into Italian-American, Black, and Hispanic organized crime (Ianni, 1972, 1974). Ianni (1974) provided a methodology for the analysis of new and emerging criminal networks that could be replicated by intelligence units (pp. 335-349). Notwithstanding the bureaucratic inertia that often infects intelligence units, "organizational intelligence analysis (rather than individual case development) could dramatically improve the ability of the criminal justice system to address the social, cultural, and economic factors that allow organized crime to survive and thrive." (Ianni, 1974, p. 331).

Reuter, one of the more ardent supporters of the use of sophisticated intelligence capabilities, contends that the failure of law enforcement to come to terms with the need for intelligence is a direct reflection of the inadequacies of the police environment, which generally excludes "civilians from positions of authority" (Reuter, 1983, p. 186). Nonetheless, Reuter calls for a more disciplined and rigorous approach to the analysis of organized criminal activities by law enforcement so that we can put to rest the myths and misinformation that cloud our understanding.

Wilson in his analysis of organized crime intelligence activities made a similar observation, finding, "the dominant ethos of (DEA), created and sustained by the central tasks of street-level investigators, does not provide a bureaucratic environment that nurtures, rewards, or pays heed to . . . intelligence analysts" (Wilson, 1978, P. 155). This was elaborated on by Moore (1977) who provides perhaps the most prophetic summary of the fundamental problem confronting organized crime intelligence units.

> There is a basic hostility toward intelligence functions in enforcement organizations. Although the exact reasons for this hostility remain somewhat obscure, one can point to a few major features of the situation. The functions of an intelligence analyst are almost wholly included in the functions of an investigator. No investigator would be happy to admit that he had not mined the files of his organization for every nugget of relevant information. Consequently, investigators think they should be doing what the intelligence analysts are doing, and also believe that they can perform this function more effectively and less expensively than analysts. A corollary of this contempt is the fear that the analysts will discover things the agent did not notice or suggest things that agents would never take seriously, or steal credit for cases that analysts helped to make. The possibility that intelligence analysts could embarrass, propose to guide, or steal credit from agents is particularly galling to agents because the intelligence analysts face no risks. They do not know how hard it is to debrief a defendant or crash a door. They sit secure in their offices to embarrass and guide street agents who risk their neck and work long and irregular hours. These bureaucratic factors may have prevented enforcement organizations from investing in intelligence systems even though their productivity could have been increased by such investments. The problem is not resources; it is a managerial problem of changing the style of an organization (pp. 168-169).

Clearly, Moore, Wilson, Reuter, et al are convinced that without a more pronounced and enlightened approach to intelligence there will be no real success in the "war against organized crime." This is not to suggest, of course, that success, however this ambiguous and rhetorical term is defined, will be achieved through intelligence alone; only that we will have a clearer understanding of what it is we are seeking to contain or control.

Contemporary Knowledge

While we often hear about integrating other relevant academic or intellectual disciplines into the intelligence function, those in law enforcement are often at a loss to appreciate how such disciplines can directly and immediately improve their intelligence capabilities. It is this lack of understanding that has inhibited the adoption of sophisticated collection and analytical techniques.

As previously discussed, the collection of information is the initial phase of this process. Its value should not be underestimated. The adage, "garbage in, garbage out" is most appropriate in discussing what types of data should be collected. Confronted with a multitude of information sources, a skillful intelligence officer should avail himself of the data that provides an understanding of (1) the illicit market, and (2) the networks that service this market. These collection requirements may, for example, seek data that address such issues:

o   Territorial Control

The data that is most useful in addressing this collection requirement is identified by examining who is providing the illicit service/product in a particular locale; whether or not "tribute" -- a form of extortion -- is paid anyone; who is being arrested and equally important, who is not; what occurs when an "independent," or, someone alien to the locale, seeks to deliver the service/product; and, have there been or are there any indications that violence (or threat thereof) or corruption has been used to enforce territorial rights?

o   Product/Service/Superiority/Exclusivity

Data of this character can be extremely important in determining market control by a particular criminal network. Essentially, the intelligence officer is searching for data that demonstrates that a particular product or service is provided at terms that are more advantageous than those of other criminal networks. For example, the quality of the cocaine being marketed may be much higher; or the technology of one criminal network may be further advanced than that of another. Perhaps a loanshark is willing to lend moneys at rates that are not as exorbitant as that of other "shys," or he need only to rely on his reputation in collecting outstanding loans, to give him a monopoly on the market.

o   Violence/Corruption Indicators

Consistent with most theories of criminal market control is the belief that, at times, violence is necessary. Moreover, because the market is regulated by the "fittest," those who have a monopoly on violence or are able to use police or prosecutorial authorities to enforce territorial domains, they are likely to control a market in a particular area. "Policy" -- a form of illegal gambling -- was once (and may still be) subject to this sort of monopoly control. Data on violence, and equally as important, on corruption are indices for determining market control.

o   Ethnic/Basic Composition of the Network
        Data of this character are consistent with our knowledge about criminal organiza-
tions and the solidarity they offer to the members. It also permits an understanding of the cultural
mores and norms of a particular network, which can be critical if one seeks to assess their proclivity
towards violence; their interaction with and among other criminal networks, the police, or other
authorities; and the symbols, values, and norms that encourage or promote their solidarity.

o   Recruitment and Career Mobility Practices
        While seemingly esoteric data, this can be very important in targeting network
members as prospective sources of information. Similar to those in legitimate organizations who
are passed over for promotion, or who are not allowed entree into the "family circle," criminal
networks also have dissidents who are vulnerable to the "right offer." By collecting data that is
indicative of favoritism, prejudice, and bias in recruitment or promotional practices, intelligence
units may become aware of potential targets of vulnerability.

o   Competitor/Complimentary Criminal Networks
        A critical piece of data that might allow for a more comprehensive understanding
of the market milieu is one that provides information about competing or complementary criminal
networks in a particular locale. Organized crime in its most basic sense, is in the business of
expanding as well as maintaining control of territory. Criminal networks that compete with one
another have a distinct interest in eliminating other criminal networks; while not necessarily
aggressively interested in expanding territorial markets, they are generally willing to assume
additional territory. Indeed, a fundamental, driving tenet of such business is expansion at the least
expense. Thus, an effective enforcement action against one competitor group may (and usually
will) open up the opportunity for territorial expansion to another criminal network (providing
demand remains constant or increases).

o   Personality of the Boss/Leader
        While data on such a subject may appear innocuous, it may provide insight into the
management philosophy prevailing within a criminal network. A violent, impulsive, or vengeful
leader is likely to relate to and attract those with similar personality traits. Conversely, a passive,
docile, and non-aggressive leader, will seek to instill such attitudes and demeanor in his
subordinates. Such data may make it possible for intelligence personnel to more accurately
understand organizational psyche and develop and modify strategies appropriately.
        If collection efforts to secure such data are precisely defined, the analytical component of
an intelligence unit will be better equipped to translate what is often perceived as discrete and
seemingly unrelated data into meaningful usable intelligence. Depending upon the analyst's
particular discipline and expertise, a variety of social science methods and techniques are
available.

Sociological and Anthropological Methods
        One formal application of sociological methods to the analysis of organized crime can be
found in Cressey's (1969) research. In describing the hierarchical and authority relationships in
the Mafia, Cressey relied upon a corporate/bureaucratic model. This suggested a rather rigid,

formalized structure, that recently has come under sharp criticism. Nonetheless, it remains the model against which other newer groups are often compared. Chambliss on the other hand, using what are referred to as ethnographic research methods, studies the environment that an organized criminal group was "forced" to operate within (Taylor, pp. 167-179). While Chambliss' conclusions were significantly different from Cressey's, his research technique (ethnography) can be of great value if we want to understand the interactive group processes at work within the organized criminal subculture.

The essence of the sociological approach to intelligence analysis is its utility for classifying networks and bringing clarity to interactive group processes. Social network analysis is an analytical technique that permits an intelligence analyst to define what are commonly referred to as "clique interests" -- the attitudes, behaviors, loyalties, and reciprocal arrangements between criminal coconspirators. Through a technique known as link analysis, individuals are linked together, and networks emerge that provide a picture -- a clearer definition -- of these criminal organizations. While this methodology is a valuable analytical tool, other equally effective methodologies are available for use in organized crime intelligence.

Anthropological research techniques have been applied to organized crime data and are available to the intelligence analyst. Ianni (1972, 1974) was one of the first to employ this discipline in the study of organized crime as an institution. By studying the basic structures of institutions and comparing these structures against one another, models begin to emerge that avoid the traditional, monolithic model as represented by the Mafia. Ianni's research combined network charting techniques with ethnographic research, to allow the development of a variety of organized crime networks.

Economic Analysis

Not until very recently have economists come to the study of organized crime with any degree of seriousness. Notwithstanding Schelling's (1967) most valuable contributions to the literature, there have been few economists who have ventured into this ambiguous terrain. Nonetheless, Schelling's insights into organized crime provide organized crime intelligence analysts with an array of working hypotheses applicable to the study of organized crime (T.F.R., p. 114.126). For example, Schelling's concept of violence in the illicit market place provides a powerful analytical tool for assessing the level of organization -- that is, how well organized a particular marketplace may be. As Schelling argues, one benefit of crime being organized is a decline in indiscriminate violence, with perhaps, however, an increase in systemic corruption (T.F.R., 1967, pp. 122.123). Moreover, because the concept of organization is central not only to defining organized crime, but equally important, in measuring enforcement impact or success, its significance can not be underestimated. As Rubin correctly points out, "less *organized* crime is not the same as less crime" (Rottenberg, P. 159). Essentially, Rubin, Schelling, and other economists and social scientists are in agreement that measuring the impact of an enforcement action through arrests alone is irrelevant. The real issue is whether monopoly control has been altered and how.

Reuter (1983), one of the few economists who has sought to test these economic theories against the real world marketplace, concluded that the organization of bookmaking (in New York City) was not a result of Mafia control, and the revenues generated from illegal bookmaking were not as significant as portrayed by law enforcement officials. Indeed, Reuter's findings have critically challenged the traditional orthodoxy, and his research methodology provides a model for economic analysis of the criminal marketplace and the respective organizations that are alleged to control these markets.

Anderson's (1979) study of the Benguerra family provides still another example of how economic principles can be used to study an organized crime network and its activities. Anderson, in studying this particular family, used confidential federal reports and employed criminal and noncriminal sources in the collection of data. Her findings, while in contravention of traditional organized crime wisdom, demonstrate the level of refinement that can be attained in developing an enforcement strategy. Assuming that her findings were accurate, that is, that they represent an accurate portrayal of an organized crime family and its activities, several policy implications follow.

First, Anderson concludes that this family's involvement in legitimate business was of a non-predatory or violent nature; that little violence was employed in the "loansharking" business, and that corruption of police to protect gambling operations was extensive (pp. 140.141). The strategies that could emerge from these findings could be contradictory and clearly demonstrate the level of analysis needed to address the organized crime problem. For example, should enforcement resources be directed toward the legitimate businesses in which this family had invested to "launder" its illicitly-acquired moneys? Or would it be more rational to allocate resources toward the corruption that appeared to be systemic and pervasive?

Second, because it was obvious that this family had a monopoly on illegal gambling in the city, what would the effects be if divestiture were attained. As Buchanan maintains, "freedom of entry (into a critical market), the hallmark of competitiveness, is to be discouraged rather than encouraged" (Rottenberg, pp. 130.131). Divestiture of monopoly control may reduce corruption, but will more than likely increase violence (since competition encourages violence in the illicit market).

Last, if investigative resources are directed toward the legitimate enterprises in which this family had invested, might not a consequence of such a strategy be the dislocation of these individuals to more pernicious criminal activities? Would this not create a more serious criminal problem? On the other hand, does not investment in legitimate business generate or enhance the ability to exercise political power corruptly, thus making an enforcement strategy that seeks to expose this shallow veil of legitimacy more beneficial in the long term? It is this sort of analysis and dialogue that must be undertaken if police resources are to be used wisely.

Of course, the answers to these issues may not be politic in the police or the political culture. Nonetheless, these questions and the accompanying dialogue are appropriate in establishing priorities and anticipating the impacts of possible or proposed enforcement actions.

Psychological/Linguistic Methods

The use of psychological research is to understand the personalities of those who are involved in organized crime. It is a method that has yet to be fully explored. While psychological profiling of foreign leaders is a norm in military and other government intelligence organizations, law enforcement has yet to develop a codified body of knowledge that brings a clear methodology to this technique.

An unpublished study of certain participants in the Federal Witness Protection Program has examined personality characteristics of organized crime members and their associates (Davis, 1984).

A research effort on psychological profiling is currently underway at Syracuse University. Miron (1984) has developed a technique commonly referred to as psycholinguistics -- the combination of psychology and linguistics (pp. 5-9). This technique relies upon the analysis of language -- sentence structure, syllables, words, pauses, inflections of the voice, etc. -- to psychologically profile or "undress" the speaker (the "target" of an investigation). It has proven to be a rather effective technique in assessing potential terrorist threats, but its application to organized crime control can be equally revealing. For example, the use of electronic surveillance is a control tactic that has been repeatedly demonstrated to be one of the most effective tools in the investigation of organized crime. The conversations that are recorded in the course of such investigations not only lead to criminal prosecutions, but equally important, can allow law enforcement to understand more clearly the nature and personalities of the persons involved in criminal activity. Combining both linguistic analysis with psychological principles could provide law enforcement with a powerful analytical tool (also see Shuy, 1981, 1984).

Political Science
Political scientists were among the early pioneers in organized crime research. Gardiner's classic study of politics in Wincanton gave us a graphic description of how organized crime and government officials conspired (Gardiner, 1967, 1970). This type of analysis is extremely useful to the organized crime analyst, and provides a rich and often persuasive accounting of how organized crime seeks to undermine government structures. Homer (1974) has devoted several chapters to analyzing the politics of criminal organizations by applying a number of organizational principles. He studied how force is used within a criminal organization to effect control; how the dispensing of favors leads to organizational unity; how loyalty inhibits growth and expansion in an organization; how secrecy both maintains dominance and breeds hostility in criminal organizations; and how respect and position are not synonymous in a criminal organization. Homer provides crime analysts with a different way of analyzing criminal organizations, examining the matrices of criminal activity(ies) rather than analyzing the criminal organization as a society. This, Homer argues, avoids the traditional Italian-dominated view of organized crime and broadens our understanding of what it is law enforcement is seeking to control (Homer, 1974, pp. 108-138).

Historical Analysis
The discipline of history is a natural foundation for the organized crime analyst. That is, historians are continuously searching out facts that were heretofore unknown or hidden from the public. They organize and distill data that have always been available but not fully analyzed. In a sense, that discipline is most appropriate to the study of organized crime. It can serve to guide the crime analyst in the analysis of organized crime and identify parallel patterns to understand contemporary criminal activities.

Humbert Nelli, one of the early pioneers of the history of the Mafia, using basic document research, provided a graphic description of the evolution of the Mafia in urban centers throughout America. If Nelli is correct when he argues, "official pressures, advancing age of syndicate leaders, and this inability to attract new local talent combined with increasing competition from Blacks and Latins mark the beginning of the decline of Italian-American syndicates," it is quite apparent that new criminal organizations will emerge to supply the continuous demand for illicit goods and services (Nelli, 1976, p. 264). What Nelli does is use history to understand the past, in order to forecast trends in the future. Given the primary value of intelligence, prediction and thus prevention, this analytical tool can be very valuable.

Block, along different lines, uses historical data to recreate the early days of organized crime's evolution in New York City. While Block offers a non-traditional view of the role of organized crime in American politics, he concludes that "the most efficient 'organized criminal' were the most individualistic, the least committed to particular structure ..." (Block, 1980, p. 265). This concept can be very useful to an intelligence analyst seeking to identify the "rising stars" within a criminal network. With such identifications, law enforcement might decide to allocate its finite resources towards those criminal entrepreneurs believed most likely to attain control of a criminal network rather than current leaders.

Operations Research

Conventional organization theory, or what is referred to as operations research, offers us yet another analytical discipline that can be applied to the analysis of criminal organizations. Smith (1978) has brought such an analytical technique to his research on "illicit enterprises." He defines this term as "the extension of legitimate market activities into areas normally proscribed, for the pursuit of profit in response to latent illicit demand" (p. 164). Smith proposes a series of theorems that allow the "illicit enterprise analyst" to bring a different evaluation to criminal roles. For example, Smith suggests that rather than organized criminal activities around "a mutually-shared "family" relationship, each role must be considered on its own terms as an entrepreneurial extension of the larger spectrum of legitimacy" (Smith, p. 171). This permits the analyst to order his/her data along "a spectrum of illicit enterprise" allowing for a "broader understanding of how to reduce the domain of the illicit power broker or enforcer" (Smith, p. 175). It is the introduction of new analytical techniques, such as those proposed by Smith and others, that will expand and maximize the capacities of intelligence units in the containment of organized crime.

In as yet an unpublished study, Maltz postulates the inadequacies of existing measures of effectiveness for anti-organized crime activity, and articulates some alternative measures that might be employed. Utilizing these new measures, analysts could probe intelligence data bases to make for more accurate assessments of claimed "successes" in the "war against organized crime." In addition, arguments for or against the maintenance of an existing strategy could be buttressed with legitimate impact analysis.

The Need for Managerial Initiatives

No statement is more precise and revealing than that of Godfrey and Harris (1971) who correctly stated, "the intelligence process is sometimes physical but always intellectual (p. 2)." Collecting and analyzing intelligence data is a unique specialty and requires a genuine commitment to rigorous intellectual skills. Tying together existing research with organized crime intelligence analysis is a task that requires at the very least, skilled collectors and analysts who have been schooled in the nuances of organized crime theory, research methodology, and policy analysis. Further, law enforcement executives must be sensitive to the dynamics of the process, know the correct questions to ask, and acquire a sensitivity and appreciation for the need to base enforcement policy and practice on empirically-supported assessments/studies. Organized crime control must be perceived as a unique discipline, distinct from other forms of crime control. It requires a cadre of specialists who have devoted a large part of their careers to mastering and furthering the state of the art. To attain this, attitudinal as well as structural change must occur.

The current ethos prevailing among most law enforcement executives is that any police officer can do any police task. The professionalism of the criminal intelligence function demands a rejection of this philosophy. Specialists are an inevitable by-product of advancing knowledge, and as our knowledge of organized crime grows it is imperative that there be a cadre of intelligence specialists that remains knowledgeable. Without this, organized crime control planning and execution will be perceived as nothing more than basic criminal investigation, with no real appreciation for the concept of strategy that is central to the decision-making process.

Training of mid-level supervisors in the art of organized crime control is the next logical step in developing this cadre of intelligence specialists. Currently, there are no training programs available that address such issues as strategy development in organized crime control, understanding market conditions and what shapes such conditions in the underground economy, and resource deployment and impact assessments, to name just a few. Rather the notion prevails and is re-enforced by management, that an arrest of one organized crime member or associate (no matter how distantly related) is as valuable as the next. Hence we find that "vice" enforcement is often synonymous with "organized crime" enforcement. Until police executives and mid-level supervisors are conditioned to think in terms of organized crime concepts, we are unlikely to experience a change in current practices.

With respect to intelligence officers and analysts, the state of the art is quite advanced, but the practice leaves much to be desired. Few programs exist to train intelligence officers to collect data. Information is the essence of intelligence work and yet it is ironic that some of the best intelligence work has come from those with the least access to intelligence data contained in law enforcement files. Studies that have been cited in this paper were conducted by researchers and students who generally had only limited access to intelligence files. And those researchers who did have access to such files were better equipped to analyze the data than those regularly employed within intelligence units. This raises clearly questions as to the role researchers should play in the analysis of intelligence data, and whether it might not be appropriate to develop mutually-desirable liaisons with researchers, subject to appropriate restraints to protect the security of data. Researchers have expertise and skill to bring to the analysis of data, capabilities that could be transferred to the law enforcement sector. Intelligence officers have the information that is often inaccessible to the researcher. An exchange of knowledge and information would undoubtedly benefit both the academic community and law enforcement.

Training intelligence officers in what to collect, and intelligence analysts in how to analyze data is critical to the success of the intelligence process. However, much of this training will have to occur outside of the traditional police environment. Police training on the whole is limited to technical knowledge, with little time devoted to developing conceptual frameworks for decision-making. If the intelligence field is to acquire the types of personnel it needs to perform these tasks properly and efficiently, recruitment of personnel with college degrees and graduate training is a must. It is essential that police executives recognize that the academic disciplines bring with them rich and powerful analytical tools that are central to the analysis of intelligence data. The lack of such trained professionals in law enforcement has undoubtedly retarded the development of organized crime containment policies and practices.

The importance of educating operational personnel to the utility of the intelligence process and its limitations should not be underestimated. Far too often investigators perceive the intelligence function as a mere service activity (e.g., obtaining telephone or name look-ups) or as a panacea for "making his case." It is neither. Operational personnel must be educated to view intelligence as a guide by which the investigator is provided with a "road map" of criminal networks. Assigning operational personnel to intelligence units for no less than two year periods, may help to overcome the prejudices and misconceptions that have developed over the years.

Nothing is more valuable for "selling" the intelligence concept than the finished project, the assessment. It is the assessment that transfers acquired knowledge in written form to management and operational units. It should save the investigator valuable time by providing the "blueprint" of where he/she should be going in an investigation. By identifying and defining with precision, the targets of vulnerability, an investigator is spared the drudgery of preliminary investigative work. The assessment, rather than being perceived as a piece of "creative writing" or a novel having no relationship to the "real world," is a working document that detects and guides investigation.

The success of the intelligence function is dependent upon a strong managerial commitment and the availability of a skilled cadre of intelligence officers/analysts. It must be perceived as a management tool, not a luxury or the waste of valuable resources. Above all, police executives must be committed to rigorous and sound methodological standards that brings credibility to its findings.

Where Do We Go From Here

There is ample reason to question whether law enforcement executives will appreciate or enhance the potential of the intelligence process. Absent a cataclysmic crisis or scandal, it is certainly a highly tenuous proposition that intelligence will ever receive the stature and allocation of resources that are necessary in a developing and implementing an organized crime policy(ies). Notwithstanding the waves of indictments of Mafia "families" throughout the country, the history of organized crime enforcement is indicative of the abysmal performance intelligence has played in this so-called "war." Rather than being perceived as a vital element in the development and promulgation of enforcement strategy, intelligence is viewed as a luxury that is of marginal utility. Moreover, policy-makers, the ultimate consumers of intelligence assessments, often rely on their political instincts, first, subjugating intelligence to an inferior role. Few agencies have integrated the intelligence concept into the operations of their narcotics and organized crime units, and even fewer have made intelligence a part of their decision-making processes. Until there is continuity and a genuine commitment to this concept, the efforts of organized crime control units will never be fully realized or recognized.

To meet this challenge intelligence units must provide products (not street information) to law enforcement executives that address critical issues in organized crime control. These intelligence products must be both relevant and timely, and provide a coherent understanding of criminal organizations and networks and the milieu in which they operate. The intelligence product must be empirically-based, not surrounded in opinion, tradition, or folklore. If we examine, for instance, narcotic enforcement control strategies (which are not synonymous with organized crime control strategies), Kleiman's research (Kleiman, 1985) coupled with that of Rand's recent study (Rand, 1984), gives support to retail-level drug enforcement as opposed to wholesale and import-level drug enforcement. Moreover, Moore's (1977) research provides law enforcement executives with an understanding of how heroin enforcement affects demand. A study of the effects of enforcement on market structures is the type of empirically-based intelligence product that law enforcement executives should have at their disposal when developing and assessing strategies.

The impact that organized criminal activities have on the social fabric of the community provides for a rich understanding of the milieu in which organized criminals function. Clearly, Lasswell's (1972) research on the narcotics and gambling rackets in Brooklyn's Bedford-Stuyvesant sections, "by 1970, organized crime was grossing more revenues from narcotics and its illegal policy operations options ... than the Federal government was collecting in income taxes from the same areas," and Reuss-Ianni's (1973) subsequent study of the Harlem rackets, "organized crime reputedly is the chief supplier of illegal goods and services to the Harlem community," are indicative of the kinds of research that can be undertaken by intelligence units.

Studies into new, ethnically-organized criminal syndicates, Mexicans, Blacks, Colombians, Vietnamese, have emerged in the last decade. Lewis (1980), provides an analysis of La Nuestra Familia; Davidson (1974) examined the "Mexican Mafia;" Ianni (1974) explored the emergence of Black and Hispanic criminal organizations; and Lupsha/Schlegel (1980) provided illuminating insights with their research on the "Herrera Family." These studies serve as a foundation for understanding of new and emerging criminal syndicates.

Market analysis has become a popular method of assessing organized criminal activity. Reuter's (1984) examination of dispute mediation in the organized crime subculture adds to the existing research on this topic (Smith, 1978; Furstenberg, 1979; Dintino/Martens, 1981; and Chambliss, 1975). Seidl's (1968) often quoted study of "loansharking" rackets provides provocative and exciting questions into the pivotal role that moneylending plays in other illicit and licit activities.

Clearly, the range and number of research projects that could be undertaken by organized intelligence units are endless. Much needs to be done to understand the mechanics of organized crime, and yet so little has been accomplished over the past two decades. Intelligence units have access to data from which most researchers have been excluded. Access to and the informed use of information could result in a more lucid and detailed understanding of organized crime and how it functions.

Reference

Furstenberg, Mark.
   (1942) "Violence and Organized Crime." In Crimes of Violence. Staff Report to the
   National Commission on the Causes and Prevention of Violence. Washington, D.C.:
   U.S.Gov Printing Off.
Gardiner, John A.
   (1970) The Politics of Corruption: Organized Crime in an American City. New York:
   Russell Sage Foundation.
Godfrey, Drexel E. and Don R. Harris.
   (1971) Basic Elements of Intelligence. Washington, D.C.: U.S. Gov Printing Off.
Goldstock, Ronald.
   (1977) "Letting the Loanshark off the Hook," Newsday. September 9.
Homer, Frederic D.
   (1974) Guns and Garlic. West Lafayette, Indiana: Purdue University Press.
Ianni, Francis A.J.
   (1972) A Family Business. New York: Russell Sage Foundation.
Ianni, Francis A.J. and Elizabeth Reuss-Ianni.
   (1974) Black Mafia. New York: Random House.
Kleiman, Mark A.R.
   (1984) Evaluation of the Lynn Drug Task Force. Cambridge, Mass.: Harvard
   University, John F. Kennedy School of Government.
Lasswell, Harold and Jeremiah McKenna.
   (1972) Organized Crime in an Inner City Community. Springfield, VA.: National
   Technical Information Service.
Lewis, George H.
   (1980) "Social Groupings in Organized Crime: The Case of the La Nuestra Familia."
   Deviant Behavior. 1:129-143.
Lupsha, Peter and Kip Schlegel.
   (1980) The Political Economy of Drug Trafficking: The HerreraOrganization.
   Albuquerque, New Mexico: University of New Mexico.
Miron, Murray S. and John E. Douglas.
   (1979) "Threat Analysis: The Psycholinguistic Approach." FBI Law Enforcement
   Bulletin. Washington, D.C.: U.S. Gov Printing Off, September.
Moore, Mark H.
   (1977) Buy or Bust. Lexington, Mass.: D.C. Heath.
Nelli, Humbert.
   (1976) The Business of Crime. Chicago: University of Chicago Press.
Reuss-Ianni, Elizabeth.
   (1973) A Community Self Study of Organized Crime. New York: Criminal Justice
   Coordinating Council.
Reuter, Peter and Jonathan Rubenstein.
   (1982) Illegal Gambling in New York. Washington, D.C.: National Institute of Justice.

Reuter, Peter.
　　(1983) Disorganized Crime. Cambridge, Mass.: M.I.T. Press.
Rottenberg, Simon (ed.). The Economics of Crime and Punishment. Washington, D.C.: American
　　Enterprise Institute, 1973.
Schelling, Thomas.
　　(1967) "Economic Analysis of Organized Crime." Task Force Report: Organized
　　Crime. Washington, D.C.: U.S. Gov Printing Off.
Seidl, John.
　　(1968) Upon The Hip - A Study of the Criminal Loan-Shark Industry. Unpublished Ph.D.
　　Thesis, Harvard University.
Shuy, Roger W.
　　(1984) "Topic as the Unit of Analysis in a Criminal Law Case." In Analyzing Discourse:
　　Text and Talk. Washington, D.C.: Georgetown University Press; "Entrapment and the
　　Linguistic Analysis of Tapes." in Studies in Language. 8:2.
Smith, Dwight C.
　　(1978) "Organized Crime and Entrepreneurship." International Journal of Criminology
　　and Penology. Volume 6, pp. 61.177.
Taylor, Ian, Paul Walton, and Jack Young.
　　(1975) "The Political Economy of Crime: A Comparative Study of Nigeria and the USA."
　　Critical Criminology. London: Roulledge and Kegan Paul.
Wilson, James Q.
　　(1978) The Investigators. New York: Basic Books.

Reports

General Accounting Office.
　　(1977) War on Organized Crime Faltering -- Strike Force Not Getting Job Done. Report
　　GGD-77-17. Washington, D.C., March 17.
National Advisory Committee on Criminal Justice Standards and Goals.
　　(1976) Report of the Task Force on Organized Crime. Washington, D.C.: U.S. Gov
　　Printing Off.
Rand Institute.
　　(1984) Strategies for Controlling Adolescent Drug Use. Calif.: Rand.
Task Force Report: Organized Crime (TFR).
　　(1967) Washington, D.C.: U.S. Gov Printing Off.

Chapter Two

The Context of Analysis

From Analysis to Synthesis: Exploring the Context of Law Enforcement Analysis

Marilyn B. Peterson

Introduction

All too often, law enforcement investigative analysis* is conducted in a vacuum. An association chart is prepared or a telephone toll analysis is done without being placed within the context of the entire investigation. Accordingly, the global view of the analytical piece (and the investigation) is lost and, with that loss, the ability to solve the puzzle is diminished.

What is lacking is *synthesis*; the weaving together of the disparate information gathered into a cohesive picture of all aspects of the case. In doing this, the analyst can better be able to bring the case to a successful conclusion, and can also learn something about investigations and analysis which will be useful in future cases.

While the proper word in definition of this process is 'synthesis' (Webster defines it as the combining of often diverse conceptions into a coherent whole), its commonly used name is 'case analysis.' This chapter will more clearly define case analysis and establish it as the context in which most law enforcement investigative analysis is completed.

Definitions and Examples

For the purpose of this article, case analysis is defined as: *The compilation, summarization, comparison and organization of all pertinent and available case materials into a coherent whole.*

To use the analogy of a jigsaw puzzle, the three steps analysts use are arranging the pieces (collection and collation), examining each one for clues about its role or placement in the puzzle (analysis), and assembling the puzzle (case analysis or synthesis). The resulting overview of the investigation leads us to draw conclusions and make recommendations about either further collection which needs to be done or what prosecutive steps should be taken.

In a simple form, case analysis can be done with limited case information. Imagine, if you will, that telephone toll records have been subpoenaed (or obtained through other appropriate legal procedure) for two local subjects suspected of being involved in a narcotics organization.

Those records are entered into a database program and sorted to see the numbers called, calls by date and time, unusual calls, etc. This is done for each subject's records and then their calls are compared to one another to see if they both called any other individuals (these are called 'interlocking calls').

---

* Investigative analysis is law enforcement analysis used to help solve or prepare cases for prosecution .

The process of comparing one set of calls to the other is the first step toward case analysis. By virtue of that comparison, a few seemingly isolated calls are shown to be important due to their interconnective nature.

Similarly, these toll records provide puzzle pieces in the larger context of the case. If they were compared to records of surveillances on the locations of the telephones, the users of these phones at the times covered by the records could be identified. If information were known about a shipment of narcotics arriving in that town on a certain date, the pattern of calls might reflect that expectation or the actual delivery. They could help identify the courier or even to predict when the next delivery could occur. Thus toll records, when compared to other investigative data, could give much greater information than toll analysis alone could do.

In a second example, we can look at the investigation of a homicide. Crime scene reports, testimony of neighbors and relatives, sworn statements, the autopsy report and related information are gathered. To make sense of it all, these pieces must be analyzed and then organized in a coherent way to support the attempt to find the murderer. Without conscious or unconscious synthesis of the material, the crime will not be solved. Using case analysis, the victim's movements as compared to those of suspects' can be charted. Suspects can be compared to one another by comparing possible motives and opportunities to commit the crime. Unfollowed leads will surface to aid the investigator in finding the solution to the case.

Methodological Distinctions

The term 'case analysis' can mislead the practitioner as it is not an analytical methodology, but rather a synthetic methodology. Synthetic is meant in its literal translation from the Greek: 'synthetikos,' meaning 'composition' or 'to put together.'

Going back to the jigsaw puzzle analogy, analysis occurs when we look at the pieces of the puzzle -- their colors, patterns, subject matter -- and compare them to the other puzzle pieces. Synthesis occurs at the moment we find the configuration to lock another piece of the puzzle into place.

Case analysis, therefore, can and does include analytical processes and products. They must be done before case analysis can be done. Synthesis occurs when those pieces are combined and logical conclusions and recommendations are drawn from them. One of Webster's definitions of synthesis is "deductive logic." For our purpose, the use of inductive logic should be included as well. Put another way, case analysis is the *organizational context* for analysis.

Inherent, too, in the process of case analysis is the element of choice and analytical decision-making. If an analyst is given a set of toll records and asked to do a toll analysis, his or her decisions on how to do that analysis are limited to the different ways to do a toll analysis. But experienced analysts are often given a more nebulous task such as: "Here are three boxes of case material -- analyze them." This can be greeted by joy or fear (or both) on the part of the analyst, who now has major decisions to make about how to analyze and organize the data.

Part of the methodology documented must also deal with how to choose methodologies as well as how to present the analyzed data and make logical conclusions and recommendations. A detail of these steps and methodologies follows.

Detail of Steps in Case Analysis

Unlike traditional analytical methods, case analysis covers the total range of the investigative analysis process. Particular analytical methods are completed on an as-needed basis, but the overall organizational steps should be done at all times.

1.   Gather Data

This is traditionally an investigative step but is, in some agencies, given to the analyst. Analysts are often used to complete records checks, public record searches, and complete other basic investigative work.

Within an organization, the analyst should make certain that all available investigative material has been forwarded by the investigators for the analysis/synthesis process. This can be difficult in situations where investigators loathe to put the facts down on paper.

The way to assure access to all data is for the analyst to routinely receive investigative reports on the case in question. In addition, investigators and support personnel should be required to prepare and submit reports in a timely manner.

2.   Reference Data

Number each page of data and make an index of all data for future reference. These reference numbers are carried through on analytical work papers and may even be present on final products. This enables the investigator or prosecutor to quickly verify all information contained in the analysis.

3.   Review Data

All material, or a representative sampling of it, should be reviewed to give the analyst an overview of the investigation. If time permits, the material should be reviewed more than once. It is through this review process that the analyst grows familiar with the material and gets a sense or overview of the case. The analyst can then better determine the analytical potential of the information.

4.   Research Criminal Context

The criminal activity area should be researched in a general way. The types of questions which may need to be answered are:

   a.   What particular crimes are alleged and what are their elements?
   b.   Were the crimes committed in a criminal environment with other crimes? What were the other crimes?
   c.   How was the crime committed?
   d.   How does the subject (or this case) compare to other known criminals engaged in this activity (or with other criminal incidents of this nature)?
   e.   What other cases of this type have been done by the department?
   f.   What types of motives are generally seen for this type of crime?
   g.   What type of opportunity is needed to commit this type of crime?
   h.   What types of familial relationships exist between victims and potential suspects?

Some, if not all of these questions can be answered by speaking to investigators who work or specialize in that particular criminal area. They can give you insights resulting from their experiences and may steer you to other sources of good information.

If there were an original complaint or investigation which was broadened in criminal scope during the investigation, that should also be noted.

5.   Separate Data Based on Methods

Data should be separated according to the type of analysis to be performed upon it.

Appendix 1 shows some uses for various types of records.

It should be noted that each type of information can be used in several different ways or products. Toll records, for example, are used to do a telephone record analysis. The resultant links uncovered can also be shown on an association or event flow chart.

Certain decisions must be made to see what types of analytical work could or should be done. And, not all of those decisions can be made at the onset of the analytical project. Experience shows that the fewer pre-conceived ideas in analysis, the better. Each batch of data should be taken on its own merit in its own form and not plugged into pre-arranged formats or conclusions. This is said in the course of a 'how to chapter' not as a contradiction, but as a reminder of the limitations of instruction. Choose and use what methods and techniques work for the particular data.

6. Perform Basic Analysis

Toll analysis and/or financial analysis are distinct forms of analysis, the results of which can be used in other forms. Any material present which would use these basic methods of analysis should first be completed.

Both, too, may lead to secondary collection efforts such as subpoenas for other phone subscribers' records, the placement of a pen register or wiretap on a phone, or the subpoena of other bank records. If these are needed, the request should be made as soon as possible. Other analyses can be worked in the interim.

7. Extract the Data

While working from original records on toll or bank records is easy, handling voluminous amounts of investigative reports, testimony, etc. can be cumbersome. Extracting the information for further analysis is a simple process and once it is accomplished, the data is in a workable form for whichever method is to be used.

These extractions are usually done in a manual or computerized format, depending on the capabilities of the department. In a manual setting, three by five cards or five by eight cards are used, with the heading of a subject or a date (or both). These can then be arranged or re-arranged to put the case in a particular perspective.

In the computer mode, standard data base management software can be used to tailor a data base with the fields and space the information requires. Such data bases can be multi-purpose (chronological, association, and biographical) if adequate information and fields are included. In either case, the documentation (record number, record date) is brought forward for accuracy. Examples of computerized data base formats can be seen in Appendix 2.

8. Decide on Other Methods to be Used

Some methods used will result from the type of case being done. If a conspiracy is to be proven, then an association analysis, showing the criminal relationships, is a given. If the case results from a specific criminal incident (homicide, arson, armed robbery, etc.), then a suspect chart or an event flow chart should be done. If the investigation relates to stolen property or financial manipulation, a commodity flow analysis should be completed.

Within this decision-making process, the analyst should not be pressured to map out all products to be done at the onset of the project. Often, the process is an unfolding one. For that reason, doing the simple analyses can springboard the analyst to the next appropriate product and so on.

Another way of deciding which products are the most appropriate is to do a rough version of all possible products and then eliminate those which seem unnecessary. If, for example, an event flow analysis explains what happened in terms of the suspects involved, you may not need an association analysis.

Aside from the outlines given in Appendix 1, you can categorize material as falling into one or more of the following bases

- chronological
- biographical
- incidental

If the chronological material comprises the largest percentage of the data, then an event flow analysis should be done. Biographical material is placed into a listing of individuals whenever possible.

A large amount of associational material would indicate the need for association analysis. Incidental material -- that is, information on a series of criminal incidents -- could require an event flow analysis, a suspect chart and a crime analysis composite chart. Again, the same data may be used in more than one analytical product.

9.   Perform the Appropriate Analyses

Examples of chart products can be seen in Appendix 3. Remember that any completed analysis is a snapshot of a case at a given time and should be dated to reflect that time frame. In some cases, products are redone at various intervals to reflect new and more complete information.

10.   Review Investigative Methodologies

Using investigative and administrative reports, compile a listing of all investigative steps that were taken and what resulted from those steps.

Some departments use this to evaluate what results were achieved during the investigation (or to date). This can be done using a visual investigative analysis chart or by other listings of investigative steps and a one or two sentence explanation of the results of each.

Completing this section might involve a round-table discussion with case investigators. The analyst could find out from the investigators what methods and techniques were proven to work. A separate discussion with the case supervisor or manager could give a different perspective on the use and success of various investigative methods. The investigators might also see, as a result of the analysts' work, what other organizational methods or illustrations could have been used in the case. This gives them and the analysts a chance to see the larger picture.

Both investigators and supervisors should give input as to what the department or unit learned from the case. This, too, should be compiled to serve as a reference in future cases.

11.   Compare Products

All the completed products should be compared for accuracy, consistency (or inconsistency) and what is missing. Write down whatever questions arise in your mind as a result of doing the products and/or comparing them. These questions form the basis of what else may be needed to complete the case or prepare it for court.

This is another time in which investigators' input is valuable. Some questions may be answered informally without the need for further data collection. Those should be cleared up at this time through interaction with the case investigators.

12.   Synopsize Analytical Products

Based on all products, listings, charts and graphs completed, synopsize the findings achieved through the investigative analysis process. These are the basis for the fact pattern and recommendations. Also to be included are what violations have been committed and what evidence supports the charges.

13. <u>Prepare a Fact Pattern</u>

A 'fact pattern' is a short summary of the facts in the case. This can be one or two paragraphs and should include the basics of all investigations: the who, what, when, where, why and how. It must reflect the findings presented in 12 above.

It is here that the current status of the investigation should be noted. This then becomes part of the executive summary in the final report.

14. <u>Use Logic to Arrive at Overall Conclusions</u>

Again going back to the findings in 12 above, use these as premises, or facts, to support logically arrived at conclusions. The type of logic used may be deductive (going no further than the facts) or inductive (going from the facts to a larger conclusion).

If, for example, a murder is the focus of the case analysis, you may see that a particular person had both the motive and the opportunity to commit the crime, but has not confessed to the crime. In the absence of other likely suspects, an analyst could conclude, *inductively*, that the person noted had committed the murder, how it was committed and why. Such conclusions would be followed by detailed direction on what additional evidence might be gathered to prove or disprove that conclusion.

With the same facts, the analysis could also state, deductively, that the killer's identity was unable to be ascertained at this time in a conclusive way. The analyst could then give the same direction on what additional evidence needed to be gathered to provide a more definitive hypothesis of what occurred.

15. <u>Recommend Further Action</u>

Most recommendations from analysts relate to obtaining more data for analysis or for integration into existing case material. If the investigation in question is a preliminary one, the analyst's list of questions cold be quite long. The nearer to prosecution the case is, the shorter (hopefully) the list is as it generally reflects what is missing.

Some less experienced analysts are uncomfortable with presenting such recommendations or questions because they fear the seasoned investigator's response to their seeming impertinence. No question is too simple to ask, provided that the tone of the asking is neither accusatory, nor fatuous, nor demanding.

Those questions can be handled as the analysis (and investigation) progresses. In some instances, the investigator knows the answers and has forgotten to include them in the written report. In others, the fresh look at the case provided by the analyst uncovers what the investigator may not see due to his/her closeness to the case.

It is best to err on the side of too many questions than too few. A question can provide a break in the case. Potential targets should also be noted. As a result of this case, new individual targets may have been uncovered or a topic for a criminal assessment may have surfaced. Suggestions on these should be listed and forwarded, in the final report, to management.

16. <u>Prepare Final Report</u>

This may include selected or all products you have completed as well as the other material detailed in the section on "Case Analysis Format. "

17. <u>Present Report</u>

Depending upon the formality of your structure and the level of the case, you may have to give an oral presentation, or briefing, on the completed analysis.

The simplest way to organize an oral briefing is around your findings, conclusions and rec-ommendations. The findings are shown based on charts and graphs which become your visual aids. The conclusions and recommendations can be handed out and discussed. The entire executive summary section of your report can be used as a handout.

Before embarking on such an oral briefing, it is important to prepare thoroughly and be able to support every conclusion with facts. The analyst can take each concluding statement and write out the facts in the case which support that statement. Where contradictory facts or evidence exist, the analyst should be prepared to state, *why,* a particular piece of evidence was believed rather than another piece. It is here that the evaluation of data sources may come into play.

Case Analysis Format

The written case analysis report should be reflective of the data analyzed and conclusions drawn during the analysis. It is here that synthesis continues to present the material in a logical and coherent way. Figure 1 is a typical outline for a case analysis which can be modified as needed.

Figure 1   Case Analysis Outline

>   A. Executive Summary
>   1. Fact Pattern
>   2. Major Findings and Conclusions
>   3. Recommendations
>   B. Criminal Context of Investigation
>   C. Analytical Products
>   D. Biographical Listings
>   E. Investigative Response and Results
>   F. Index
>   G. Bibliography

Information to complete each of these points should be obtained from the work papers compiled using the steps on previous pages, except for the Index and the Bibliography. The Bibliography should reflect the research done for Section B. The Index, on the other hand, shows all names mentioned in the report and the page(s) on which they are mentioned. The indexing process is often an interesting one as it gives you a final analysis of frequency of distribution of particular people (or groups, or businesses) in the analysis. In some cases, additional conclusions may result from the indexing process.

Conclusions

While this chapter attempts to de-mystify the process of law enforcement investigative analysis, it can do so only with certain caveats. These processes, methods, and ways of choosing them are merely a reflection of one analyst's thinking process; one analyst's way of doing the job. They are shared with the intention of provoking thought and discussion, not with the intention of becoming dicta regarding analysis. If other practitioners are willing to compare it to their ways, or to consider it as an alternative when doing analysis, then its purpose will have been served.

Appendix 1

ANALYTICAL USES OF DATA
A Partial Listing

Record Types	Analytical Methods Used
A. Telephone Bills or Pen Register Records	1. Telephone Record Analysis 2. Association Analysis to show links between people and/or businesses 3. Event Flow Analysis to show occurrence of calls in context of other events.
B. Bank Account Records	1. Financial/Check Analysis 2. Commodity Flow Analysis 3. Association Analysis to show links between people or businesses 4. Net Worth Analysis to estimate annual expenses 5. Event Flow Analysis to show payments or deposits in context of other events.
C. Investigative Reports or Patrol Reports	1. Association Analysis- surveillance of meetings 2. Event Flow Analysis to show unfolding conspiracy or criminal activity 3. Suspect Chart 4. Biographical Listing 5. Visual Investigative Analysis 6. Crime Analysis Composite Chart
D. Crime Scene Reports	1. Event Flow Analysis 2. Suspect Chart 3. Crime Analysis Composite Chart
E. Public Records - Deeds Incorporation Papers, Tax Reports	1. Financial Analysis 2. Association Analysis 3. Event Flow Analysis 4. Commodity Flow Analysis
F. Interviews, Sworn Statements Testimony, Wire, Transcripts	1. Event Flow Analysis 2. Association Analysis 3. Suspect Chart 4. Content Analysis

Record Types	Analytical Methods Used
G. Corporate Records	1. Financial Analysis 2. Association Analysis 3. Event Flow Analysis 4. Commodity Flow Analysis 5. Biographical Listing
H. Refuse and Personal Records	1. Association Analysis 2. Event Flow Analysis 3. Financial Analysis 4. Biographical Listing 5. Suspect Chart
I. Administrative Records of Agency	1. Visual Investigative Analysis

Appendix 2

COMPUTERIZED DATA BASES FOR ANALYSIS

Types of Data	Fields
Associational	Name 1, Name 2, type of association, date of association, record number, record date
Chronological	Date, time, description of event occurring , person(s) involved, record number, record date
Associations and Events	Name 1, Name 2 , type of association, date of association or event, time of association or event, event, record number, record date
Multi-Purpose	Name 1, ID Number 1, Name 2, ID Number 2 , association, event or ID description, date of event, time of event, source of information or other comments, record number, record date
Biographical*	Name, date of birth, identifiers, other materials
Incidental	Date, time, location, weapons, violator descriptors, victim descriptors, related data

---

* This is more easily done in word processing but should be double-checked by comparing information in the format against a concurrent data base. A field for *type of information* in any data base can segregate types of data for sorting and reporting. Biographical information could be included in a multi-purpose data base and could be extracted for comparison to the list in Appendix 3.

ANALYTICAL PRODUCTS

Association Analysis
    A compilation of the known or potential criminal links between subjects and/or their businesses. The product generally includes an association chart and conclusionary statements. This is accompanied by a biographical listing. See Chapter Four for a detailed look at association analysis.

Association Chart

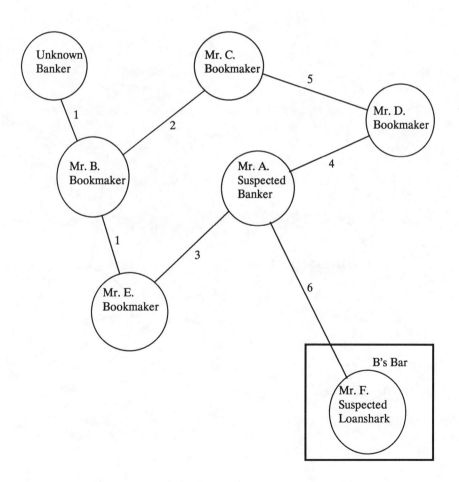

Telephone Record Analysis

Telephone record analysis dissects telephone bill or pen register (non-audio intercept) data to ascertain primary numbers called, normal calling hours, geographic spread of calls, unusual calls, etc. When multiple subscriber data is analyzed, charts can be made (see below). Often, this analysis is used to help establish probable cause for an audio wire intercept. Also see Chapter Five for complete details, examples and samples.

Telephone Record Analysis Chart

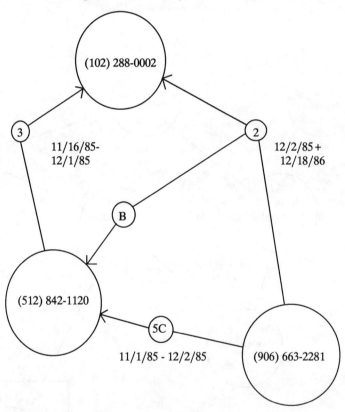

B = Billed to
C = Collect

Flow Charts

Flow charting tracks the passage of events leading to criminal activities or the movement of goods or commodities. They are usually termed 'event flow charts' or ' commodity flow charts.' The primary distinction between them is that event flow is based on chronology and commodity flow is based on the movement of goods. Presumed events or movements are also tracked.

Event Flow Chart

Insurance Fraud

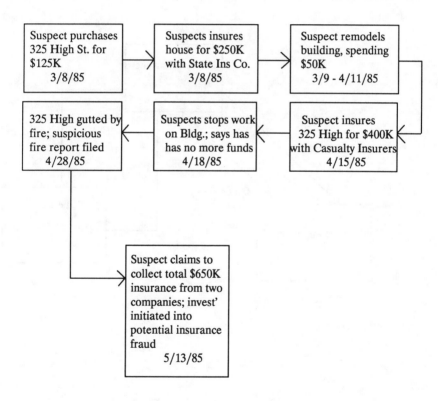

Commodity Flow Chart

Trail of Goods Stolen in Residential Burglary

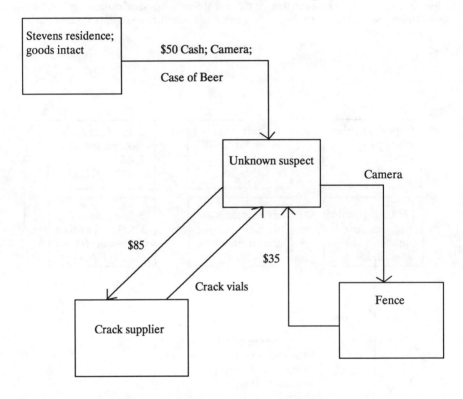

Visual Investigative Analysis

Visual Investigative Analysis is the step-by-step laying out of the actions taken in an investigation and the results of each action. It includes primary, secondary, and even tertiary action lines with space for additional data as it is gathered. It is used in multi-jurisdictional investigations and can aid in the elimination of duplication in the case.

Visual Investigative Analysis

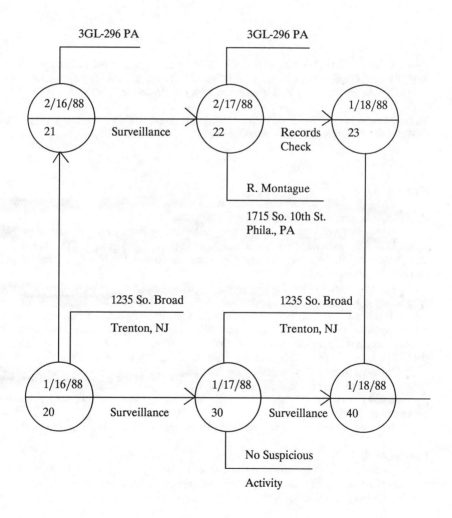

Biographical Listing

An alphabetical listing of subjects under investigation which includes all information known about them. This material is fully referenced within the listing. If the investigation is complex, a special listing of targets may be compiled and/or a listing of victims may be compiled. A third listing may be designed to support the prosecutive effort and would include all information by source. This is especially effective in surfacing contradictions in statements. Document reference numbers appear in parentheses.

*   *   *   *   *

Sample Listing

Jones, Andrew J. "Andy" dob 10/23/61. Res: 2601 South Seventh Street, Philadelphia, PA 19146. Tel: 581-2290 (75-6) Works at Jim's Deli, 24th & Washington Sts. (63-2) Seen meeting with Raymond Ciaciattore 7/12/86. Left meeting with manila envelope in hand. (51-5)

Martin, Lewis dob 7/3/54. Res: 21 West Evergreen Avenue, Philadelphia, PA 19118. Tel: 242-0001 (75-4) Self-employed (62-5) Associate of Luigi Ciaciattore (72-3)

*   *   *   *   *

Financial Analysis

Financial analysis is a term used to cover at least three types of such analysis: net worth analysis, check analysis and business record analysis.

In net worth analysis, the assets and liabilities of a person over at least three years are analyzed to determine the person's net worth and any changes in that net worth. Those figures are then compared with the person's declared income to determine the possibility of undeclared (and possibly illegal) income.

In check analysis, the checking account records are compiled and analyzed to determine where the funds went -- to major payees, to other accounts in what amount and when. Account activity is summarized to show what went into the account and what went out, and highlights any relationships between deposits and withdrawals. Unusual payments are also noted. Check analysis can show money laundering, tax evasion, and other white collar crimes. It is also used as the basis for determining what a person's estimated living expenses were in the net worth format.

Business record analysis takes the financial and/or sales records of a company and compares them to determine the possibility of fraud, tax evasion, skimming, or other forms of white collar crime. It is almost inevitable that certain white collar crime violations occur in concert with organized crime violations.

Because of their complexity, no examples of financial analysis appear in this chapter.

Content Analysis

Content analysis is used in the course of reviewing written or oral information which requires some summarization, interpretation, comparison, and conclusion drawing. It may be done on transcripts, testimony, written documents, periodicals or books.

It can also include quantitative analysis in terms of space devoted to particular topics, frequency distributions of particular items, etc. No example is shown here due to its complexity.

Crime Analysis Composite Chart

A Crime Analysis Composite Chart is produced by breaking down incident data into its elements and then performing frequency distribution analysis in reference to those elements.

The incidents are reviewed for what elements are common to the particular type of data being treated. Common crime analysis elements include date, time, location, violator data, victim data, method of operation, use of weapons, etc.

The information is placed into the composite chart for ease in reviewing and analyzing it.

Crime Analysis Composite Chart

Narcotics Sale Incidents

Day	Time	Amount	Purity	Seller Age	Buyer Age	Seller Sex	Buyer Sex
TU	1217	1 gm	75-80	17	16	M	M
SA	1419	1/8	70-80	28	19	M	M
FR	1515	1 gm	80	16	15	M	M
FR	2224	2 gm	80	26	21	M	M
WE	1907	1/8	75-80	24	20	M	M
MO	1235	1 gm	65	16	14	M	M
TU	1520	2 gm	75	15	15	M	M
FR	1250	1 gm	70	17	16	M	M
MO	1518	1 gm	80-85	15	16	F	F
TH	1218	1 gm	85	16	17	M	M
FR	1516	2 gm	70	15	15	M	M
SU	1310	1/8	60-70	23	28	F	M
MO	1255	1 gm	65-75	17	17	M	M
TH	1201	2 gm	75-80	15	14	M	M
SA	0112	1/8	65	25	27	M	M
WE	1322	1 gm	65-70	16	16	M	F
SA	2315	1/8	70-80	32	28	M	M

Suspect Chart

A Suspect Chart may be used to compare the possible suspects in an investigation, such as a homicide or robbery, along with their potential motives and their opportunity. It facilitates the comparison among the suspects by arranging the data into a simple format.

Suspect Chart Sample - Homicide

Suspect Name & Identifiers	Motive To Commit	Opportunity To Commit	Rec # Date
Jarrell, Thomas SBI#241-783	victim owed money	seen near victim's home night of murder	79-3
Williams, Mabel 132-78-1008	former girlfriend	no alibi night of murder	79-25
Burch, Liz 145-63-7110	current girlfriend	with victim night of murder	79-31
Hall, Mark 121-73-9231	business partner	last person to see victim alive	79-17

Chapter Three

Collection And Analysis Plans

Paul P. Andrews, Jr.

Introduction

Intelligence is a management tool. It is meant to facilitate planning, decision making and policy development. One of the best reasons for intelligence is that it serves to systematically look ahead to develop a set of alternatives with which to meet unforeseen or dimly lit future eventualities. Yet, for this to become reality, and not merely rhetoric, the conceptual as well as the pragmatic aspects of intelligence, i.e., as a process and as a product, must be understood.

Intelligence has been described in many different ways. For example, intelligence has been described as an organizational resource serving policy decision makers; intelligence is organized and managed information; it is information that has been subjected to a process and transformed; it is a function; intelligence is an end product; intelligence is an information system; it is a model for processing data into judgments.

The task of intelligence, most simply stated, is to develop knowledge. Such knowledge materializes through developed human behavioral activities, such as: senses, perceptions, images, inquiries, insights, formulations, reflections, affirmations, judgments and communications. These human behavioral activities though do not just occur, nor should they. They should occur, however, as a result of planning and direction, and collection, distinct phases within the intelligence process.

Often defined in a cyclical context, intelligence as a process contains five phases: planning and direction, collection, processing, production and analysis, and dissemination (Johnson, p. 1). Within this process of continually evolving and interconnected phases are two components that vastly effect major phases of the intelligence cycle, to the extent that determines whether or not resources are properly directed, whether or not relevant information is collected, and whether or not intelligence as knowledge is produced. The two important elements are the collection plan and the analytical plan. Each type of plan plays an important role in the planning and direction phase, the collection phase, and in the production and analysis phase. Collectively, they identify information requirements, focus and direct collection resources, and direct production and analyses.

A fundamental intelligence problem within the law enforcement community is not collecting information, but rather what to collect and for what purpose. Law enforcement intelligence units can not afford an ad hoc or nonsystematic practice of gathering and analyzing information. Such practices not only hinder, for example, organized crime control strategies and policy development but may also degrade existing strategy and policy. Dintino and Martens (p. 77) have stated:

> Initiating a collection plan clearly represents one of the most impor-
> tant phases in the intelligence process. The collection plan articulates the
> information needed to develop or test a particular hypothesis and provides
> intelligence personnel with the parameters for their collection efforts. The
> collection plan represents the only rational mechanism to manage the intel-
> ligence officer's collection effort. It establishes precise pieces of data
> necessary to accomplish the overall goal of the project and provides the in-
> telligence officer with an understanding of how the data fits into this bigger
> puzzle.

Without employing a collection plan, intelligence officers are left with their own predilec-
tions, collecting data that they believe are relevant to the organization and intelligence unit. The
results are non-direction, misdirection and a totally inefficient and ineffective utilization of
collection resources.

Similarly, without an analytical plan, a key means of supervision is removed from the
production and analysis phase of the intelligence cycle. Moreover, absent an analytical plan,
analysts will examine data relying upon intuition or "seat-of-the pants" methodologies, and
perhaps not question data relevancy and adequacy.

To exemplify the significance in particular of the collection plan to intelligence collection,
a case of industrial espionage, today commonly referred to as business competitor intelligence, will
be briefly touched upon. Computer companies are highly technical, constantly modifying and enhancing their products to meet consumer demands and to become industry product leaders. IBM
has always been considered one of the leaders within the computer industry. As a result, during
the early 1980's, IBM became a competitor intelligence target of Hitachi, a Japanese electronics
firm seeking to obtain design information for several new IBM computers and ancillary components. To meet its objective, Hitachi generated a "shopping list," i.e., a collection plan, that
specifically specified the type of IBM information that was desired. For example, the list included:

> Design information for the IBM 3081 computer.
> Components of the 3081.
> Tapes containing source microcode and test and maintenance programs
> for the 3081.
> Design information for the IBM 3033 computer.
> Design information for the IBM 3380 disk storage unit.
> Components of the 3380.
> Documents containing maintenance information for the 3380.
> Automated logic diagrams for the 3380 and the IBM 3380 storage control
> unit.
> Tapes containing source code for the MVS/SP.
> Version 2 operating systems program (Sammon, p. 49).

Competitive business intelligence occurs within each and every major market sector in the
world. Most often business intelligence production results in more effective and less vulnerable
business strategies, and in strategic planning. Such intelligence on the one hand attempts to
preclude rambling and compulsive management, and on the other hand, offer sound information
to support corporate strategy and policy development. The IBM story clearly points out that

Hitachi knew what to collect and for what purpose.

Collection and Analytical Plans

Collection and analysis planning are subordinate to overall direction and planning, but are no less important. Knowing the objectives of intelligence planning, i.e., to optimize personnel and equipment, to sustain the progress of intelligence production evenly and systematically, to have intelligence available when needed, and to disseminate intelligence promptly and accurately, one clearly observes the intentions supported by both the collection and analytical plans.

Equally important is understanding the purpose for which intelligence may be used. First, for example, from the National Drug Enforcement Policy Board, a coordinating body tasked to organize national and international drug law enforcement strategies: "reliable and timely intelligence allows law enforcement resources to be applied more effectively" (p. 49). Within the context of strategic, tactical and operational intelligence, the collection and analysis plans would establish information requirements, for example, to determine drug cultivation, production, availability, trafficking patterns, smuggling targets, money laundering activities, violations of currency reporting laws, the identity and activities of organizations, establish relationships, and reveal conspiracies (Ibid., p. 51).

The International Association of Chiefs of Police lists numerous purposes of intelligence in a policy manual on criminal intelligence. The manual points out that intelligence should be utilized:

> To identify criminal principals and their associates, including current and emerging criminal leaders.
>
> To provide their descriptions and activities within a given jurisdiction.
>
> To identify the extent to which organized crime has developed within a given jurisdiction and its relationship to organized crime participants and activities to other jurisdictions.
>
> To assess organized crime's capabilities, its direction and growth potential within given jurisdictions.
>
> To determine the nature and extent of criminal infiltration into legitimate business.
>
> To identify those business enterprises and public officials which are controlled or directly influenced by criminal elements.
>
> To identify the economic, social and governmental problems created by organized crime and suggest methods by which these may be impacted (pp. 39-40).

Hence, to meet the aforementioned goals, well developed plans must focus the collection and analytical efforts.

It has been stated in general terms that intelligence ". . .is a prerequisite for an effective policy or strategy,. . .It can identify options and probabilities and illuminate the consequences of action or the failure to act" (Laquer, pp. 31 and 34).

In essence, intelligence facilitates the management and employment of law enforcement resources and provides a range of end products that support strategic, tactical, and operational decision making.

One would expect intelligence unit supervisors receiving specific requirements from their

Chiefs detailing what they need or want to know. This, however, is probably the exception. Hence, one asks, "How is production generated?" By knowing what generates production, the analyst is better prepared to develop both the collection and analytical plans. Important to remember is that production needs information requirements. It has been pointed out that ". . . production is the end game of intelligence. Without production, the collection of intelligence. . .would be virtually useless" (Hulnick, p. 332).

Defined, production represents a number of elements that take into account intelligence management, developing information requirements, analytic tasking, analysis, intelligence production (i.e., end product and packaging), evaluation and dissemination. Production may be initiated in several ways. First, law enforcement executives themselves may provide general requirements or ask questions to support a policy initiative. For example, a Chief may demonstrate serious concern about the rapid increase in automobile thefts, or question the level of activity of a particular gang operating in a specific area of a city.

Second, requirements may be generated by the intelligence unit supervisor and analysts. The supervisor and analysts should be knowledgeable about the activities the Chief is concerned about. They should ask themselves: "What types of information would I want, if I were the Chief?" They should consider what might be wanted as well as what might not be wanted.

Third, requirements may often be generated by criminological events. These are activities unanticipated by the intelligence unit but that require coverage beyond requirements of the day. For example, a prominent member of a La Cosa Nostra organization is assassinated, or a multi-ton cocaine seizure is made at a local airport. This type of situation creates an informal or ad hoc production demand and is often under rigid time constraints. Generally, later, the analyst will be able to review the event and the surrounding circumstances.

Fourth, production requirements may be generated by previous intelligence products. This may occur in at least two ways. A particular intelligence assessment, for example, on outlaw motorcycle gangs, their structures and activities, may be undertaken and updated every two years. Also, analyzing the influence a criminal organization has on a particular labor union might cause the intelligence unit to examine all labor unions, or perhaps conduct a comprehensive analysis of the industry to which that particular union provides labor.

Fifth, production requirements may also be a matter of standard operation procedure. For example, the intelligence unit may also be responsible for providing tactical intelligence information each time there is organized crime related violence, i.e., a homicide or attempted homicide. Collection resources may be required to ascertain minimally the motive, modus operandi, who is most likely to benefit from the violence, and identify possible suspects. Given this circumstance, intelligence would be directly supporting the investigation into the violence.

Regardless of the way intelligence production is initiated, the analyst must be prepared to focus his energies on developing collection and analytical plans. These plans may take on a multi-dimensional and multi-disciplined approach that ultimately lead to intelligence products that are timely, relevant and useful.

The collection and analysis plans may be devised by more than a single analyst on an assigned project. This is particularly true in the case of developing a strategic assessment. Specifically, within this context considerable research might have to be conducted to become familiar with prior research, concepts and appropriate analytical methodology. On the other hand, collection and analytical plans involving tactical or investigative assignments are more direct in that they may become slightly routine, though this is not an absolute. For example, an analyst who has been developing tactical intelligence assessments on a specific La Cosa Nostra organization is now tasked to develop such an assessment on a Colombian cocaine distribution network. One would not expect the analyst to use the identical collection and analysis plans, though some of the information requirements and analytical methodologies may be similar.

The collection and analysis plans do not follow any prescribed format. Individually, they can range from single worksheets to long, detailed plans. The type and format of each type of plan will depend upon the size of the intelligence unit, to include the analytical component, the unit's mission, and the situation.

To more fully understand the uses and objectives of the collection and analytical plans, the following provides clear delineations. Since intelligence collection is a process that involves the gathering of information from all available sources, the collection plan serves as a management tool that directs and focuses collection resources. It should reflect information requirements that satisfy the intelligence requirements of the Chief or the intelligence unit supervisor. The collection plan provides a breakdown of an objective into meaningful component parts, i.e., relevant items of data, but places them into the context of information. It identifies relevant from irrelevant information required for analysis. Additionally, the collection plan provides collection management, i.e., the intelligence operations officer, and the analyst, with the ability to evaluate requirement satisfaction, provide requester and consumer feedback, identify additional requirements, and to adjust collection requirements.

The collection plan may be likened to an on-board navigation system that guides a ship from one point to another. Without the correct coordinates to guide its course, the ship will veer off course, perhaps becoming lost, losing valuable time, and perhaps not reaching its destination. The collection plan is a navigational aid, with the information requirements serving as the coordinates, each having the function of steering information collection resources to a selected and defined objective.

Intelligence requirements may be stated in the form of a question, e.g., "Have the Yakuza entered our jurisdiction? If so, when, where, and in what strength?" Additionally, intelligence requirements may be stated as an imperative. For example, "Ascertain the scope of the retail crack cocaine sales in our jurisdiction."

The question, concerning the Yakuza, implies the possibility of the presence of a situation in which an effort will be made to determine. The imperative, on the other hand, implies that a crack cocaine distribution problem is evident and its scope must be determined.

The Chief or his intelligence unit supervisor may know what he wants or the objective he desires to achieve. Nevertheless the analyst must also recognize what needs to be known in more specific terms and clearly define and delineate the information requirements that must be collected to support analysis and intelligence production.

The purpose of the analytical plan is to define the types of analyses that will be applied to specific types of data obtained. It precludes unnecessary trial-and-error analytical efforts. Additionally, the analytical plan encourages analysis rather than mere "report-gisting." It also alerts consumers of potentially new material that may be factored into what is currently known.

An analytical plan may also identify the hypotheses that are to be tested. However, if hypothesis testing is not initially integral to the analytical effort, perhaps then the analytical plan may indicate that other specific types of inferences will be generated and tested. Also the analytical plan will vary in scope and detail based upon the nature and complexity of the criminological issue or target being examined.

To develop a good analytical plan, the analyst must have a firm background in research, analytical methodologies and the types of data required to support the methodologies that are associated with crime-related issues. Information and methodology are complementary. To adequately examine an issue, sound methodology must be applied to relevant and adequate data. A weakness in either element results in the creation of false or fragile intelligence.

Like the collection plan, the analytical plan is not static. It should be updated as new types of information are required, identified and collected, or when additional methodologies are required to examine data for an added perspective.

The collection and analysis plans are the analyst's research plans. Together they provide a model, or framework, for collection and analysis, and provide management and accountability.

The following illustration depicts the steps that are integral to developing the collection and analytical plan.

COLLECTION PLAN	ANALYTICAL PLAN
Identify the criminological issue or target in specific terms.	Identify the criminological issue or target in general/specific terms.
	Research and review literature, prior assessments, investigations, relevant reports.
	Refine and define criminological issue(s), concepts and targets.
	Format hypotheses.
	Define Unit(s) of Analysis(es).
Formulate specific information requirements	Identify general information requirements.
	Identify applicable methodologies.
Evaluate information	Evaluation.
Modify and update	Modify and update.

When these plans are developed, they are reviewed for thoroughness. They are reviewed at several levels of supervision and generally approved by the analytical unit supervisor, the operations officers and/or the intelligence unit supervisor. Following approval, the collection plan is distributed to the field.

At this juncture, both the collection and analytical plans have advanced through a series of decision points. These central decisions determine the following: whether or not adequate and objective information have been indicated as requirements; whether or not terms and concepts have been defined to the degree that they are understood and useful to the collectors as well as to the consumers of the final product; and the applicability and adequacy of methodologies to be used.

Briefly, to comment on each of the above mentioned points, it is not uncommon for the intelligence analyst to build into the collection plan requirements for more than sufficient information. Yet, critical to the analyst's analysis is whether or not adequate data are received from collection resources. Suffice it to say, analysts never have enough data. Here the analytical plan comes into play. Knowing beforehand the methodologies to which collected information will be applied helps the analyst to recognize when sufficient data has accumulated to develop inferences that go beyond emotion or sentiment. Moreover, the analytical plan inhibits extraneous data being probed by analytic methodologies.

Next, the collection plan is supported by the analytical plan since to a large degree it serves as a preamble to the criminological issue or target to be examined. This is particularly true relative to strategic assessments. The analyst defines issues, concepts, terms of reference and units of analyses within the analytical plan which results in an analytical plan of action and which impacts upon the collection plan.

Within the context of tactical assessments, the analytical plan is much less formal and may define merely target entities, units of analyses and general information requirements, in support of the subsequent collection plan, and methodologies to be applied.

Generally within the context of investigative analysis, the analyst does not prepare an analytical plan since most criminal investigations are reactive in nature. Hence the assigned analyst will have to proceed with the investigative data that have been collected. Yet, this would not preclude the analyst from generating a collection plan.

Deciding beforehand on the analytical methodologies to be applied to the requirements bearing on the issue or the target entity is simply efficient for at least two reasons. First, the analyst may learn early in the project that a particular methodology is less suitable than expected. Since there are a wide variety of ways to approach an issue or problem, several methodologies may be exploited using the same data, to determine which methodology is more effective. Second, information that may have once been considered extraneous may take on a new significance. If this situation occurs, there might well be a need to incorporate additional methodologies to the analytical plan.

Lastly, and particularly important for the analytical and collection plans is the review. For both plans, the following questions must be asked: Are the requirements adequate and objective?; Do they reflect the issue being addressed?; Are issues, concepts and targets defined and understood?; Is the analytic methodology effective? For the analyst, next to defending the final product, i.e., the intelligence assessment, this review can be positively disquieting. The analyst must remember that the goal of intelligence analysis is to produce a defensible, objective intelligence product.

To reiterate an earlier point, neither plan is static. Each of them is subject to modification for several reasons. For example, issues or targets have been narrowed or expanded; requirements have been added or deleted; information collected impacts on either plan; applied methodologies change. The collection and analytical plans attempt to preclude the notion "garbage in -- garbage out" situation, yet provide boundaries within which information is collected and analyzed. Moreover, the collection plan, in particular, strengthens intelligence planning and directing in general, which provides the means for determining what must occur, in proper sequence, to complete a task by the time required. The collection plan facilitates the intelligence process via a constant review of present and future requirements thus knowing what to do in the present. Planning emphasizes prevention rather than correction of delays in intelligence production.

To assist in developing strategic and tactical collection and analytical plans in the areas of organized criminality, the following items, through not all inclusive, are offered:

1. Membership of group: All members with biodata available on them. Length of membership if available. Note any trends such as criteria for membership regarding number of members, geographic range of their legal and illegal activities.

2. Geographic data on group: Headquarters, location of members, geographic range of their legal and illegal activities.

3. Hierarchy of group: Past and present. Is there a known philosophy of current or past leaders relative to violence or criminal activities? Who appears to be rising through the ranks?

4. Criminal activities of group: All known or suspected illegal activities. Dates of criminal activity occurrences should be included to show possible changes or trends.

5. "Legitimate" business activities of group members: All known or suspected involvements with "legitimate" business including employment history, ownership of or investments in businesses, past and present. Look for hidden ownership through fronts and paper corporations. Again, look at possible trends or changes.

6. Financial health of group members: Any information that shows evidence of financial condition of members or group -- real estate, vehicles, travel, and any other things of conspicuous consumption. Analyze tax and/or bank records of group leaders. Trends and changes should be noted.

7. Connections to other groups: Is this group working and another group equal, superordinate, or subordinate? Is "tribute" paid to another group? Does each group have an established territory? Have any changes occurred in these network conditions?

8. Connections to the government structure: Are there agencies or governmental bodies that regulate the general activity area in which the types of crime being committed occur (police, licensing, and regulatory agencies)? Do any known connections/relationships exist between group members and persons involved in these agencies or governmental bodies?

9. Previous work in the system: Have any enforcement actions been taken

against the group, either for criminal or civil violations, by any agency?

10. Has any agency conducted tactical investigative or strategic analysis on the group? If yes, what were the results?

11. What has been and is the social, economic, political, and criminal climate in the area(s) in which the group operates? Are other groups perpetrating the same criminal activities? Is there a strong enforcement presence? Is there strong community opposition to the criminal activity (Sommers, pp. 34-35)?

Likewise the following items, though not all inclusive, are offered to assist in assembling strategic and tactical collection and analytical plans relative to assessing categories of criminal activity:

1. Statistical data: Occurrences of crime over past "X" years. Trends? Changes?

2. Geographical range of criminal occurrences. Where is it the heaviest? Weakest? Have there been changes? Trends?

3. Criminal techniques used: Modus operandi. Are there new techniques? Is violence a key or ancillary ingredient to the crime?

4. Known relationships between this crime and any other crimes.

5. Individuals and/or groups involved in this criminal activity: Is this enterprise shared by several groups, perpetrated by unconnected individuals or part of a monopoly? Changes? Trends?

6. Connections to "legitimate" business: Are businesses used as fronts for illegal activities? Are they used to launder illegal profits?

7. Financial: What is the estimated monetary value of this crime per year in this jurisdiction? Are profits rising or falling? What are the costs of doing business? Are the costs rising or falling?

8. Where do the profits go? Is there a criminal hierarchy to which a "tribute" is paid? Have there been changes in this?

9. What is the market for this criminal product? Who buys or uses the product? Is the market shrinking or expanding?

10. Connection to the government structure: Are there government agencies or bodies that regulate the activity area in which the crime is being committed? Are there any known or suspected connections between perpetrators and persons involved in these government agencies or bodies?

11. What has been and is the social, economic, political and criminal climate in the area in which the crime in occurring? Is there a strong enforcement presence there?

12. Has any agency conducted an investigation, tactical or strategic analysis on this criminal activity? If yes, what were the results (Sommers, p. 36)?

Though the foregoing items are generalized suggestions, the analyst must prepare the analytical and collection plans to support the proposed intelligence demands. The analyst will find that in time requirements become more refined and specific. Hence, the analyst should strive early on to generate both collection and analytical plans that are as specific as possible. To meet this objective, researching the criminological issue or investigation thoroughly but quickly is imperative. A generalized analytical plan and in particular collection plan will likely result in delay and in duplicative collection efforts.

The following analytical and collection plans represent actual works that were developed to support both strategic and tactical intelligence assignments. Moreover, it will become evident to the analyst the relationships that analytical plans have to collection plans, and the relationships that strategic analytical and collection plans have to tactical analytical and collection plans.

The first example presented is a work that combines both the analytical and collection plans together into a single composition. The plans were composed to manage and focus limited intelligence and investigative resources examining organized crime (LCN) involvement in the solid waste (garbage) industry, from a civil and criminal anti-trust perspective.

Example 1. <u>Racketeering In the Solid Waste Industry</u> [*]

In consonance with the major objectives of the State solid waste investigation, the following analytical plan is being formulated to provide organization and a systematized approach to the collection, collation and analysis of information required for a successful product delineating the current organizational arrangements of the solid waste industry and the extent in which racketeering exists. Analysis will focus upon the dynamics of the solid waste industry and focus away from the common images or patterns of criminality. This is not to say that as antitrust or criminal violations are recognized they will be placed aside. On the contrary, as antitrust or criminal violations are recognized, analysis will pursue those activities and determine why particular activities exist at points within the structural organization of the solid waste industry and what elements, either social or economic, support the presence of those transgressions. The results of the analytical study of the solid waste industry will produce an assessment of the industry, elaborating upon labor racketeering and additional matters, both legal and illegal in nature, that create situations not conducive to the viability of many enterprises, i.e., carting firms, and the solid waste industry.

Methodological Approach

First, a conceptual framework will be developed. Contained within the conceptual framework will be a conventional description of the organizational structure of the solid waste industry. The presented image will be compared against the organizational arrangements that currently exist in the State. This will familiarize the reader with the structural elements of the solid waste industry.

Also included in the conceptual framework will be the genesis of the current investigation with its current status and a presentment of what other investigations of the past have disclosed and the consequences of those investigations.

Because of the dimensions and complexities of this investigation, one association -- the Municipal Cartmans Association (MCA) and two personalities -- Carlo Rossi and Anthony Francci have been chosen as focal points of the investigation. The reasons for choosing MCA, Carlo Rossi and Anthony Francci will be discussed later in this paper. However, by focusing the solid waste investigation around the association and personalities, it is felt that major questions will be answered.

---

[*] Names of particular entities have been fictionalized to maintain confidentiality.

To develop the most accurate portrayal of the solid waste industry and racketeering as it exists within the industry, the following data will be extracted from information collected:

1. The organizational structure of the solid waste industry in terms of organizational arrangements.

2. The economic framework of the solid waste industry.

3. The size of the market in terms of clients or customers.

4. The size of the industry market in terms of licensed carting firms.

5. Landfills -- the number currently in use and their significance to the industry.

6. The regulatory inputs that the Public Utilities Commission (PUC) and Department of Environmental Protection (DEP) furnish the solid waste industry and the impacts of existing regulatory statutes upon carting firms.

7. The mechanism of the industry in terms of gaining entry into the solid waste industry and the methods by which carting firms remain viable.

8. The mechanisms found within the solid waste industry that challenge new carting firms from gaining entry into the industry or remaining viable in the industry.

9. The means by which carting firms expand their sphere of influence within the industry.

10. The means by which infractions or violations are redressed within the organizational structure of the industry.

11. The scope, characteristics and function of labor racketeering within the solid waste industry.

12. The specific aspects or structural elements of the industry that lend themselves to racketeering and the support means that maintain the presence of racketeering.

13. The role Teamsters Local Union No. 459 plays in the solid waste industry.

14. The role carting associations play within the industry.

15. The impact SCA and Browning-Ferris (BFI) have upon the solid waste industry.

In analyzing the data, the following questions will be examined:

1. Does the current market structure in terms of clients or customers support the number of licensed carting firms?

2. Does the economic or organizational structure of the solid waste industry make it a target of labor racketeering?

3. Employing investigative complaint-reports as a barometer, what types of complaints have emanated from both customers and carters?

4. How many "certificates of public necessity and convenience" (licenses) have been issued by the PUC between 1970 and the present? Of those, who were awarded licenses, were they in any way related to persons, at that time, active in the industry?

5. How many "certificates of public necessity and convenience" have been denied by the PUC between 1970 and the present? Those who were denied a license, what reasons were offered to support denial. Were they in any way

related to persons, at that time, active in the industry?

6. What types of racketeering and/or corruption exist in the solid waste industry?

7. To what extent is violence, threats or sabotage employed toward those who "don't play the game?"

8. To what extent is there an organized crime presence within the organizational structure of the solid waste industry?

9. Assuming the presence of organized crime, is it totally responsible for labor racketeering in the solid waste industry?

10. Would labor racketeering exist in the industry without the presence of organized crime?

11. How many carting firms have left the industry; and if obtainable, for what reasons?

12. Is there evidence of corrupt alliances between political structures and those persons engaged in labor racketeering?

13. Is there evidence of monopolistic control over particular geographic areas and/or particular segments of the market in terms of services provided to customers or accounts? Is there evidence of carting firms having to pay tribute to operate in a particular area?

14. What is considered to be acceptable behavior in the industry? How are deviations from the norm adjudicated?

15. What benefits are derived via affiliation with a trade association?

16. How has the emergence of SCA and BFI impacted upon the solid waste industry as a whole and the individual carting firm?

17. What are the derived benefits for employees belonging to Local Union No. 459? Is management the recipient of any benefits or liabilities via union affiliation?

18. How many carting firms have employees in Local Union No. 459?

19. What are the noted operational differences of carting firms located in Northern, Central and Southern parts of the State? What are the differences attributable to?

20. Do activities associated with the solid waste industry, that occur in the Northern part of the State, also occur in the Southern part of the State?

21. What are the positive and negative impacts regulatory agencies currently have upon the industry?

These questions are not meant to be all inclusive. As the study into the solid waste industry matures, probably more questions will be generated as information gaps appear. Consequently, this analytical plan will be modified from time-to-time.

Earlier, the Municipal Cartmans Association (MCA), Carlo Rossi and Anthony Francci were alluded to as focal points of this investigation/study. They were chosen for numerous reasons. First, because of the dimensions and complexity of the industry and the size of the staff dedicated to this investigation/ study, the scope had to be narrowed so not to dilute the image of the industry. Moreover, the limited investigative staff precludes an in-depth investigation, tackling the State as a whole. Second, MCA aligned carting firms, Rossi and Francci are known to be strongly involved in all aspects of the solid waste industry, legal and illegal. This has been reflected in intelligence reports, investigative reports and transcripts. Furthermore, Rossi and Francci have known links to organized crime through Local Union No. 459. Finally, it is firmly believed that by concentrating upon MCA, Rossi and Francci, all aspects of the solid waste industry will be touched upon as well as the extent and nature of racketeering in the industry.

Inasmuch as the Municipal Cartmans Association (MCA) is being focused upon via bid patterns, territory/customer allocation and complimentary bidding, relationships among the individual carting firms will be developed. Relationships will be translated through familial ties or business transactions, e.g., blood relatives and marriage, stock ownership, financial transactions and other business transactions. Provided relationships exist among MCA affiliated carting firms, the following questions will be examined:

1. What carting firms are affiliated with the Municipal Cartmans Association?

2. Do they present "threatening relationships (monopoly control, corrupt dealings, shifts in economic and political power)" within the geographic boundaries they conduct their services?

3. Are "values (equity, free enterprise, honesty, moral rectitude)" threatened because of the "threatening relationships" that exist?

With regard to data (extracted from the Civil Investigative Demands) examining bids, municipal and school board awarded contracts, the following questions will be examined:

1. Have MCA membership firms held municipal contracts with particular municipalities for an extended period of time, i.e., longer that five or six years through either competitive bidding or sole bid?

2. Observing municipal contracts held for an extended period of time via sole bid by the same contractor, what other carting firms, in terms of proximity, had the opportunity to submit a contract bid but did not bid? Why did they not submit bids?

3. Observing municipal contracts held for an extended period of time via competitive bidding by the same contractor, were competitive bids "in line" or out of line" in relation to the carting firm being awarded the contract? (Note: Some contractors may undercut other bidders thereby accepting a loss only to acquire the contract).

4. Upon the rejection of a sole bid by a municipality on a contract, what other carting firms bid for the contract against the initial sole bidder? What were the amounts bid? Is there a relationship between or among the subsequent bidders? Why did they only submit bids during the rebid?

The manner by which this particular analysis will occur is through:

1 . Determine which municipalities each MCA affiliated firms submitted contract bids between 1963 and 1977.

2. Collate all awarded contracts by municipality and contract period to each MCA aligned firm.

3. Collate all municipal contracts not awarded to each MCA connected firm.

Furthermore, the Municipal Cartmans Association will be scrutinized as an entity employing subpoenaed meeting minutes, letters, association constitutions and other information developed by the investigators. The product will be a composite of the organization.

Inasmuch as MCA affiliated carting firms operate out of the Northern part of the State, it will be interesting to observe non-MCA aligned carting firms, located in the North, and the types of garbage contracts they maintain. Furthermore, it will be determined whether or not those carting firms submit bids for municipal solid waste contracts. If they do not, the question -- why? -- will be explored.

A number of reasons exist for converging the sights of the investigation on Carlo Rossi and Anthony Francci. Rossi's name continues to appear in intelligence and investigative reports. For example, it is documented that Rossi and Fred Nardi were antagonists owing to Nardi's winning the two year contract of Roselle Park, in November of 1975, which had been held for a number of years by Waste Company Incorporated operated by Carlo Rossi. The contract bid submitted by Nardi was for in excess of $358,000. Nardi's firm, Custom Waste, was also involved in an attempt to bid on the New Brunswick garbage contract which Waste Company Incorporated was also involved in during 1975. The New Brunswick contract involved more than $2,000,000. Waste Company Incorporated won the contract with a bid of in excess of $2.1 million with a contract period of June, 1976 through May, 1981. Lastly, with regard to Nardi's relationship to Rossi, documented is the fact that according to an officer in Custom Waste, the Rossi's, among others, may have wanted Nardi killed. Although Carlo Rossi is not currently listed as an officer of Waste Company Incorporated, currently a subsidiary of SCA, he continues to act as an intermediary for Waste Company Incorporated. Through his father, Pietro (Peter) Rossi, Carlo is reportedly close to Ernest Pazzuto, a business representative to Local Union No 459, who has confirmed organized crime connections. Furthermore, it has been ascertained that Waste Company Incorporated has the largest number of employees represented by Local Union No. 459 in the State. Consequently, both the union and Waste Company Incorporated have a stake in each other that would naturally develop a close relationship. Recently, Mrs. Van Farro (via transcript) related that Carlo Rossi is acting as a mediator for Waste Company Incorporated. She indicated this with regard to her deceased husband having to "make peace" after winning a number of "stops" (commercial accounts) away from Waste Company Incorporated. Eventually, Waste Company Incorporated received the accounts back from Van Farro (Van Farro Carting).

Concerning other carting firms, sources in the carting industry indicate that Carlo Rossi controls Meadow Carting Incorporated and Essex Disposal Incorporated. Through corporate checks, Rossi only appears to be the registered agent for Essex Disposal Incorporated. Interestingly, on one occasion, observed was a Waste Company Incorporated garbage truck picking up a stop owned by Essex Disposal Incorporated in Hazlet. Essex Disposal Incorporated is located in Livingston, a considerable distance from Hazlet. In 1972, a George Post and his son, Richard, appeared before the Public Utilities Commission to apply for a Certificate of Public Convenience and Necessity for solid waste collection. Also appearing at the same public hearing was Carlo Rossi and his lawyer (name currently unknown) to challenge the awarding of a license allowing the son of Post to start his own carting firm. Consequently, the license was not awarded. Reportedly, Post and his son will be re-applying for a carting license within the next few months. Currently, information concerning Carlo Rossi is of the nature that many people within the carting industry know who he is, fear him and believe that he is strongly aligned with Ernest Pazzuto.

Anthony Francci, President of the Trade Waste Association (TWA), was chosen because of his close ties with Ernest Pazzuto and association with Tino Fiumo. Moreover, there have been allegations of Francci influencing other carting firms not to bid on specific contracts, i.e., Roselle Park and Piscataway School Board. Francci is the President of Trade Waste Association (TWA), which replaced the Central Cartman's Association. Currently, it is being hypothesized that TWA is a "front" for Local Union No. 459 since many of the carting firms of Central Jersey are not presently unionized. Interestingly, the vast majority of the Central part of the State carting firms are smaller in terms of personnel and equipment than those located in the North. With Francci controlling TWA and fronting for Local Union No. 459, this may be the manner in which Local Union No. 459 plans to extend its sphere of influence. Lastly, Custom Waste Service Corporation, currently operated by Irene Nardi, wife of the deceased, Fred Nardi, is reportedly being assisted by Francci in operating the firm. This association has been on-going since Fred Nardi's death on June 3, 1976 in New York City.

Included are two collection plans pertaining to Carlo Rossi and Anthony Francci, the purpose of which is to guide the investigative efforts of this study.

Figure 1

COLLECTION PLAN - CARLO ROSSI

The following information will be developed by the investigators assigned to this personality:

1. Develop a complete background on Carlo Rossi to include familial ties, business associations and organizational affiliations.

2. Determine the role Rossi performs for Waste Company Incorporated.

3. Identify all business holdings to include solid waste related, landfill and resource recovery related, trucking related, any miscellaneous interests in business enterprises.

4. Establish the type of relationship Rossi maintains with Local Union No. 459 and the strength and basis for that relationship.

5. Determine whether Rossi maintains strong alliances with either political or administrative structures (police, mayors, freeholders, PUC, DEP).

6. Determine whether Rossi maintains any organized crime connections. What is the strength and function of these associations?

7. Determine whether Rossi engages or has engaged in any corrupt practices.

8. Determine whether there was a relationship between Rossi and Thomas Varone, prior to Varone assuming his current status -- President of SCA and prior to Waste Company Incorporated becoming a subsidiary of SCA.

Figure 2

COLLECTION PLAN - ANTHONY FRANCCI

The following information will be developed by the investigators assigned to this personality:

1. Develop a complete background on Anthony Francci to include familial ties, business associations and organizational affiliations.

2. Determine Francci's business sphere of influence. That is to say, demonstrate the scope of the Anthony Francci Company, Incorporated and other solid waste collection, landfill or transfer related enterprises.

3. Determine other business interests Francci may have interest in other than the collection, disposal or transfer of solid waste.

4. Establish the type of relationship Francci maintains with Local Union No. 459 and the strength and basis for that relationship.

5. Determine whether Francci maintains strong alliances with either political or administrative structures (police, mayors, freeholders, PUC, DEP).

6. Determine whether Francci maintains any organized crime connections. What is the strength and function of these associations?

7. Determine the organizational structure of the Trade Waste Associates (TWA), its purpose, its membership and other organizational ties.

8. Determine whether tariff violations are in evidence with regard to Francci's scavenger business.

9. Determine the extent of public use of Francci's solid waste transfer station. That is to say, does Francci's transfer station provide services to other carting firms? If so, what firms use it and for what unit price?

This analyst estimates that a preliminary assessment of the solid waste industry will be completed during December, 19XX. Contained within that assessment will be a conceptual framework discussing the organizational structure of the industry with the different organizational arrangements and economic framework of carting firms. Additionally, much of the analysis on the Municipal Cartmans Association should be completed.

Shown should be the Association's spheres of influence in terms of municipal contracts and scavenging work and any patterns that may exist between collection firms and municipal contracts.

Lastly, information that has been developed on Rossi and Francci, at that point will also be presented. Modifications to either the analytical or collection plans will also be delivered at that time.

This first example represents an analytical plan and collection plans composed to focus specifically on two persons, their businesses and an industry. As the investigation progressed, additional collection requirements were generated and disseminated that addressed local unions, trade associations, industry market dynamics, insurance bonds and political corruption. Important to remember is that information requirements must support the needs of the consumer, i.e., Chief, intelligence unit supervisor or case supervisor.

The next example of an analytical and collection plan concerns organized crime violence. You will notice that organized crime violence is defined, and further refined, to mean homicides. Two major parameters are established; they are organized crime homicides in New Jersey and those specific homicides that occurred within a specific time frame. Moreover, specific variables to be analyzed are introduced by the analytical plan. The actual collection plan consists of itemized statements that identify the specific information requirements. Yet, to ensure continuity and completeness, a collection outline is designed. This facilitates not only uniform collection, but also collation and data entry, particularly if computer assisted analysis is available.

Example Two. Organized Crime Violence in New Jersey
Pursuant to a memorandum emanating from the Executive Office entitled, "Organized Crime Violence in New Jersey," the following presents a detailed analytical plan that will guide the development of the assessment that will examine". . .organized crime violence in New Jersey or affecting New Jersey."

Introduction
It has been suggested that organized crime groups are capable of limiting and controlling their need for violence. In addition, pointed out have been several forms of organized crime violence -- external, internal, and secondary. Associated with organized crime violence, particularly organized crime homicides, also have been distinct motives that are generally placed into the following categories: that which results from territorial and economic expansion, that which effects internal discipline and "justice," that which intimidates and/or eliminates witnesses or informants, and lastly, that which is employed to resolve disputes between or among individuals.

Between March of 1980 and January, 1983, observed have been fifteen organized crime related homicides, recently referred to as the "Bruno War." These deaths, attributed to a schism among members of the "Bruno Crime Family," presently represent a fraction of the organized crime related homicides which have occurred in or have affected the State of New Jersey in recent history.

In an effort to update information currently held within the Intelligence Bureau, on organized crime violence, and to meet the requirements of an assessment, a rigorous examination covering a five year period -- January 1979 through December 1983 -- will be undertaken to facilitate an assessment of homicides internal and external of organized crime groupings, both traditional and non-traditional. The purpose of the study, in addition, is to substantiate, expand upon, or challenge historical findings with fresh empirical data.

Methodology and Scope
The methodology will center upon the victims of organized crime homicides, and the offenders or suspected offenders of the homicides. The selection of organized crime homicide victims and offenders (and suspected offenders), will be predicated upon an exhaustive examination of the State's leading newspapers, and records of federal, state, and county law enforcement authorities. Also criminal history records both of the victims and of the offenders will be inspected

for criminal proclivities. A formal collection effort by intelligence officers in the field, by examining federal and county law enforcement records to collect specific information, must also be undertaken.

Moreover, numerous variables will be gathered and correlated against victim and offender related data, to discern any demographic or criminal behavior patterns. The variables will include the following:

> The age of the victims relative to that of the offenders, or suspected offenders.
> The sex of both the victims and offenders.
> The race and ethnicity of the victims in relation to the offenders.
> The marital status of the victims and the offenders.
> Prior criminal involvement of the victims and offenders, including their arrest records specifying the type(s) of crime(s) for which they were arrested.
> The apparent or known motives for the homicides.
> The type of weapon used, and the location where the victims were found.
> The status of each homicide case under scrutiny, and a statistical percentage of cases cleared by arrest and those that ended in a conviction.
> The organized crime associations maintained both by the victims and offenders.

To facilitate capturing, indexing, and correlating the volume of information anticipated, the Organized Crime Analysis Program (OCAP) will be employed to assist in the preparation of the assessment. The Computerized Intelligence Data System will be used to develop profiles of the victims. Appropriate charts and diagrams will be employed to depict the findings.

Organization

The arrangement of this assessment will take the form of a strategic intelligence assessment.

Collection Plan

To ensure the continuity and completeness in collecting specific demographic and criminal related data on victims and offenders, the following plan is submitted.

> 1. Identify all victims of organized crime (traditional and non-traditional) violence for the years January 1979 through December 1983.
> 2. Provide each victim's name, residence, age, race, ethnicity, date of the homicide, location of the homicide, type of weapon, and "crime family" affiliation.
> 3. Identify the criminal activities of each victim at the time of the violence.
> 4. What was the apparent or known motive for each homicide? For example, was the homicide a result of internal discipline, territorial expansion, intimidation, or dispute resolution? Explain.
> 5. Identify those missing persons who are suspected of being victims of organized crime violence, and provide their residence, age, race, ethnicity, and date reported missing.
> 6. What is the status of each homicide case, or missing persons case?

7. Identify the perpetrator(s) or suspect(s) of the violence.

8. Name of each perpetrator(s) or suspect(s) residence, age, race, ethnicity, and crime family affiliation.

To facilitate the collection of demographic and criminal-related information, relative to the victims and offenders a uniform format figures entitled "Organized Crime Violence Study," is shown in Figure 3.

A rather detailed collection plan is depicted in Figures 4 through 6, "Colombian Organized Crime Survey."* This collection plan, as most plans, holds a couple of very useful utilities. First, since this collection plan requests information within a narrow time frame, i.e., one year, the results of the data collection effort will provide a base line analysis. Second, in three years for example, the same collection plan, with obvious modifications, may be disseminated to support a comparative analysis of the Colombian organized crime problem within the same jurisdictional areas.

Moreover, it should be evident that many collection plans are enduring instruments that may be reused or institutionalized. This greatly diminishes the amount of research and critical thinking that goes into developing collection plans. For example, a standard collection plan may be developed to support the collection plan on persons and businesses affiliated criminally. This is illustrated in Section II of the "Colombian Organized Crime Survey."

---

* This plan was prepared by the Middle Atlantic Great Lakes Organized Crime Law Enforcement Network in 1987 to support a report for member agencies.

Figure 4

Organized Crime Violence Study
January 1979 - December 1983

Victim's Name: _____

Address: _____
_____

Age:_____Race:_____Ethnicity:_____

Crime Family Affiliation: _____Status:_____

Date of Homicide: _____

Location of Homicide: _____

Weapon(s): _____

Location of Body: _____

Date Reported Missing: _____

Criminal Activities: _____

Motive: _____
_____

Suspect or Perpetrator: _____
    (Circle One) _____

Address: _____

Age:_____Race:_____Ethnicity:_____

Crime Family Affiliation: _____Status:_____

Criminal Activities: _____

Status of Homicide Case: _____ Solved
    (Check One) _____ Unsolved

Court Disposition: _____
    (Explain) _____

Figure 4

Colombian Organized Crime Survey (Section I)

Respondent's Title and Name:_____Phone:_____
Division:_____Town:_____
Agency:_____State:_____

1) Are there Colombians residing in your jurisdiction? ( )Yes( )No( )Don't Know

If yes, as of 12/31/86, what was the estimated number of known and suspected Colombians?

_____
_____

To the best of your knowledge do these individuals have contact with the Colombian Cartel families? ( )Yes( )No( )Don't Know

If yes, to which families?

_____
_____

(Some of the following questions may not apply to your jurisdiction, if your response to question 1 is no or the estimated number of Colombians is low. If either case is true, simply record N/A -- not applicable).

2) In 1986, how many Colombians were arrested in your jurisdiction?

_____
_____

How many of these arrests were for attempted/actual assault or murder of a law enforcement officer?

_____
_____

3) During 1986, what was the estimate value of currency and property seized in your jurisdiction from Colombian investigations?
$_____

Continued Next Page

4) From the list below, CHECK those illigitimate activities in which Colombians are known or suspected to be involved in your jurisdiction. CIRCLE those crimes for which Colombians have been arrested..

_____ Absconder		_____ Fraud	
_____ Assault		_____ - Confidence Scams	
_____ Bribery		_____ - Credit Card	
_____ Burglary		_____ - Insurance	
_____ Clandestine Labs		_____ Immigration	
_____ Corruption		_____ Kidnapping	
_____ Counterfeiting		_____ Liquor Violations	
_____ - Documents		_____ Murder	
_____ - Money		_____ Obstructing Justice	
_____ Drugs		_____ Perjury	
_____ - Cocaine		_____ Racketeering	
_____ - Crack		_____ RICO	
_____ -Heroin		_____ Robbery	
_____ Quaaludes		_____ Smuggling	
_____ - Marijuana		_____ Stolen Property	
_____ - Other_____		_____ Goods for Payment	
_____ Explosive		_____ Tax Evasion	
_____ Extortion		_____ Terrorism	
_____ Financial Crimes		_____ Theft	
_____ Firearms		_____ - Auto Chop Shop	
_____ Forgery		_____ Other_____ Shop	

5) From the list below, CHECK those "legitimate" activities in which Colombians are known or suspected to be involved in your jurisdiction?

_____ Restaurant	_____ Travel Agency
_____ Bar	_____ Export/Import Co.
_____ Automotive	_____ Real Estate Co.
_____ - Repair Shop	_____ Notary Public
_____ - Auto body shop	_____ Insurance Company
_____ - Sales	_____ Translator
_____ Livery Services	_____ Other_____

If known, describe the connection between the "legitimate" businesses checked above and those illegitimate activities checked in Question 4.

_____

_____

_____

Continued Next Page

6) List regional and local groups that are associating with Colombians in your jurisdiction. If known, identify the group's role (transporting/distributing, money laundering, informant, use of "legitimate" business" in their association with the Colombians and the nature of their activities.

Group	Role	Activities

If for the following questions, your agency has collected data too excessive or detailed to list do not attempt to record it in the spaces provided. If available simply attach informational sheets (handwritten documents are sufficient) or briefly describe the data and provide the name and telephone number of an individual to contact.

7) During the past three years has your agency been involved in any multi-jurisdictional Colombian investigations? ( )Yes( )No If yes, record below:

Group or Cartel Investigated	Agencies Involved	Activities Investigated

8) What law enforcement methods of investigation or prevention have your department found most effective in the discovery and elimination of illegal Colombian activity?

9) Describe indicators, that is, characteristics that are unique to Colombians and that enable one to differentiate Colombians from other Hispanic groups.

Method Of Operation:_____

Street Slang/Language:_____

Continued Next Page

Tattoos: _____

Use of Weapons and Violence:
_____
_____

10) Describe Colombian color codes, symbols, or signs which have been discovered on packages or in a Colombian's possession by your department. A hand drawn sketch may be attached.
_____
_____
_____
_____
_____

Figure 5

Colombian Subject and Business Profile (Section II)

Name:_____(Include Photo)
      (Paternal)   (Maternal)   (First)   (Middle)
Aliases:_____

Date of Photo: _____   INS#:_____

Sex: _____   SSN#:_____

DOB/POB: _____   FBI#:_____

Height/Weight::   _____   DL#:_____

Hair/Eyes: _____   FPC:_____

Tattoos: _____   Other:_____

Criminal Speciality: _____   LKA:_____

Role in speciality, if drug related indicate amount and frequency moved (Omit those dealing 1 kilo or less a month):
_____
_____

Related to:_____Cartel family:_____
         (See Section III)
Distributor family:_____Local family:_____
Position in family/organization:_____
Last date of contact with Criminal Justice system:_____
Type of contact: _____Under Investigation
  (Check one)   _____Arrested
                 _____Bailed
                 _____Transferred to Correctional System
                 _____Deported

Three most serious crimes with which subject has been charged:
1._____2._____3._____
Three most serious crimes for which subject has been convicted:
1._____2._____3._____

Figure 6

Businesses Associated with Colombians

Name:_____ Phone Number:_____ Type:_____

Address:_____

Owner:_____
                                    (nationality)
Address:_____Phone Number:_____

Manager:_____
                                    (nationality)
Address:_____Phone Number:_____

Role of business in illegal Colombian activities (storage, money laundering,
business negotiations, transportation):

_____
_____
_____
_____
_____

Columbian Family Organization Chart (Section III)
    In this section, data regarding organizational relationships or familial relationships are
requested. This data may be presented by a hand drawn link chart, family tree structure, or sketch
of an organizational chart. If your information is not stored in this way a brief written explanation
of how you think the groups and individuals operating within your jurisdiction are connected or
related is sufficient.

Conclusion
    The importance of analytical and collection plans is their significance to the planning and
direction, collection and production, and analysis phases of the intelligence process. Each type of
plan plays a vital role that ensures that accurate, up-to-date, and relevant information is sought and
properly analyzed. Additionally, each type of plan provides collection and analytical management
over the two most labor and intellectually intensive aspects of the intelligence process. Without
these internal controls and directions, the managerial aspects of intelligence, the finished product
in the context of strategy and policy development would be weakened. Good planning begets good
collection and production.

References

Dintino, Justin J., and Martens, Frederick T.
(1983) Police Intelligence Systems In Crime Control. Springfield, IL: Charles C. Thomas.
Hulnick, Arthur S.
(1988) "Managing Analysis Strategies For Playing The End Game." International Journal of Intelligence and Counterintelligence, Vol. 2, No. 3, (Fall), pp. 321-343.
International Association of Chiefs of Police.
(1985) Law Enforcement Policy on the Management of Criminal Intelligence. Gaithersburg, MD.: IACP.
Johnson, Loch K.
(1986) "Making The Intelligence 'Cycle' Work." International Journal of Intelligence and Counterintelligence, Vol. 1, No. 4, (Winter), pp. 1-23.
Laquer, Walter.
(1986) "The Future of Intelligence." Current, March/April 1986, pp. 25-34.
Meyer, Herbert E.
(1987) Real World Intelligence. New York: Weidenfeld & Nicolson.
National Drug Enforcement Policy Board.
(1987) National and International Drug Enforcement Strategy. Washington, D.C.: Government Printing Office.
Sammon, William L.; Kurland, Mark A.; and Spitalnic, Robert.
(1984) Business Competitor Intelligence. New York: John Wiley & Sons.
Sommers, Marilyn P.
(1986) "Law Enforcement Intelligence: A New Look." International Journal of Intelligence and Counterintelligence Vol. 1, No. 3, pp. 25-40.

Chapter Four

Network Analysis

Francis A.J. Ianni and Elizabeth Reuss-Ianni

Analytical tools must be both useful and usable in accomplishing a particular task. Analysis has traditionally been viewed and all to frequently dismissed as a theoretical rather than an applied tool. However, any thinking about data that goes beyond the isolated fact or incident itself and imposes some history, pattern or theory, is performing an analytical function. Police officers, detectives and other law enforcement operatives are continuously "analyzing" or interpreting new information in order to clarify, expand, or replace previous information. Intelligence analysts are doing the same thing in a more systematic and self-conscious way although somewhat more constrained since they must usually depend on information or data developed by others. This observation is not meant to trivialize the role of the intelligence analyst, but to both assure and reassure those who perform the analysis and those who eventually must use it in an investigation, that while the analytical function is an abstraction, it nevertheless relies on the same facts and activities which structure the real world.

Any analytical technique, no matter how elaborate or elegant, will not replace good data or make up for poor or inadequate information. The truism that garbage in produces garbage out is generic to all analytical techniques. Those collecting the information and those analyzing it (usually two distinct roles as well as functions) must communicate and in a very real sense complement each other. Data collection and data analysis are not isolated functions although those responsible for each generally hold different titles in the organization, and each will suffer as a result of inadequate, infrequent or untrustworthy exchanges of information.

Recently, the mathematical application of network techniques in order to facilitate macro analysis of large social groups seems to have gone a long way towards complicating, if not confounding, its use and usefulness in law enforcement's attention to micro analysis of interaction in small groups. In its original inception, network analysis involved a representation of reality based on plotting points for persons, connected by lines to other persons (represented by other points), thus depicting a relationship between and among those so connected or linked. The resulting pattern of lines resembling a web or a net was characterized as a network. A total network would theoretically include the population of the entire world, since by definition, there is no one that is not connected to someone else. However, for the purposes of using network data to aid in a particular investigation, we can and should take care that we limit the range in which the net is cast. The reason for using network construction as a tool in intelligence analysis is not in the furtherance of some theoretical application, but in its usefulness as a means of developing alternate hypotheses to direct or facilitate current or future investigations.

At its simplest level, a network implies that one or more individuals interact with other individuals who in turn interact with still others. At this basic level, no assumptions must or should be made about the nature, scope or scale of these interactions or relations, only the fact of some relationship or interaction. In a very real sense, network analysis at this level is largely an art and not yet a science that should serve to guide not constrain its user. Network construction should serve as a tool that is comfortable, that works for the analyst while making optimal use of the data available, and not one that limits vision and subsequent analysis as a consequence of trying to fit facts into a proscribed structure or theory.

The metaphorical use of the term network has been common in anthropological literature since 1940, when Radcliffe-Brown first wrote of social structure as a "complex network of social relations" (1940, pp 1-12). But in 1954, when Barnes used the notion of network to elucidate his study of class, kinship and friendship in a Norwegian community, its significance as a tool for visual as well as conceptual depiction of the structure of relations became apparent.

Barnes's original description of a network is perhaps still one of its clearest and simplest.

"Each person is in touch with a number of other people, some of whom are directly in touch with each other and some of whom are not. I find it convenient to talk of a social field of this kind as a network. The image I have is of a net of points, some of which are joined by lines. The points of the images are people, or sometimes groups, and the lines indicate which people interact with each other". (p.43)

Thus, a network can be represented by a diagram; a map in which each person or entity is represented by a point, and in which lines are drawn between points to indicate when two people

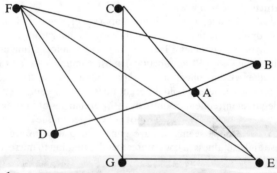

Figure 1

or entities are related, connected, or linked. A simple network can be mapped as in Figure 1.

Here, "G" directly interacts with "C", "E", and "F", but not with "A", "B", or "D". "A" directly interacts with "B", "C", "D", and "E", but not with "F" and "G". Of course, network maps may become much more complex than this, which prompted Barnes to point out that when the lines criss-cross one another often the "resulting pattern looks slightly like an untidy net and is appropriately called a network" (Barnes, 1968 p. 111). Barnes' notion of a network soon became quite useful to anthropologists as a means of depicting and analyzing the relational contexts which form the basis for social action.

As network analysis has developed and broadened in its application, attempts have been made to develop a consistent language so that those using the technique could be assured that they were speaking about the same phenomenon. Such standardization has not quite come about, but there is at least a minimally acceptable vocabulary for describing networks. Since terms cannot be relied on to be used consistently, any report utilizing network analysis should always clarify how specific technical terms have been used. Some of the most common terminology include:

a) Network. A representation of all the links, all the interactions among persons or entities in a defined social field where every point is reachable from every other point.

b) Partial Network. An aspect or an extract of the total network, based on some externally imposed criterion.

c) Field or Set. To look at a network from the point of view of one member or actor. While a network may persist over time, a set or field focuses on a particular individual, entity, activity, event or incident at a particular point in time.

d) Bounded Social Network. Implies that there are individuals or entities "outside" of the network or that membership is limited and finite.

e) Action Set. Relationships or linkages activated by one member of the network for a particular purpose at a particular time.

f) Groups. In theory, networks have no boundary until some specific criterion is imposed which sets boundaries. Groups are bounded networks in the sense that there are distinct insiders and outsiders. In a group, everyone has a relationship with everyone else. In a network, only some of the members have direct relations with one another.

g) Maps. The visual depiction, in terms of lines and symbols, of the network, field or action set.

h) Link. A connection represented by lines between two points suggesting the fact of some relationship. An arrow at either end of the line shows direction or flow of the relationship, event, product, information, etc. Arrows at both ends of the line depict a reciprocal relationship.

i) Points. A visual representation of individuals, groups, organizations or events. Also referred to as nodes.

j) Density. The proportion of theoretically possible direct links that do exist.

k) Cluster or Clique. Persons whose links with one another are comparatively dense, or a highly cohesive subset of actors in a network.

l) Connectivity. The degree to which members of the network are linked to each other through direct or indirect ties.

m) Path. An alternating sequence of points and lines, beginning and ending with a point. Also, a connected sequence of lines by which one can move from one point to another.

n) Path Length. The number of lines in a path so that the distance between two points is the length of the shortest path.

o) Position. How a particular point is situated in a pattern of ties or linkages.

p) Isolates. Points not connected to other points.

q) Centrality. A point location such that it is near to all other points or on the shortest path to all other points.

r) Matrix. A means of representing network data in the form of rows and columns equivalent to the total number of points and relations.

s) Multiplexity. The presence of multiple relations between units.

Charting or mapping a network and analyzing a network are two distinct but related processes as well as products. Once again, the eventual usefulness of a network chart is heavily dependent on the accuracy and comprehensiveness of the identification of the points or units and their relational content. Because of a kind of domino effect of interdependent units, mistakes in the units or points have ramifications well beyond that single error by suggesting relations that do not exist or failing to be aware of relations that do exist. For example, considerable care must be taken by the analyst to assure that individuals who are identified by their street names -- such as "Iggy" -- are not included until additional identifying information is obtained. This is a common problem with individuals identified through conversations picked up on "taps" or "bugs". Critical to the usefulness of network analysis is representation of the data in a form that facilitates and enhances analysis but does not preclude alternate or further interpretation or expansion as a result of additional information. A social network comprises all of the linkages or relations that connect two or more individuals. A network is represented by a diagram, or map, in which points most frequently represent persons, but can also be used to define an organization or any other entity or collective unit. Lines connect or link points to indicate where two or more individuals (or entities, etc.) interact or intersect. These linkages can be based upon kinship, friendship, occupation, business relations or any commonality that serves to tie, both literally and figuratively, one or more individuals to each other.

As we map or chart the network of relations, however, care must be taken that we clarify the nature and the timeliness of the connecting links. That two people are connected does not tell us anything about the form, content or permanence of that connection, but simply that at this point in time there is some connection between them. Taking the next step, or performing the analytical function is based on knowing or suggesting a reason for that linkage or relation and making assumptions about current or future actions or activity based on what is known about the nature, frequency and duration of that relationship.

Defining or delimiting a network is the first step in constructing a network. This is done by depicting all the individuals you know or believe to be somehow related or linked to each other as a result of a particular activity as points with lines connecting any two individuals who have a direct relationship. Suspected, but unconfirmed relationships can be noted as dotted rather than continuous lines. At this point, there may be little or no information about the reason for the connection, the identification of any roles (such as leader, broker, etc.), for particular individuals, or even a focal point to the network. There is simply information on the fact of an observed or reported set of relations among all those individuals contained in your network.

Thus Figure 1, for example, represents a network chart containing 7 individuals or units identified as "A" through "G". There are no characteristic shapes or designs to a network map. Rather the shape is dependent on the number of points and linkages. Moreover, both artistic and perceptual skills are involved in drawing network charts that capture the entire "net" of relations, particularly in a readable and usable manner. A matrix representation of Figure 1 would take the form as shown in Figure 2 on the next page.

In order to chart or map a network, boundaries must be drawn. While there has been much discussion in the literature about the importance of defining bounded (finite) or unbounded (infinite) networks, it is essentially a theoretical concern relying on mathematical formulas to account for linkages involving large numbers of points. Most investigations are not concerned with

Figure 2

	A	B	C	D	E	F	G
A	0	1	1	1	1	0	0
B	1	0	0	0	0	1	0
C	1	0	0	0	0	0	1
D	1	0	0	0	0	1	0
E	1	0	0	0	0	1	1
F	0	1	0	1	1	0	1
G	0	0	1	0	1	1	0

Matrix

0 = absence of direct link
1 = presence of a direct link

networks of such scale so that while theoretically everyone can be connected to someone else, the process of defining meaningful boundaries will always be somewhat arbitrary and subjective. Limits or boundaries are always and necessarily imposed by available and current intelligence or information, yet always open to expansion or contraction based on additional information. Since the analyst will primarily be looking at portions of total networks as a function of focusing on a particular person or activity, then networks will be bounded because of the focal point of interest. While network maps commonly depict individuals represented by points, those points can also be used to designate specific entities, such as key locations or institutions involved in a money laundering operation.

The most common type of network map is one that includes all interactions or linkages that are relevant to the current field of interest within a certain distance from a particular individual or point. Thus, a first order network would directly limit the focal point (referred to as "ego") to some other individual. Referring again to Figure 1, if "A" is the focal point of our investigation, then "A's" first order limits would be "B", "C", "D", and "E". "F", who has no direct link to "A", but has a direct link to "D" is a second order tie to "A", as is "G" and so on for third, fourth, and other order ties.

The two basic types of network diagrams are *egocentric* and *non-egocentric*. The non-egocentric diagram is a classical network map as depicted by Figure 1. Here one can clearly determine who is in direct or first order contact with whom, and who is connected through an intermediary or linking individual. An egocentric network consists of links drawn to a certain distance from a given individual or ego who is the central figure of interest in that network and may include a criterion such as links of economic transactions, face-to-face interactions, or common membership in an organization. A very simple egocentric network chart has been called a star (Mitchell, 1969). This chart also depicts first order ties from ego. In Figure 3, "B","C","D","E","F", and"G" are "A's" primary or first order contacts.

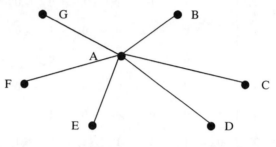

Figure 3

A <u>second order</u> egocentric network would contain some members who are not directly connected to ego, but to whom ego has indirect access because he can reach them through no more than one intermediary or connecting point. If we expand "A's" network to second order ties in Figure 4, "H" is connected to ego through "C", and "I" is connected to "A" through "F".

From this point, more creativity and artistry is required in order to better incorporate more information, and address more complex questions. For example, with "A" (ego) as our focal point of power, we may want to know about relationships of those individuals who bear a first order relationship to "A", but who may in themselves constitute power sources. Here we can depict a network with various centers or denser concentrations of relationships. Figure 5 represents such a network diagram.

Figure 4

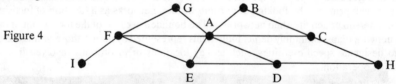

The next step is to identify *sets* of people on the basis of *links* provided by the network. A set differs from the network because it is centered on a particular individual and looks outward from his classification. Thus, while an organized crime network would include all "made" members, associates, and outsiders who may be peripherally involved as clients or providers of services, a set might contain only the "made" members of the organized crime group, or a gambling operation run by members of a particular clique or crew, or a labor union, some of whose officials are members or associates of the criminal organization. *Sets* are defined by the relations or activities which bring them together regardless of duration. Usually, of course, this will be some illegal activity or operation that is the basis for the investigation. It becomes more complex if some relations are totally legitimate and others illegitimate.

Figure 5

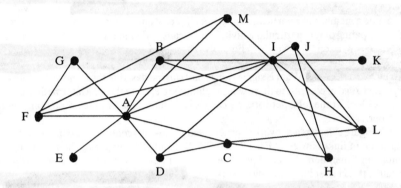

Figure 6

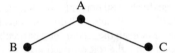

The notion of the *density* of a network is based on a measure of how *close knit* or *loose knit* it is. Since density is a hypothetical measurement, its usefulness for the purposes of intelligence analysis is limited. It is most commonly defined as the proportion of the direct links that are theoretically possible to links known to exist. (Barnes, 1968 P.117). For example, in Figure 6, ego "A" has known links to both "B" and "C", although theoretically there are 3 possible links; "A" to "B", "A" to "C" and "B" to "C". Since individuals in this network are not connected to everyone to whom they *could* be connected, it is not complete. According to Barnes formulation, the density would be 66.7 percent. The density formula developed by Barnes is written:

Figure 7

$$D\% = \frac{100 \times na}{1/2n \times (n-1)}$$

D = Density
na = # of actual relations
n = # of persons
1/2 n x (n-1) = # of theoretically possible relations

$$\frac{100\,(2)}{1/2\,(3) \times (3-1)} = \frac{200}{1.5 \times 2} = \frac{200}{3} = 66.66\%$$

More useful for our purposes is Barnes' notion of *cluster*. *Clusters* contain individuals, all of whom are adjacent to each other and also contained in a larger network of relations. Thus, *clusters* are sets of individuals with relatively dense linkages, while *cliques* are sets of individuals who are all connected to each other and thus have 100 percent density. An individual need not always be a member of a particular cluster or clique. Membership can change over time as a result of participating only in particular activities, or because other members may or may not be involved. The determination of cluster or clique membership is very important since those involved in organized crime networks are increasingly known to have varying allegiances to different groups and at different times. What is significant is that *clusters* describe those individuals who are always adjacent to ego in contrast to those whose relations to ego are through intermediaries. In addition, when we look at the total network, we can visually determine to which *clusters* any individual is a member.

Figure 8 depicts a network (Barnes, 1968 p. 118-119) containing a comparatively dense con-figuration of links between "F","G","H","I","J", and "K" suggesting the possibility of a cluster containing 6 members. Of the 15 possible linkages, there are actually 13 present. Using the density formula, this cluster has a density of 87 percent. In Barnes' formulation, a *cluster* is defined when there is a density of 80 percent or more, a somewhat arbitrary but still useful standard. If "A" is added with only 1 link to "F", the density is reduced to 66 percent which suggests that "A" is not a member of the cluster containing "F", "G", "H", "I", "J" and "K" since the density calculation has fallen below the theoretically established 80 percent level. Saying that "A" isn't a member of the cluster containing "F", "G", "H", "I", "J", and "K" does not necessarily mean that "A" may not still be a very important operative or even the leader for a particular activity. Rather it raises a variety of possibilities or hypotheses about the role or function of "F", for example, as a mediator between "A", who may be a member of another cluster, and his own cluster. Again, the reason for mapping or charting the linkages at different points in time and for different activities is to suggest alternate hypothesis about when and why different connections or relations are established, maintained or eliminated.

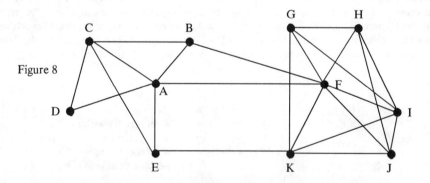

Figure 8

Barnes goes on to explain the usefulness of the concept of clusters as a means of identifying who is a critical actor or who is a peripheral member at a particular point in time. He writes: "Not all members of a cluster make the same contribution to its density. Thus, for example, in the cluster shown in figure 9, "Q" is linked to all seven members; "D", "P", "R", "T", and "X" each have six links, "S" has five and "C" has only four. We may describe "Q" as a core member of the cluster and "C" as a peripheral member. We may also describe "Q" as an essential member, since by removing "Q", the density of the set formed by the remaining seven members drops to 76 percent, which is below the critical value of 80 percent. None of the other members of the cluster is essential in this sense." (1958, p. 119)

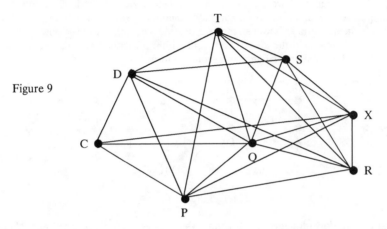

Figure 9

Within a network it is also often useful to distinguish the degree of *connectedness* between and among points, especially in terms of the flow of communication or authority. There are several standard network maps that illustrate the range of possible communication linkages. Figure 10(a) depicts a situation where there are 4 links, and each individual or point can reach another in two or less steps. Figure 10(b) is a chain with four links but where 1 and 5 can only reach each other through 4 intermediaries. In figure 10(c), each point is connected to two others, while in figure 10(d), each point is linked to each other.

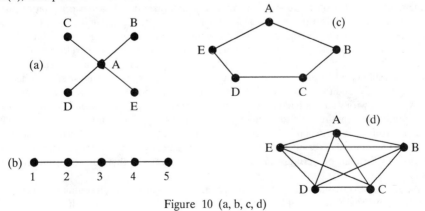

Figure 10 (a, b, c, d)

Disconnected groups can create problems for control and communication. The maps in Figure 11 (a, b, c, d) are illustrative of disconnected networks.

The process of depicting or constructing network charts and maps enables the analyst to provide a framework within which to describe interactions and identify members or participants. The intention is to depict a system in process and not to describe a permanent structure. While theoretically the first step in network construction is to determine its boundaries or limits, in an applied setting and especially during an on-going investigation, the analyst rarely knows the extent or boundaries of the network. If, however, the investigation is completed and no new information is expected or available, than the analyst can work within prescribed boundaries, and with a network that has taken on a final (if only provisionally) form.

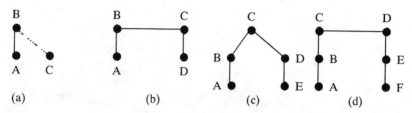

Figure 11 (a,b,c,d)

What can we do with network charts and what can network analysis tell us? Network construction provides a necessary framework from which to speculate or hypothesize about the function, frequency and substance of particular known or suspected interrelationships or linkages. Analysis occurs as we make assumptions or develop hypotheses about the content or meaning of linkages or relationships in order to arrive at the best possible explanation of known or suspected activity. The network displays the composition of fields of activity in which individuals participate or interact. Following the permanent or changing composition of networks or fields of activity and relations over time will provide important information on the changing character and process of group membership, cohesion, and disruption in criminal organizations. In a very pragmatic sense constructing network charts provides a method and means of not only managing and processing all available information but, perhaps just as important, highlighting missing information.

Once a total network is displayed, we can more clearly visualize and therefore explain or hypothesize when and how relationships or connections are operationalized and when and how relationships established in one context may be useful, unnecessary, or even dysfunctional in another context. In addition, we can better describe how relationships or contexts change or persist over time, with what individuals and in what contexts. Even more useful, would be the ability to predict or hypothesize about the impact on the network (or group, cluster, set) of the removal or "turning" of particular individuals (by death or arrest, for example). Further, mapping the effects of the removal of certain individuals either permanently or temporarily from particular groups or activities can be very useful in clarifying the nature of their function, power and influence.

A network has no center until a criterion of focus is imposed. Instead, it contains all the units and combinations that will or could constitute groups, fields, sets, or cliques. If a center is to emerge, it will be based on prior information or because a particular individual is the focal point of an investigation. Assume that a certain ego "A" is particularly important to an operation or group of operatives. "A" then becomes the focal point from which to look outward to the rest of the network or action set; from which to cast the net. As limits on the range of "A's" relationships or interactions in the context of a particular activity or operation are set, boundaries also become clarified, as a result of the quality and quantity of available intelligence.

The notion of *network centrality*, or proximity to the core of a system of linkages or transactions is useful in determining focal points of power and influence. Here ego's position in the center of radiating points or paths suggests increased power as a result of his ability to access if not also control, large numbers of paths or points. In addition, strategic locations at intersections of paths are suggestive of important functions such as "mediator", "broker", or "coalition builder". Centrality is measured by the shortest distance of one point to all others. To the extent that ego is close to all points in the network, he or she is less dependent on intermediaries for communication or control.

Typically, or at least traditionally, analysts have focused on identifying or labeling particular organized crime members in terms of fixed roles or positions in a predetermined organizational structure. This has severely limited our ability to analyze and hypothesize about the nature of changing patterns of relations between members and associates who, although holding no formally recognized position, are nevertheless important to the success of particular operations. Charting relationships or linkages through network analysis, however, enables us to better explain when individuals who are believed to hold particular positions in a criminal organization seem to deviate from expected behavior; or to interact with members of other criminal enterprises; or to associate with non-members at particular times or in particular patterns of relationships. Further, the focus on relationships among individuals enables us to demonstrate if not always verify the range of opportunities or constraints under which an individual operates because of his links to others who are also linked to other fields and action sets.

The principal use of a network chart in law enforcement applications has been to look at relationships or linkages from the point of view of a targeted member of that network, i.e. ego. Once ego has been identified as the focal point, the boundaries of the network become clear and it also becomes possible to display ego's field(s) of action and to determine the cluster(s) to which he belongs. We can also begin to develop hypotheses about ego's behavior and relative importance based on the strength of his network connections to others and why certain linkages are chosen in particular situations and not in others. Strength in this context refers to both the quality and quantity of interactions over time. Here again, the distinction between the value of looking at networks rather than enduring or presumed permanent structures (as in organized crime "family" charts) is in our ability to clarify empirically, the scope and scale of relationships as a process of power and control and as they occur in particular operations or activities. Ego's relative position in the network is also significant as an indication of his value as a partner with access to other groups, clusters or coalitions.

The charting of fields or action sets is another important dimension of network analysis. A social activity field or *action set* is defined and determined by its central focal point or ego. It is not permanent, and care must be taken that as we map the field, we do not include linkage or relations developed in other contexts or at other points in time. While all linkages are part of the total network, they may not be part of a particular field or action set. The field itself is composed of the actors immediately involved in the operation or activity under investigation. A field will change in different situations or as a result of the inclusion or exclusion of particular members. It also allows us to identify individuals whose participation in an action set will vary. For example, Figure 9 represents a cluster but occasionally, "T" might also become involved with stolen merchandise that is moved to various discount outlets by "P" and "X" because they have connections in the discount business. The action set is the stolen merchandise activity, which "T" controls. While "P" and "X" are involved, other members of the cluster are not.

The notion of *exchange relations* or *reciprocity* is another important aspect of network analysis. Here we are concerned with developing hypotheses about how individuals relate to each other through known transactions which have implications beyond a particular exchange or activity because it creates a set of reciprocal expectations and obligations.

Thus, an exchange network consists of actors or points, links as information, resources or items, and a choice of alternative partners or points in the exchange field. Tracing paths at different points in time can provide clues as to who is obligated to whom and the direction of the exchange or transaction. In addition, analysis of exchange networks can provide information on multiple alliances and exchange opportunities over time, as relationships established in one context are utilized in another. Finally, some exchanges occur between unconnected individuals in an exchange network when they are mediated by an intervening link or links. If the same mediating point is always used by the same actors and in similar transactions, then one can develop hypotheses about the relative power, influence or "respect" of that mediator. It may indicate that we trace out connecting points with the mediator as the central focus of an action set, rather than always treating him as an associate in the path of another ego's action set. Similarly, if ego always goes to individual "X" for a particular resource although other participants in the network could also provide that service or product, this provides useful information about the relative power and position of "X".

Network analysis can also provide some sense of how connected particular individuals are to each other and how this changes in different contexts or with the addition or elimination of certain individuals. A fully connected network allows every actor to reach every other one through some available path, while any disconnection in the network raises the possibility of disrupting communication or exchange as well as giving rise to problems of control. Analysis of the *connectivity* of particular networks or action sets is very important in terms of predicting change in activity as a result of the elimination or exclusion of particular members.

Clearly, there is information that network analysis can not provide. For example, network analysis alone can not provide information on the quality or intensity of relations. However, given additional information on the participants and on the frequency of their interaction, we can at least suggest alternative hypotheses on the nature and content of those interactions. For example, while a high interaction rate among three individuals does not necessarily imply a permanent or structured relationship among the three, it does suggest a degree of mutual trust or reliance based on prior experience and precedent.

Figure 12 on page 80 is a chart depicting an illegal drug network.

Analysis of this network should enable us to clarify terminology, techniques and procedures discussed earlier in this chapter. Moreover, such a network chart should assist the analyst to generate hypotheses concerning how a criminal enterprise operates and which positions or persons are more or less powerful or controlling within the entire operation, or within particular criminal activities.

We have reliable intelligence on connections among individuals that are alleged to be involved in the financing, supplying, transporting and selling of illegal narcotics. Again, recall that the use of mapping is *artistic* rather than *scientific*. It should be useful and adaptable to the information available in this investigation. Analysts should be able to manipulate the map visually in order to better capture key centers, intermediaries and clusters. Information charted on this map should be located at a specific point in time; hence a network chart should be dated. Changes in links or points over time as a result of the arrest or elimination of any of the actors or new intelligence information will not only change paths and patterns of relations but is important longitudinal data for observing the relative power and influence of individuals, groups and clusters.

The variety of information that can be included in the chart is limited only by the imagination (and possibly time) of the analyst. For example, relationships can be coded by different colors or numbers to suggest different contexts, contents and time periods, and arrows can be used to designate the direction of transactions. Several charts of the same network might be developed to highlight the different aspects of the individuals, relationships or activities under investigation, as well as changing patterns of relations over time.

This network is a map of all known relationships among particular individuals. Analytically, the task is to connect different groups or networks to each other through links between and among points. By displaying these linkages we may also identify groups or clusters or higher or lower density which enables us to tentatively develop hypotheses about relative degrees of power and influence among individuals and groups. While our intelligence is reliable in terms of demonstrating *some* linkage between identifiable points or persons, we are less certain that the linkage is *always* related to the drug operation. Similarly, while we know the identity of the individuals involved, we are *less certain* about the content and direction of the linkages connecting particular individuals and groups.

Points "A" through "Z", including numbers "1", "2" and "3" represent persons and the lines connecting particular points or individuals represent some known link or relationship. Suspected relationships are represented with dotted lines. The analyst may, of course, indicate the degree of verification of a "known" versus "suspected" linkage with different colored lines, or a code noting whether the basis for knowledge is observation, informant, or electronic surveillance, for example.

If the analyst wants to focus on individual "H" for example, and look at the network from the point of view of ego, then, of course, the resulting action set would include those points (individuals) and paths that are linked or connected to "H", by first, second, third, etc. order linkages.

The degree and range of connectivity is also important information. For example, "I" can reach "L" directly, but can reach "M" only through "K", "H" or "L". In fact "K" is the only person in the partial network that has a direct link to everyone else, which suggests that he may be the leader or the person with the most power (not necessarily synonomous) in the group.

Since there is only one known link between the motorcycle gang and the O.C. Family I, it is possible that other gang members may not be involved in this particular activity consequently it may not be worth an investigator's time to focus on gang members "O", "N", "M", "L", "I", and "J". In fact, it is possible that the path should connect "P", "K", "H", and "A", and those four points would then constitute a field or set for the purpose of the drug operation. Also "A"'s action set for the purposes of the drug operation would contain "D", "H", and "K". "A", "B", "C", "D", represent a cluster in the O.C. network "A", "B", "C", "D", "E", "F" and "G". It is possible that "T" may be a yet unknown member of that "family". "T" may also be the key player in the drug operation because of his position and connection to both the money and the drugs.

	O.C. Family I -	A, B,C,D, E, F, and G
	Motorcycle Gang -	H, I, J, K, L, M, N, and O
Details for Figure 12	Lawyers in Firm -	P, Q, R, and S
	O.C. Family II -	U, V, W, X, and Y
	Stock Broker -	T

Figure 12

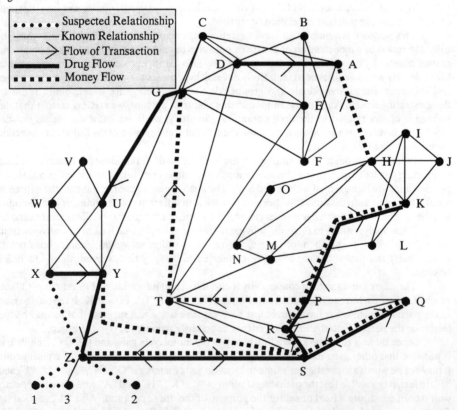

There may be multiple linkages among or between particular points or individuals. For example, we know that "G's" son is married to "U's" daughter and that "C" is godfather to "Y's" son. While knowing this is important in terms of assumptions which can be made about the intensity of the linkages, care must be taken that such a relationship is not by definition assumed to *always* link "C" and "Y". That is to say, that while the kinship link may be meaningless in explaining activity in the illegal drug operation it may provide very important information on the nature and strength of the relationship in other contexts, and other activities. It is critical that the two kinds of information not be confused.

While being part of a network provides opportunities because of either direct or indirect access to others, it also imposes constraints as a result of those same connections. It is useful as one follows changes in networks over time, or in different activities, to note consistent or random changes in participation by certain individuals and if the same individuals are always directly tied (first order ties) or tied through the same intermediary or intermediaries (second, third, etc. order ties). For example, in order to understand the workings of a partial network such as "H", "K", "P", and "I", it is equally important to take into consideration the configuration of links or ties that are several steps removed from "H". If we can develop a series of network charts over time and in the context of different activities in which "H" is always involved, such as selling stolen motorcycle parts, contract arsons, and part ownership in several "legitimate" motorcycle shops (through which he receives and sells stolen parts and bikes), then it would be very useful to determine if or how his relationships or links differ especially with "A", for example in any or all of those activities. Similarly, network analysis can provide useful albeit tentative hypotheses about why individuals chose certain contacts or linkages and not others among all or any possible relationships and when or in what context those choices are made.

In the drug network, there are a few cross linking relations, "T", "Z", "S", "Y", and "G". This suggests that, for example, while neither "T" nor "G" seem to hold central positions in their respective partial networks, they may be crucial intermediaries within the context of the drug network. Therefore, in any cost/benefit consideration of who to "turn", where to concentrate law enforcement efforts, where to place undercover operatives or who to eliminate in order to disrupt if not destroy this drug operation, those individuals must be viewed as vulnerable. It is possible, however that removing one of these links can have a detrimental effect leading to a stronger total network or one more resistant to law enforcement efforts .

The reason for using network charting in intelligence analysis is to get the best possible use and meaning from existing investigative data. Yet while drawing conclusions or positing definitive answers to questions is usually seen as the objective of any analytical tool, developing or generating hypotheses or inferences based on what we know about current relationships or linkages is equally important to on-going investigations. Network analysis is better designed to accomplish the latter than the former as a tool to both visualize and interpret a continuing and changing system of relations, alliances, and coalitions.

Network theory is an alternative to viewing relationships as essentially static roles or positions. It assumes that relationships at any point in time are a function of alternative choices made to select one point or path over another. It does not assume that an individual's choices are constrained by group membership, but that even as a member of a group, a person may more frequently or always choose to relate to some members and not others, and knowing which members of a total network are selected more frequently by another member provides valuable information concerning power, influence, and access to resources and leadership. Choice is then a function of position in an ever changing network of relationships, rather than some permanent attribute.

We began the description of network analysis by admitting that there is little consensus not only on the concept of network as an analytical tool, but on terminology and form. While this may produce some concern about methodological rigor, it is nevertheless an advantage in terms of allowing the analyst maximum creativity and flexibility. In the final analysis, network construction provides a framework to look at interactions and transactions as a function of both permanent and temporary relations. Within law enforcement intelligence analysis, it is an invaluable tool for amalgamating and translating the often disparate bits of information and observations into an understandable pattern of behaviors and social action, and determining the logic or "rules of the game" which structure those relations.

References

Alba, Richard D.
(1982) "Taking Stock of Network Analysis: A Decade's Results." Research in the Sociology of Organizations,Volume 1, p. 39-74.

Barnes, J. A.
(1954) "Class and Committees In a Norwegian Island Parish" in Human Relations, 7:1, pp.38-39.
(1968) "Networks and Political Process." in Marc. J. Swartz, Local Level Politics, Aldine Publishing Co.
(1979) "Network Analysis: Orienting Notion, Rigorous Technique or Substantive Field of Study?" in P. Holland and S. Leinhardt (eds),Perspectives on Social Network Research. New York.

Boissevain, Jeremy.
(1974) Friends of Friends. St. Martin's Press, New York.
(1979) "Network Analysis: A Reappraisal", Current Anthropology, Volume 20.

Boorman, S.A. and H.C. White.
(1976) "Social Structure from Multiple Networks",American Journal of Sociology 81: 1384-1446.

Burt, R.S.
(1980) "Models of Network Structure." Annual Review of Sociology 6: 79-141.

Cook, K.S. and R.M. Emerson.
(1978) "Power, Equity and Commitment in Exchange Networks." American Sociological Review 43: 721-739.

Davis, Roger.
(1981) "Social Network Analysis: An Aid in Conspiracy Investigations." FBI Law Enforcement Bulletin, December.

Fisher, C.S.
(1982) To Dwell Among Friends: Personal Networks in Town and City. Chicago, University of Chicago Press.

Jay, Edward J.
(1964) "The Concepts of Field and Network in Anthropological Research." Man, No. 177, September-October.

Knoke, D. and J. H. Kuklinski.
(1982) Network Analysis. Sage University Paper N.28. Sage Publications, Beverly Hills.

Laumann, E.O. et.al.
(1982) "The Boundary Specific Problems in Network Analysis" in R.S. Burt and M.J. Minor (eds.) Applied Network Analysis: Structural Methodology for Empirical Social Research. Sage Publications, Beverly Hills, California.

Lincoln, J.R. and J. Miller.
(1979) "Work and Friendship Ties in Organizations: A Comparative Analysis of Relational Networks."Administrative Science Quarterly 24: p. 181-199.

Mitchell, J. Clyde.
        (1969) Social Networks in Urban Situations.Manchester University Press, Manchester,
        England.
Radcliff-Brown.
        (1940) "On Social Structure." The Journal of the Royal Anthropological Institute, Vol.
        LXX, pp.1-12.

Chapter Five

Telephone Record Analysis

Marilyn B. Peterson

Introduction

The analysis of telephone records is a key tool for officers involved in any conspiracy investigation. This analytical methodology has, in some form, been utilized by investigators for decades. And it is, by far, the most often requested analytical product in law enforcement agencies across the United States.

In a narcotics investigation, for example, out-of-state suppliers or distributors can be ascertained by analyzing long distance telephone records. In a gambling case, the local bookmaker's "lay off" or "banker" may be identified. In a theft ring, calls between thieves and fencing operations can be found. With the aid of dialed number recorders or pen registers, local co-conspirators can be identified, thus broadening the individuals under investigation.

Telephone record analysis can be an exciting uncovering of the criminal puzzle and has aided in the investigation and prosecution of countless criminal cases.

Previous documentation of the methodology of telephone record analysis has been limited. Within law enforcement agencies, the methods are passed from senior investigator to recruit. Analytical training vendors have developed only rudimentary training on this topic. This chapter is a attempt to bring forward methodologies developed by the author in the course of performing telephone toll analyses. Where possible, varying methodologies utilized by other agencies are additionally noted.

The chapter gives a step by step process for doing telephone record analysis manually. The application of this process to computers is also discussed. The variations between telephone company record analysis and that of data tapes from dialed number recorders are discussed. Charting techniques and samples of charts and written reports are included.

Definition

Telephone record analysis is the compilation and review of telephone company, long distance service and/or dialed number recorder information to show the strength and patterns of relationships between the subscriber and numbers called. The underlying methodology of telephone record analysis uses the tools of association analysis, frequency distribution and link charting techniques.

The products of a telephone record analysis include a written report, charts, listings, matrices, oral briefings, conclusions and recommendations.

Background

The initial efforts at telephone record analysis are easily traced. Investigators, seeking to determine potential associates of a criminal figure, obtained monthly telephone bills of the criminal. The bills were then read and each different phone number recorded on a three by five card or a list. The investigator would then contact the phone company or other agencies to determine the identity of the subscribers called. Often, criminal checks were done on the subscribers to ascertain possible criminal links.

The net result was information on other individuals, but little on their associations to each other or to the original suspect. This method, while effective in cases involving residential phones with a limited number of calls, was hard to use in dealing with business phones. Businesses may have hundreds of calls per month to large numbers of different subscribers. To identify each subscriber is time consuming. By gleaning out potentially important numbers from the telephone records, the analyst or investigator can minimize the investigator's work.

Also, the subscriber identification method gives little information relating to the suspect's calling habits. This knowledge is important when an agency is considering placing a wiretap on the telephone. The cost of running a twenty-four hours a day, seven days a week wiretap is high. If the analyst finds that the suspect only makes calls between 6 p.m. and 10 p.m., Monday through Friday, that knowledge allows the department to run a more cost-effective intercept.

Further, a closer look at the records can give the investigator more insight into the relationships between the subscribers contacted. If a suspect's records show a pattern of calls at particular intervals, this could indicate a chain of command or other associational links.

Telephone record analysis bears a strong relationship to association analysis. The association matrix, used to determine the concurrent relationships of co-conspirators, is also a tool of telephone record analysis. Link chart techniques used in association analysis are also used in telephone record analysis.

	Figure 1 Steps in Telephone Record Analysis
1	Collect the records to be analyzed
2	Define the scope of the calls
3	Determine the frequency of calls by date and day of the week
4	Determine the frequency of calls to specific numbers
5	Determine the length of time spent on calls
6	Develop a primary listing of numbers called by frequency in steps (4) and (5)
7	Analyze frequently called numbers for patterns
8	Review records of collect and third party calls
9	Analyze calls by time of day of the call
10	Review all records for geographic distribution
11	Prepare charts if applicable
12	Make recommendations for further investigation
13	Combine all of the above in a comprehensive written report

Steps in Telephone Record Analysis
The basis of telephone record analysis is a thirteen step process which views and analyzes the records to provide the investigator with as much data as possible.

The following pages detail the steps in that process. Practitioners are cautioned, however, that each telephone record analysis is separate and must be treated individually. Going through a predetermined format with each analysis in an unthinking way could cause one to miss important data. Each analysis should be done with a questioning eye. This process merely represents guideposts to aid the analyst in covering all the possible information to be gleaned from the analysis.

Collect Records
Records to be analyzed may include copies of telephone company monthly bills, long distance line service bills (MCI or Sprint), car phone bills or copies of tapes from dialed number recorders or pen registers.

Telephone company bills vary among the companies providing them. In general, they provide a listing showing the date of the call, the time, the direction of the call, the number called to, the city and state called, the length of the call in minutes and its cost. Figure 2 shows a sample telephone bill. For charged (credit card) calls, they show the authorization number of the credit card and the number called from. The latter is generally marked with the prefix "FR" (from). For third party calls (generally without credit card use), both the number called and the number called from ("FR") are listed.

On typical telephone company bills, only long distance calls are listed. This limits the analysis to calls outside the immediate calling area. Telephone companies do keep records of every call made, even in the local calling area, but only once has this author seen those made available to enforcement. One way to pick up all outgoing calls is the use of a wire intercept such as a pen register.

When telephone company bills show little to no telephone toll activity, the investigator may want to inquire into alternative long distance service as possibly being used by the suspect. MCI and Sprint are two examples of long distance services available to residences and businesses. These companies have been willing to provide investigators with information on subscribers' calls. The type of information given is similar to that on a telephone company bill.

Mobile car phones have come into greater use in the past few years and the companies which serve them are another source of telephone call information. Even local calls are listed and charged for, so investigators have access to all calls made from such phones.

Figure 2   Sample Telephone Bill

No.	Date	Time	Place	Area-number	*	Min	Amount	T
Bell of Pennsylvania			March 21, 1983					Page 1
1.	2-23	959am	To Worthington OH	614-555-4010	DC	2	2.02	D
			FM SHLBVL IN	317 555-1552				
2.	2-23	253pm	Cincinnati OH	513 555-3722		1	1.62	D
3.	2-24	1051am	To Cincinnati OH	513 555-7731	DC	3	2.36	D
			FR WRTHGTN OH					

It should be noted that most records sought from these sources will require a subpoena or other formalized request. It is further important to make certain the telephone company does not make the subscriber aware of your interest in the records. A law enforcement agency can get the company to agree to not notify the suspect for a certain period of time; usually sixty to ninety days. If the investigation is a complex one, the agency must then send a second request to the phone company to extend the non-notification period.

The fourth source of telephone calling records is through a dialed number recorder (DNR) or pen register. Such a wire intercept usually records the following information and places it on a paper or magnetic tape:

- the date. May be regular calendar or Julian (1 - 365)
- the time the phone is taken off the hook (is picked up). This is expressed in hours, minutes and seconds
- the number called. Older DNR models only allowed up to 17 digits to be recorded. With the advent of MCI and Sprint codes, newer models track up to twenty-four digits
- the time the phone is placed back on the hook; also expressed in hours, minutes and seconds
- the length of time spent on the phone (time elapsed)

It should be noted that incoming calls are recorded with date, time off hook, time on hook and length of time, with no information in the number called field. It is important to include such calls in your analysis even though it is unknown by whom the call is made. Often conspirators may receive instructions or information on an incoming call which is then relayed to other conspirators via outgoing calls.

For the purposes of the remainder of the steps, it will generally be assumed that telephone company records are being analyzed. The same techniques and format can be used for MCI or Sprint bills or for car phone bills. Special attention to DNR records analysis will be given in a separate section.

Defining the Scope of the Calls

The first pieces of data to be obtained from the records are the total number of calls made and the dates between which calls were made. Simply, one counts each call record to get the total calls made. The dates are found by reviewing, in the case of phone bills, the first and last call on each bill, as calls are generally in chronological order.

Depending on the number of calls per month, you may want to work with three months to a year's worth of records. Another factor influencing this decision is the type of case being investigated and whether it involves a specific criminal incident or an ongoing pattern of crime.

On an average residential phone, there may only be a dozen toll calls per month. On a business phone, there can be hundreds of calls in the same period. And, if DNR records are used, the number of calls per day is considerably higher, thus making the analysis of data more complex and time consuming.

In general, it is recommended that any telephone record analysis with greater than 1,000 records be computerized. While many agencies now have this capability, others which do not can gain access to computerized analysis through working with state agencies and/or regional intelligence sharing systems such as WSIN in California and MAGLOCLEN in the Middle Atlantic area. Methods of using computerized telephone records for analysis are discussed later in this chapter.

Frequency by Date and Day of the Week

With the two pieces of data found under scope of calls - - number of calls and first and last dates of calls - - one can determine the average number of calls billed to that phone per date. By then counting the number of calls made on each day the records cover, one can see the frequency of calls per date. From this distribution, we can also see:
- what days of the month were without calls
- what dates had the highest calls
- if there were blocks of days without calls, which might signify out of area trips by the
    suspect

The information gained from this can be checked against investigative reports to see if peak calling times occurred on significant dates.

By using a calendar, the analyst can see what days of the week the calling dates fall upon. For a business phone, it is not unusual to have few to no calls being made on weekends and holidays. In a sports betting operation, peak calls are placed up to the games' starting times. Thus, the day of the week of the calls can be an important factor.

This exercise also brings significant calls to light. If the subscriber shows a general pattern of no weekend or holiday calls, then calls which are made on these dates should be brought to the attention of investigators.

Frequency of Direct Calls to Numbers

The telephone records are then reviewed to determine what specific numbers were contacted and how many times. This is a painstaking process to do manually. The simplest way to organize this data manually is to put each number called on a three by five card and arrange the cards in numerical order. For each card, the following data would be included:
- area code, phone number and state (at top of card)
- date, time, length of call, and direction for each call made to or from that number

A sample card is shown in Figure 3. You should note that the times are written in military (24 hour) time. This avoids the use of a.m. and p.m. and adds clarity to the analysis process.

Figure 3.

Three by Five Card

305	555-5555	FLA	
2/11/82	908	3	
3/07/82	1043	2	
4/12/82	1433	3	C
4/27/82	1307	5	

The three by five card method reduces the possibility of miscounting the number of calls made to a subscriber and also provides a basis for collecting other data in a logical way. Once these cards have been completed, those with a higher number of calls than average can be sorted numerically. These are the primary numbers and form the basis for the Primary Listing.

Calls by Length

Other important numbers can be those with high lengths of calls. By checking the call lengths on three by five cards, you can determine what the average length of this subscriber' s calls were . On an average, calls last between two and four minutes . Those numbers with greater than average lengths of time could be considered worth noting and should be added to the primary numbers list.

Primary Listing

The Primary Listing is derived from those cards which show a greater than average number of calls or longer lengths of calls. The numbers can be arranged either numerically or by decreasing frequency of calls.

The data included in the primary listing is shown in Figure 4. It includes the number called, the total number of calls made to the number, their aggregate length and the beginning and ending dates of the calls.

The number of numbers contacted which should be shown in the Primary Listing varies from case to case. In cases with small telephone activity, all numbers contacted can be shown. In larger cases, the analyst may pick an arbitrary cut-off (e.g., "three times the average number of calls") and list only those which meet that criteria.

With this primary listing, as with all pieces of the analysis, it is important to analyze the data shown. Listings and charts are merely compilations of data. It is the human interface that provides the actual analysis of the data by looking for its meaning. The analyst should look at the time spans listed. Are they similar to the beginning and ending dates of the records being analyzed? Or does the incidence of calls cover a smaller time span? Such information gives the analyst more insight into the relationship between the caller and the person called.

Figure 4.

Primary Listing

Number Called	# Calls	Total Length	Time Span
(305) 555-5555	20	97	2/11-6/24/82
(609) 999-8888	17	52	2/17-6/15/82
(716) 222-1111	12	34	4/15-6/24/82
(817) 333-9876	09	25	2/12-4/14/82

Any trends which are noticed here should be pointed out to investigators in the written report. A flurry of calls may surround a conspiratorial activity. An abrupt end of calls to one number , followed by the beginning of many to another, could be indicative of a change in contact person, or the location of the contact, or a change in territorial agreement.

Collect Calls

Each collect call to a criminal suspect is potentially significant. A collect call implies that the target wants to hear from the caller as he is willing to pay for the call. It suggests a closer than average relationship between the caller and the subscriber.

Collect calls come from both numbers called directly and numbers with no other apparent contact. For the purpose of the analysis, collect calls should be looked at in terms of frequency of calls, dates called, etc. Any collect calls of note should be included in the written report. In some instances, every collect call might be highlighted, e.g., when there are only a few numbers calling collect or if one suspects the collect calls are from conspirators in transit. In other cases, a primary listing of collect calls, following the Primary Listing example shown on the previous page, could be used.

Third Party Calls

This type of call includes credit card and non-credit card calls billed to the subscriber in which neither the number called to nor the number called from is the subscriber's number.

Only authorized persons would generally be making calls billed to a subscriber thus all these calls are important to note. It is also important to check both the "to" and the "from" numbers to determine if any direct or collect calls were made to or from these parties. As with collect calls, the frequencies, dates, lengths, etc. of third party calls should be noted. In a single subscriber analysis, third party calling activity provides a basis for link charting. See Figure 9 for an example of this.

Frequency by Hour

Just as the frequency of calls by date is done, so should the frequency of calls by hour be done. Either the phone records or the three by five cards can be used for this. A simple listing of hours (0100 to 2400) can be placed on the left side of a sheet of paper, with "tick" marks added for each call in any given hour. This is later translated into a formal calls by hour listing, an example of which is seen in Figure 18.

When the subscriber has a significant number of collect or third party calls, the listing might have separate columns across to the right -- "direct calls," "collect calls," and "third party calls." This enables the analyst to see if the subscriber's collect calls occur at a time of day which differs from the direct calls.

An even more sophisticated way to look at calls per hour is through constructing an hour/day of week matrix as depicted in Figure 5. This pinpoints the calling activity two ways.

Once the calls by hour have been identified, the listing (or matrix) should also be analyzed. What periods are highest in calling activity? Are there "regular" calling hours? This should be noted and calls made during "unusual" hours should additionally be listed. "Unusual" hours would be hours in which little to no calls are made. On a business line, this might be nights and weekends.

If you construct an hour/day of week matrix, are there peak calling hours on particular days? In one football betting investigation, for example, peak calling hours were between 1100 and 1400 on Saturdays and Sundays, plus between 1800 and 2000 hours on Monday nights. The calling pattern, then, substantiated the suspect's involvement in football betting. Further analysis of the pattern of calls made during those hours enabled the investigators to identify potential "lay off" persons whom the bookmaker was using. Thus, it was important to analyze calls within the hours

Figure 5

Hour/Day of Week Matrix

Hour	SU	MO	TU	WE	TH	FR	SA	TT
0100	-	-	-	-	1	1	-	2
0200	-	-	1	-	-	-	-	1
0300	-	-	-	-	-	-	-	-
0400	-	-	-	-	-	-	-	-
0500	-	-	-	1	-	-	-	1
0600	-	-	-	-	1	-	-	1
0700	-	2	1	1	2	1	-	7
0800	-	-	1	-	1	2	-	4
0900	-	9	2	1	3	4	-	19
1000	-	12	7	9	8	10	1	47
1100	-	15	10	12	11	17	-	65
1200	-	10	6	5	7	11	-	39
1300	2	9	7	8	6	9	3	44
1400	-	14	12	11	13	18	-	68
1500	3	16	14	16	18	20	2	89
1600	-	13	9	7	6	8	1	44
1700	4	6	3	5	4	7	-	29
1800	-	7	2	4	-	1	4	18
1900	1	5	4	-	1	4	-	15
2000	-	3	3	1	-	4	-	11
2100	2	-	-	2	1	2	-	7
2200	-	2	-	1	1	3	-	7
2300	-	-	1	-	2	2	-	5
2400	1	-	-	-	-	2	-	3
TOTALS	13	123	83	84	86	126	11	526

they were made.

Geographic Distributions

The final way in which telephone records can be analyzed is by their geographic distribution. Using the three by five cards, one can separate the numbers into their respective states to see what areas were in contact with the suspect.

The contacts by state can be listed or, if significant changes occur during the time span, can be placed within a matrix along with respective months in the time span. In a narcotics distribution case, for example, it was seen that several suspects had calls to Florida which ended, abruptly, in June, followed by increasing calls by suspects to New York. This led investigators to believe that the middleman of the narcotics had changed from Florida to New York.

Patterns

There are several ways to uncover patterns in telephone records. Time span changes were mentioned in an earlier section as one potential pattern. Calls might also be seen at the same time of day, day of the week, or day of the month. Two or more persons might be contacted in close order repeatedly. In another case, certain numbers would be contacted after placing calls to a foreign number.

Through reviewing the records relating to geographic distribution, certain patterns may be seen. In an investigation involving another narcotics distribution network, calls were seen to Florida, followed by collect calls from various points between Florida and the Mid-Atlantic region. The investigators then deduced that the collect calls were from the narcotics courier as he made his way up the coast with the drugs.

Charting

As was earlier mentioned, link charts are sometimes used to graphically depict telephone associations derived from a telephone record analysis.

Charts resulting from telephone record analysis are especially effective when the investigative results are to be presented to a prosecutor or in court.

In a single subscriber analysis, charting may be foregone unless there is a significant number of collect or third party calls. In that case, the charting can show these in a simple, yet complete manner.

The techniques of developing a chart for a telephone record analysis is similar to that used in association analysis. A modified association matrix as shown in Figure 6 can be used, with numbers contacted occupying the spaces names in "calls to" and subscribers analyzed occupying the spaces in "calls from."

The symbols used include circles (for individuals), rectangles (for businesses), lines with arrows (depicting the calls) between the geometric shapes. These are all shown in Figure 7. The lines are solid between direct or collect calls, and dotted when connecting a third party call to the billed subscriber.

Small circles are used on the connecting lines to contain the number of calls placed. If both direct and collect calls occurred, then two circles are used in the connecting line, with a "C" connoting the collect calls.

For added information, the time span of the calls can be taken from the appropriate listing and placed near the subscriber on the chart.

Various examples of link charts are given on later pages. Figure 8 shows a simple link chart which could be used in a single subscriber analysis to show primary numbers and some collect call activity. Figure 9 shows a single subscriber with interlocking direct, collect and third party toll activity. Figure 10 depicts a single subscriber analysis with heavy credit card calling.

Figure 11 shows a three subscriber, with direct calls to the same subscribers. Figure 12 presents a four subscriber analysis with some collect and third party calls interlocking among suspects.

Conclusions and Recommendations

It is the aim of every analytical product to provide both greater information and investigative direction to the investigator for which they are performed.

Figure 6

Telephone Record Matrix

Calls From:

Calls To:

Figure 7

Telephone Record Charting Symbols

Subscriber or person called is shown in circle

Arrows show calls made and direction. Solid arrows show direct or collect calls;
dotted lines show billing links of third party calls

Circle shows number of calls made   The C indicates collect calls made

One automatic recommendation which arises from a telephone record analysis is to
identify and run criminal record checks on the noted subscribers contacted by the suspect.

In the case of substantial involvement in calls by a subscriber other than the suspect,
coupled with a reasonable suspicion that the individual may also be involved in criminal activity,
the agency may wish to subpoena the telephone records of that individual.

On occasion, a recommendation may be made to initiate contact with another law
enforcement jurisdiction to proceed in a joint investigative manner. And, the analyst may always
encourage the investigator to collect and submit further data for analyzation.

Writing the Report

The final step in assembling a telephone record analysis is composing a written report.

The report is merely a summation of the findings uncovered in steps one through twelve of
the analysis. A sample of one such report is found in the Appendix.

Included in the report are listings of primary numbers, important collect and third party

Figure 8

Single Subscriber Link Diagram Showing
Direct and Collect Calls

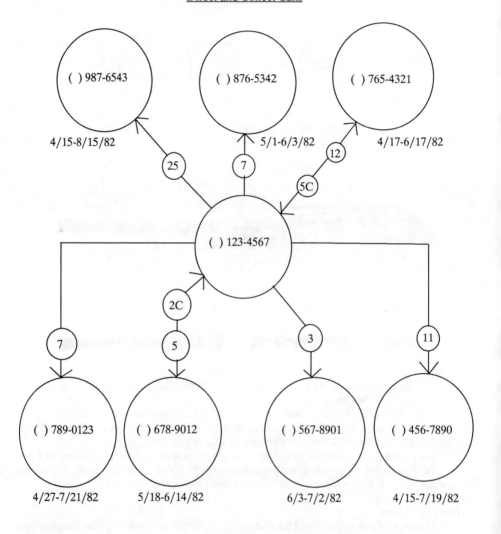

Figure 9

<u>Single Subscriber Link Diagram Showing Interconnecting</u>
<u>Third Party Calls</u>

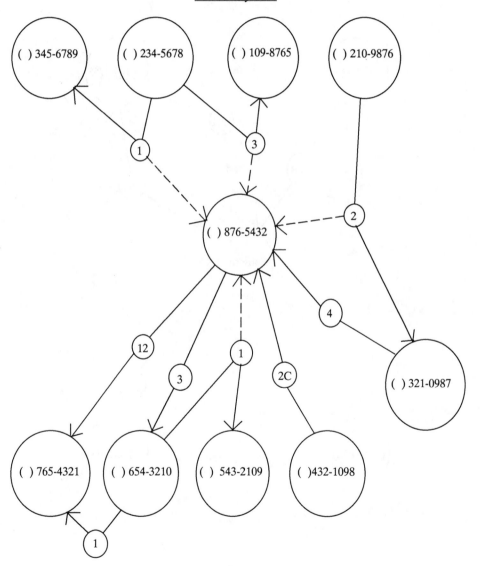

Figure 10

Single Subscriber Link Diagram
With Credit Card Calls

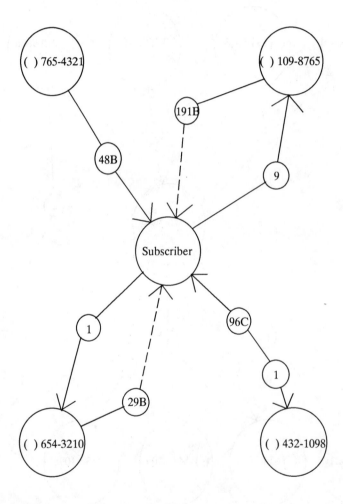

Figure 11

Three Subscriber Link Diagram
Showing Common Contacts

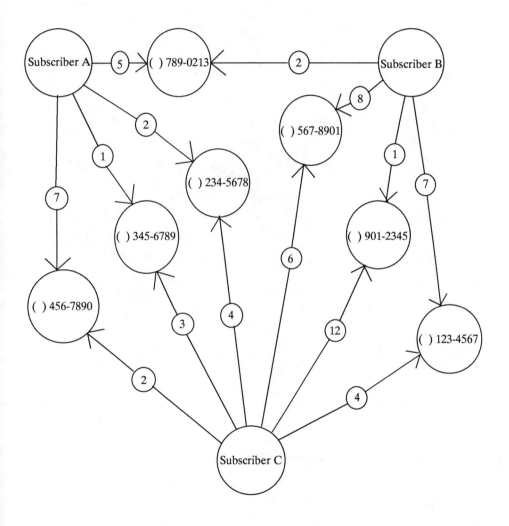

Figure 12

A Four Subscriber Link Diagram
With Collect And Third Party Calls

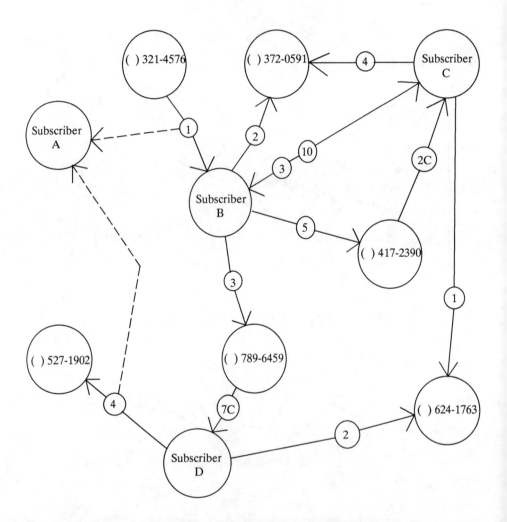

calls, calls by state, date and hour, and unusual calls. Each of these receives its own section and comments relating to data of interest to the investigator. The report is ended with the conclusions and recommendations.

The techniques of report writing are covered, in detail, in a later chapter of this text. It is important, however, to be aware of three factors in writing the report:
- the audience
- the data
- potential questions

The audience includes investigators, investigative supervisors, prosecutors and, potentially, judges and juries. Accordingly, the report should be written in concise, easy to understand language. Heavy reliance on academic/statistical language is not effective in such a report.

The report should be reflective of the data included. It should explain the listings, matrices and charts. This explanation does not have to be an involved one, but should guide the reader through the data.

The third factor is potential questions that could arise from reading the data. If, for example, the analyst writes that four calls were made on Saturdays over a three month period, the reader will wonder to whom the calls were made and when. All material included in the analytical report should be reviewed for such questions. All answers available to the analyst should be included. Questions not answerable by the analyst may form part of the investigative recommendations.

Multiple Subscriber Analysis

In a conspiracy case, agencies will often subpoena the records of several subscribers and forward those to the analyst. When this occurs, each step as listed on page 86 is taken for each subscriber. In addition, the records of the various subscribers are compared to learn:
- if any subscribers have been called by two or more suspects
- if patterns of calling exist among suspects and subscribers
- what hierarchical or associative inferences can be drawn relative to the associations
        among suspects and subscribers

If a conspiracy exists, there will be evidence of suspects contacting various subscribers. The knowledge that several conspirators are in communication with an individual can cause the agency to broaden the investigation to include that individual.

A hierarchical relationship may be determined by the associations found among suspects. If suspect A communicates with B, while B communicates with C, D, and E, A may be the head of the organization, effectively buffered from broader public contact by B.

In multiple subscriber analysis, charting is key. It is in this instance that previously unidentified co-conspirators may surface, as those relationships become quite evident through the charting process. Figures 11 and 12 are examples of multiple subscriber link charting.

Dialed Number Recorder Record Analysis

The analysis of dialed number recorder (DNR) or pen register data is similar to that of telephone company records, but has some distinctions.

To begin with, DNRs produce a printed tape which are cumbersome to work with, if one attempts to do the analysis directly from the tapes. A worthwhile intermediate step is to have the tapes photocopied, or listings typed from them. The latter puts the data in a much more workable format for analysis or data entry.

The second largest concern with DNR records is their number. By its nature, a DNR will record volumes of calls which toll records do not pick up. There are significantly more data to analyze.

The advent of independent long distance service providers created a challenge for the analyzation of DNR records. To make a long distance call, the subscriber must dial the provider (generally a seven digit number). Then, he may have a two or three digit access code. If he is not utilizing his home phone, an additional code may be required. Finally, the long distance number (ten digits) is entered. In total, twenty four digits have been entered. DNRs manufactured several years ago could only record up to seventeen digits. Following the twenty four digit scenario, one would end up with a string of numbers which did not include the actual phone number called except for the area code.

Some manufacturers now provide models that can record up to twenty four digits. They have also developed the facility for converting older models to the longer number strings. The twenty four digit capability covers most cases except where a subscriber misdials and notices his error while punching in the numbers. He can then punch in another code to indicate the error and then punch in the correct number, for a final tally of over 30 digits. Thus, even newer models can lose the last digits of a call.

Interpreting numbers logged on a DNR can be difficult for the analyst. Sometimes, it can be hard to tell what is going on, especially if two digit area codes are used or a long distance service provider is used. In the first case, some foreign calls use only two digit codes. Since the DNR picks up all numbers in a string, a two digit code would make the number harder to read. In the case of the subscriber using other codes including long distance service entry numbers and codes, the analyst must search through the string of numbers for the potential number called.

One potential solution to the long distance service problem would be to subpoena the company's telephone records and compare them to the DNR tapes. This could clear up any mis-interpretations that may arise.

Other difficulties inherent in the records are differences in calendar and time. The Julian calendar is used on some DNR models. This calendar numbers the days from 1 to 365. The analyst must convert the dates to 12 month calendar dates to provide an understandable picture of the time frame. Also, DNRs track minutes and seconds with exactness. Accordingly, minutes may be rounded off to avoid a lot of calculations.

Finally, DNR tapes do not identify the city or area being called. Analysts who work often with phone records begin to know what area code matches what city or group of counties but this takes some experience.

Other Techniques

Agencies across the country use varying techniques to perform telephone record analysis. Some agencies, for example, prepare charts for use by the investigator and give an oral briefing relating to the charts. Seldom do they complete a written report. Other agencies keep huge data banks of numbers analyzed and can tell the investigator if any number in the current investigation has surfaced in a previous investigation.

In some instances, an investigator will only want the analyst to look at calls made to certain telephone numbers which have already been identified as criminal targets. Or, they may only want to know the hours the phone is in use, in preparation for setting up a wiretap.

Some investigators or agencies are not familiar enough with toll analysis to know what they can get; what the analyst can do. The analyst should explain to the investigator what is available and give what is requested and possibly more. When an investigator sees what data a full telephone record analysis can give, the importance of the analytical function is better understood.

Computerization of Telephone Record Analysis

The greatest advance in telephone record analysis has been the development of computerized techniques. As is shown by the thirteen step process of telephone record analysis, several of the steps involve tedious counting work. The computer alleviates this tedium by counting and arranging the records in a cogent way and provides key summary reports on the data.

Computerized telephone record analysis is now being done on micro to mainframe computers. Many computer systems offer shelf software which can easily be adapted to analytical use. At the micro level, programs such as D Base III + and R:Base are used. Virtually any database relative software can be adapted to analytical use. Telephone record analysis in the computer is simple and time saving.

Telephone Record Database

One example* of a telephone record data base is a fifteen field data base for telephone company records and a separate one for DNR records. The fields of the telephone company records are shown in Figure 13. An explanation of each field and its relationship to computerized telephone record analysis follows.

1. Code

Each subscriber whose records are entered into the computer may be given a code, either two or three digits. This is done to eliminate the additional entry work of putting in that subscriber's phone for each record. It also differentiates between that set of records and any other records in the database. Thus, for a multiple subscriber analysis, each subscriber's set has a different code, giving the analyst the ability to look at all three records and determine common calling links.

2. Month

Month is a two digit numeric one through twelve. When the telephone records were originally computerized, month, day and year were in one field. The computer was unable to retrieve the records by month, so the field was re-defined to break it up.

3. Day

A two digit numeric from one to thirty one.

4. Year

A four digit numeric. It should be noted that records can be entered in one field for date and the computer separates the fields for us. Also, date can be entered as 2/24/84, which the computer then converts to 2/24/1984.

---

* This database was developed by the author and other analysts while working at the Middle Atlantic-Great Lakes Organized Crime Law Enforcement Network (MAGLOCLEN) project, a federally-funded multi-state information sharing system.

5.   Hour

A two digit numeric field for numbers 01 to 24. As was true with date, this was originally set up as a four digit 'time' field, but experience found that the computer would not then count by hour. The fields were altered to hour and minute. Data can still be entered as 1108 and the computer will break it into hour and minutes.

6.   Minute

A two digit numeric field for numbers 01 to 60.

7.   Area Code

A three digit numeric field for area codes, abbreviated AC.

8.   Phone Number

A seven digit numeric field for the phone number called.

9.   Length

A two digit numeric field for the length of the call.

10.   Direction

This is a one digit alpha field for the direction of the call. We use C = collect; G = charged; A = telegram; T = third party; F = foreign.

11.   Frequency

This field was used under an older release of our INFO software at MAGLOCLEN. It was always a one digit numeric, always '1'. It enabled the computer to count the records in the reporting function as we needed it to. A later INFO release eliminated the need for this field.

12.   Area Code 2

This is a three digit numeric field used in collect, charged and third party calls, for the area code called FROM.

13.   Phone Number 2

This is a seven digit numeric field used for the phone number called FROM.

14.   State

This is a two digit alpha field for the common state abbreviations. This is not entered with each record. One can instead, establish a separate database with two fields: area code and state. After records are entered, one can command the computer to relate the records entered in the area code/state database to the records. The computer then automatically places the proper state name into the records when they are reported.

15.   Day Name

This is a three digit alpha field for names of days of the week. This also is not entered to each record. In another separate database, one can establish a calendar which lists the dates of the past three years and the appropriate days of the week. As with the state file, this is related to the records entered, relating off the month/day/year field. Again, it is automatically placed in the records and reported.

An example of a print out from the above data base is displayed on Figure 13 on page 106.

DNR Record Database

With data from Dialed Number Recorders or pen registers, computerization faces additional concerns. A separate database can be developed for DNR records that covers the specific needs of this type of data. A listing of the fields in a sample DNR database is found in Figure 14.

As was mentioned in the section on DNR analysis, there are certain differences in the way in which data are reported in the DNR. For example, on some DNRs, the date is listed as the Julian date. Using the technique of relating databases mentioned earlier in this section, one can make a separate data base with a field for Julian date and a field for calendar date. By relating the database to the records entered, the computer automatically places the calendar date into the records.

Also, the DNR lists time by hours, minutes and seconds. So, the field previously used for time in the telephone company record database has to be expanded to include seconds. Also, work has to be done to allow the computer to add the seconds and minutes based on sixty seconds equals one minute, etc., for the totalling function to work properly.

As was true in the telephone company database, one can have two files for day of week and state name which are related to the records and then that data is automatically entered into the records.

There is one final field in the sample DNR record database which helps with difficult records. It is a numeric field of 30 characters into which one can 'dump' any strange number strings that are found in the DNR records. This is used for number strings that seem to bear no relation to telephone numbers. An area code or local long-distance prefix is found, for example, in a string of numbers greater than seven. Information on these unusual numbers may be important and is passed on to the investigator through the analytical process.

Computerized Reports

Once all the records from the telephone bills have been entered, they are checked for accuracy. Then, the data entry people have the computer generate certain reports on the data. The first report is a primary number report. This lists each subcriber called, with each call detailed. It adds up the number of calls made per subscriber and the total length of the calls made to each subscriber. An example of this type of report is seen in Figure 15.

The second basic report is a calls by day report. This lists the same data shown in Figure 15, but in chronological order, by date. The final basic report is the calls by hour. The calls are sorted and reported according to the hour and minute they were made. The computer adds the number of calls for each hour.

These three basic reports give the detail needed for a toll analysis. In addition, one can formulate various summary reports which the computer can run and give several types of data in summary. For example, the computer can give a summary listing of all subscribers called, the number of calls made to each, the total length of time spent on the phone and the first and last dates of calls. From that, a summary of only those subscribers with more than average calls or length of calls can be made, as shown in Figure 15. Another summary can give the total number of calls made by state (Figure 16), by day of week (Figure 17), or by hour (Figure 18).

The listing of primary contacts shows the most frequently called numbers or those which have been contacted with unusually long call lengths. The time frame of calls is important to note as some subscribers may be contacted in a concentrated time frame which may have some bearing on the investigation.

Figure 16 shows the geographic distribution of all calls. While the primary calling area of this analysis appears to be New York, New Jersey, Pennsylvania, and California, lesser number of calls to other areas should also be noted, particularly if they are out of country.

Figure 13

Calls By Number Called								
Code # 1	Date	Time	L	F	#2	Dir	St	Day
123 215 459-6720	3/23/88	1018	2	1			PA	Wed
123 215 459-6720	4/21/88	1027	5	1			PA	Thu
123 215 459-6720	4/18/88	1052	2	1			PA	Thu
			9	3				
123 217 320-1975	2/15/88	2153	2	1			IL	Tue
123 315 572-4391	3/18/88	1418	2	1			NY	Fri
123 412 687-7519	4/12/88	1821	5	1			PA	Tue
123 412 687-7519	4/14/88	1907	3	1			PA	Thu
			12	4				
123 617 235-1935	5/02/88	0925	7	1			MA	Mon
123 617 621-5970	6/17/88	1203	5	1	215 244-7390	T	MA	Fri
123	3/09/88	1422	4	1	212 371-2959		NY	Wed
			16	3				
			37	10				

Figure 17 shows the incidence of calls by day of the week. From this data, Friday appears to be the most important calling date. Weekend calls, because of their unusual nature, should be noted.

Figure 18 shows the distribution of direct, collect and third party calls over the twenty-four hour period. The numbers represent the aggregate of all calls made during the time frame analyzed. Another summary report developed is an hour/day of the week matrix which is shown in figure 5 on page 92.

New Developments in Computerized Telephone Record Analysis
   1.   Pamco/Epson

One DNR vendor, PAMCO, has come up with a computer aided program which could be of great help to analysts. Working with the Epson computer company, PAMCO has developed a DNR interface which puts the DNR data on a magnetic recording tape. This tape can then be loaded into a EPSON micro computer and placed on floppy disks. The data is then available for computer aided analysis programs.

Figure 14

DNR Computer Database

Field	Character Width	Contents
Hour S	2	Starting hour
Min S	2	Starting minute
Sec S	2	Starting second
Type	1 (alpha)	Incoming or outgoing
Code	3	Subscriber code
J Date	3	Julian date
ACl	3	Area code
PN1	7	Phone number called
L-H	2	Length in hours
L-M	2	Length in minutes
L-S	2	Length in seconds
Day-NM	3 (alpha)	Day of week
State	2 (alpha)	State called
Freq	1	Frequency (1)
Year	4	Year of call
Month	2	Month
Day	2	Day of call
String	30	Unidentified number string

Figure 15

Primary Contacts

AC	Number Called	Total Calls	Total Minutes	First - Last Call
( )	441-4000	25	81	1/11/82 - 3/27/82
( )	561-2359	21	36	1/26/82 - 3/21/82
( )	646-2100	12	54	2/01/82 - 3/24/82
( )	822-8482	09	47	3/11/82 - 3/29/82
( )	739-2690	08	12	2/01/82 - 2/12/82
( )	432-2954	06	29	1/11/82 - 1/15/82
( )	251-4420	04	20	2/13/82 - 2/24/82
( )	329-2874	02	46	1/27/82
( )	357-7496	02	35	3/13/82 - 3/17/82
( )	986-4592	01	14	3/27/82

Figure 16

Calls by State

State	Number Calls
California	44
District of Columbia	03
Florida	07
New Jersey	51
Pennsylvania	17
Colorado	02
British Columbia	03
New York	36

Figure 17

Calls by Day of Week

Day	Number Calls
Sunday	05
Monday	39
Tuesday	43
Wednesday	38
Thursday	47
Friday	86
Saturday	12

Figure 18

Calls by Hour

Hour	Direct	Collect	Third Party
0100	0	0	1
0200	1	0	0
0300	0	0	0
0400	0	0	0
0500	2	0	0
0600	3	1	0
0700	6	2	0
0800	24	7	2
0900	37	10	5
1000	54	9	0
1100	49	8	3
1200	34	3	0
1300	35	2	1
1400	67	9	3
1500	85	16	2
1600	58	9	0
1700	27	6	6
1800	13	4	5
1900	8	2	0
2000	7	3	2
2100	4	0	0
2200	3	1	1
2300	6	2	0
2400	0	1	1

2. Optical Character Reader

Optical character recognition (OCR) is another potential aid to computerized record analysis. While expensive, some OCR scanners can read several type fonts. The use of OCR scanners to input records could increase data entry efficiency.

3. Computer to Computer

All major telephone service providers have their records on computers. The phone bills investigators subpoena or request are simply printouts of computerized data.

As computer usage continues to grow, the potential for universal operating systems (such as UNIX) will also increase. Eventually, it could be possible for telephone companies to provide law enforcement with the data on floppy disks or tapes which could be put directly into the agency's computer.

4. Broadening Services

Telephones now have the capability to do several things previously impossible. Speed dialing, call forwarding, and banking by phone, will all begin to have a greater impact on telephone record analysis, particularly when working with DNRs.

Just as DNR technology has expanded to allow longer number strings to be recorded, so also must new developments occur to meet the challenge of broadening telephone services.

Analysts must, likewise, be flexible to new methods and technological developments. By pacing the changes, the analyst can continue to provide investigators with valid and timely telephone record analyses.

Conclusions

This chapter represents a detailed look at telephone record analysis in its varied forms. It shows both manual and computerized techniques for such analysis. From it, analysts and investigators should be able to provide as complete a telephone record analysis as their case requires.

In conclusion, it should be reiterated that telephone record analysis is easy to make into a standard format or formula where only the numbers change inside the form. But this is a disservice to the case and to the data. Caution should be exercised to approach each new batch of records as a completely new analysis. Otherwise, important facts will be missed.

Appendix

SAMPLE

Individual Subscriber Activity Synopsis

Smith Construction Company
237 Yale Avenue
Philadelphia , PA
(215) 907-2222*

The telephone records for the Smith Construction Company from January 1, to December 1, 1983 were subpoenaed and reviewed. The following data was taken from these records.

1.   Direct calls
Two hundred and thirty seven calls were billed to this number between January 1, 1983 and November 27, 1983. Eighty-eight numbers were called direct. The average number of calls made to a number was 2.5. The ten numbers called most frequently appear in the primary contact listing.

Figure 1

Primary Contacts

Number Called	Total Calls	Total Minutes	First Call	Last Call
201-502-3519	05	45	5/14/1983	6/19/1983
212-534-5326	05	40	1/20/1983	3/12/1983
212-534-5326	08	46	5/05/1983	8/19/1983
212-741-2700	53	428	2/04/1983	11/19/1983
215-799-8139	05	119	5/14/1983	7/07/1983
305-395-6805	12	25	2/05/1983	11/01/1983
513-766-0794	05	05	1/06/1983	1/26/1983
609-422-2605	05	31	1/20/1983	1/27/1983
609-422-5344	08	42	1/20/1983	2/25/1983
717-423-1412	06	18	1/20/1983	4/15/1983

2.   Collect Calls
There were 63 collect calls billed to this number. Those subscribers with more than one collect call are described in Figure 2.
The first number, in New York, also received 53 direct calls (see Primary Contacts listing). The Washington, D.C. number received no direct calls. The California number received one direct call on 2/9/83.

---

* All telephone numbers in this sample are fictitious.

Figure 2

Frequency of Calls Billed

Called From	Total Calls	Total Minutes	First Call	Last Call
212-741-2700	14	193	3/17/1983	7/1/1983
202-746-0332	02	004	2/12/1983	
203-881-8888	06	054	2/1/1983	4/8/1984

3.   Third Party Calls

There were five third party calls charged by 212-687-9503 to this number. They occurred between 7/11 and 7/13/83 and contacted four numbers: 202-532-9864; 305-371-3756; 305-371-3654; and 201-884-6252 (2 calls). The chart on the last page of this paper graphically depicts these calls.

4.   Other Unusual Calls

Other unusual types of calls were a "verify busy" call made 3/16/83 at 1955 hours by (717-558-1291 and a telegram, destination unknown, sent on 5/7/83.

5.   Calls by State and Foreign Calls

Calls from this number or charged to it connected to eleven states, countries, or provinces. They included: New York - 94 calls, Florida - 74, Ohio - 16, Colombia, S.A. - 4, Ontario, Can - 1, Washington, D.C. - 5 ,Wisconsin - 3, Virginia - 1, Connecticut - 1, New Jersey - 18, and Saskatchewan - 1 call.

The foreign calls were to the following numbers:

Figure 3.

Foreign Calls

AC	Number Called	Total Calls	Total Minutes	First Call	Last Call
( )	535-5860	04	57	4/27/1983	9/19/1983
( )	564-0519	01	04	8/13/1983	
( )	982-3600	01	14	8/19/1983	

6.   Calls by Hour

Calls were made by this phone between 0600 and 2400 hours. The times with the highest number of calls were between 1100 and 2400 hours. Calls by hour are shown in Figure 4.

Figure 4

Calls by Hour

0100	3	0600	2	1200	15	1800	15
0200	3	0700	4	1300	19	1900	13
* * * * *		0800	7	1400	20	2000	16
		0900	8	1500	21	2100	15
		1000	9	1600	19	2200	13
		1100	20	1700	17	2300	12
						2400	3

Approximately half of the calls made between 2400 and 1100 hours were made to five numbers. The following matrix indicates the distribution of these calls.

Figure 5.

Off-Hour Matrix

Hour	201 623 1412	212 475 2770	609 382 2605	609 936 3519	201 721 6805
2400	1	-	-	-	1
0100	-	1	-	-	-
0200	-	2	-	-	1
0300	-	4	-	-	-
	*	*	*	*	*
0600	-	-	1	-	-
0700	-	-	3	1	-
0800	-	-	-	2	-
0900	3	-	-	-	-
1000	-	4	-	-	-

7.   Calls by Date
    There were three hundred twenty nine days in the calling period. Calls occurred on both weekdays and weekends. There was an average of less than one call per date. Two hundred seven dates had no calls. Periods of four or more days without calls were:

1/09-14	7/23-8/2	9/20-27	11/15-18
1/28-2/3	8/04-14	9/29-10/6	11/20-26
2/26-3/2	8/16-8/23	10/08-11	
3/05-11	8/28-9/2	10/16-19	
7/14-21	9/04-11	10/25-31	

    The months of July (15 days), August (23 days), September (20 days) and October (21 days) had the most dates without calls. There were calls every day from March 12 to July 13. When we relate the states called by the month of the call, the following matrix occurs:

Figure 6

Calls by State and Month

Month	Ohio	New York	Colombia	Canada	Florida
Jan	-	4	-	-	15
Feb	4	8	-	-	9
Mar	-	8	-	-	13
Apr	1	27	1	-	11
May	-	17	1	-	7
Jun	-	21	1	-	3
Jul	-	8	-	-	6
Aug	-	3	-	3	1
Sep	-	7	1	-	-
Oct	-	5	-	-	1
Nov	-	-	-	-	9

It is shown in the above matrix that New York calls peaked from April to July. There was a concurrent peak of calls to Colombia, South America. The Canadian calls fell in the only month of five months in which a call to Colombia, S.A. was not made. It should be noted that calls shown on this matrix for July through November account for 85% of the total calls made during this period.

8. Calling Patterns

The date/time listings were analyzed to determine potential patterns or connections. Foreign calls were reviewed to ascertain calls made prior to or after certain calls on the same date. The listing shown in Figure 7 resulted.

9. Conclusions and Recommendations

a. All numbers identified in this report should be checked for subscriber identification and any possible criminal records of the subscriber.

b. Investigative reports should be checked to ascertain any activity on dates of particular note in the report.

c. Further data gathered should be submitted for other analysis.

d. The New York authorities should be contacted to obtain telephone records for (212) 741-2770.

e. A background check of this number's subscriber should be done.

Figure 7

Calling Patterns*

Date	Time	Called To
4/27/83	1253	212-747-5051
	1346	535-5860
	1952	718-977-3592
5/14/83	1829	212-799-8139
	2140	535-5860
6/19/83	0755	535-5860
	0942	212-799-8139
7/1/83	1927	212-741-2770
	1943	535-5860
	2221	212-741-2770 (collect)
8/13/83		212-799-8139
		564-0519
		212-741-2770 (collect)
8/19/83		212-747-5051
		982-3600
		212-278-4240
9/19/83	1325	212-741-2770
	2248	535-5860

---

* It should be noted that calls surrounding foreign calls are all to New York.

Figure 8

Third Party Calls
Smith Construction Company

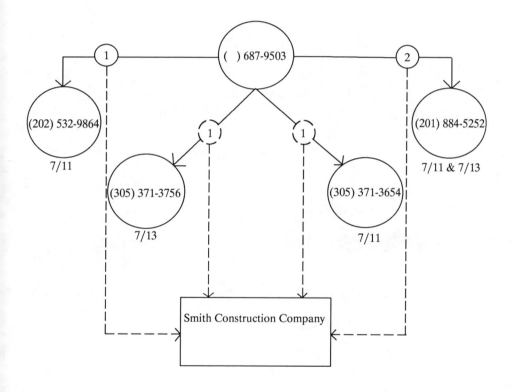

Chapter Six

The Analysis of
Tape Recorded Conversations

Roger W. Shuy

Language Crime

Much of the crime or alleged white collar crime that is ongoing in the United States is a crime of language. That is, no physical act is committed; no bodily injury takes place; no material is physically stolen. Instead the crime is one of agreement to do something, promising, offering or threatening. Linguists consider such events as speech acts (Searle 1969, 1979, 1983). There are several types of speech acts. One type involves performatives, speech acts which accomplish the act by their utterance. Such performatives include christening ("I hereby name you John"), arresting ("You are under arrest"), and employee dismissal ("You're fired"). Such acts are direct and clear. They are called performatives because they perform the event by saying it. Other speech acts are more indirect, such as: "Do you have a bathroom?" which usually serves to request permission to use the bathroom even though it contains none of the language forms usually associated with such a request (as in, "May I use your bathroom, please?"). Indirect speech acts are subject to misinterpretation by their hearers, depending on a number of factors including shared assumptions, culture and context.

Whenever a law enforcement agency tape records conversations of suspected persons, there is a potential for misunderstanding both in the production of the speech acts themselves as well as in the interpretation of the speech acts by other conversational participants, and by later listeners such as juries. As a result, investigators may sincerely believe that they have captured on tape incriminating evidence of a crime or an intent to commit a crime, when a more careful analysis of that conversation can reveal no such act or intention. An indictment based on such misperception can be wasteful of both prosecution and defense resources, time and psychological well-being.

To compound the problem, a trial jury faces the task of listening to these taped conversations in order to try to reconstruct the actual event, as it originally happened at some point later in time, after which additional knowledge is accumulated, and in a physical context, in the courtroom where the setting is quite different from the original event. If the taped language is indirect, rather than performatively direct, as is the case in most conversation, the jury will rely on either the prosecution's ability to convince them that a crime was indeed intended or committed, or on the defense attorney's ability to convince them that it was not. Years ago, communication theory averred that all communication consists of three components: 1) a Sender, 2) a Message and 3) a Receiver. These three components are analogous to the three types of understanding available in the courtroom.

The Sender of the message has his or her own agenda, intentions or purposes. The Receiver, likewise, has his or her own conversational agenda, intentions or purposes; often not the same as those of the Sender. Traditionally in court, the perceived meaning of the event under discussion is described and interpreted by witnesses for the prosecution and the defense based on the memory of the event as it happened.

With the advent of tape recorded evidence, however, a third component of communication theory also becomes available for analysis: the message itself. Now, there are three ways to understand the event in question--1) the prosecution's interpretation, 2) the defense's interpretation and 3) the text of the event itself. Similar possibilities exist in other areas of the analysis of meaning as well. In the field of literacy analysis, for example, at least three types of literacy criticism have existed for years. "Historical criticism" treats the poem or fiction under analysis by considering what it must have meant to the writer at the historical period when it was written--a Sender-based analysis. "New criticism" treats the poem or fiction from the Receiver's perspective, ignoring the historical intentions. New critics look for the meaning only in themselves: "What does it mean to me at this current time, regardless of whatever it may have meant to the writer?" The "Textual critic" takes a Message oriented analysis, ignoring both the Historical-Sender and New Criticism Message oriented viewpoints. The textual critic examines only the text itself, and looks for clues to meaning that are self-contained in that text.

All three types of analysis are useful and important, both to literature analysis and to courts of justice. It is important to know what the antagonists in a law case believe to have been true about the event in question. But it is also important to let the text (in this case, the tape recording) of the actual event provide its own clues. Such evidence, in fact, gets at the core of the areas of dispute between litigants. For example, in a criminal case in Oklahoma in 1982, a businessman was tape recorded by the FBI as he telephoned a former accountant who had left the company with shares in a racehorse which the businessman felt were his. The gist of the conversation was an attempt by the businessman to set up a meeting with his ex-accountant to discuss the matter. The tone of the conversation was firm, but not angry. During the conversational closing, the businessman asked about the accountant's son, whom the businessman knew well and had taken to races on occasion. The text is as follows:

Businessman:	By the way, how's Frankie?
Accountant :	Don't threaten my son!
Businessman:	I just asked how he was, I'm not threatening anyone.

On the basis of this sentence, the businessman was indicted and tried for threatening the accountant. The prosecution claimed that the sender of this message was making a threat. The defense claimed that he was politely asking about the health of Frankie. If there had been no tape recording of the event, there would have been no clear resolution of the dispute. Both parties sincerely believed what they apparently perceived to be true.

To the accountant, who was very much afraid of the businessman, having run off with shares in a successful racehorse, it might seem logical that he was being threatened. To the businessman, who felt wronged by the accountant's action, and whose conversation was an effort to get together to talk through their dispute, it might seem logical that these words about Frankie were no more than peace making politeness.

But since there was a tape recording, it was possible to put these isolated words back in context. There were no other hints of threats uttered by the businessman throughout the conversation although it is possible to see evidence of the accountant's fear throughout. It was clear from the conversational evidence that any "threatening" on this tape was Receiver based and generated, not Sender oriented. The message analysis, therefore, played a major role of describing how the charges brought against the businessman were generated in the receiver's mind. Although linguistic analysis cannot determine exact intentions, it can point out the clues to a person's intentions that are residual in the language that person uses. But, in order to be able to do this, an exact record of that language, the message itself, must exist and be made available for linguistic analysis.

The important point here is that there was an incredible waste of time and money in the threat case of the Oklahoma businessman. He was acquitted, of course, once it became clear to the jury that the accountant's inferences about the alleged threats were not based on anything that the businessman said, but were instead generated out of the accountant's fears about what he had done with the shares in the racehorse.

A careful analysis of the tape recording *before* the indictment would have saved both the prosecution and the acquitted businessman money, time and emotional strain. An indictment should never have been made at all. If, as Harris points out, the end product of intelligence is an informed judgment (Harris 1976, p. 3), one can only conclude that the judgment in this case was not informed.

Of the four major steps in the intelligence process: (1) collecting (2) evaluating for usefulness (3) analyzing for meaning and (4) reporting findings, this paper primarily concerns the steps of evaluating and analyzing, with implications for feedback to intelligence collecting as well. Thus, these first three steps in the intelligence process will frame the remainder of this paper. Since evaluation and analysis of tape recorded intelligence informs methods of collecting such information, the normal chronological sequence of these three steps will be reversed here.

Evaluating Tape Recorded Intelligence
In an effort to capture white collar and organized crime, various federal, state and local government agencies have been using surreptitious tape recording techniques for over a decade. The invention of the tape recorder has opened the door to a new kind of legal evidence with vast implications for both intelligence gathering and trial practice. Five evaluation tasks are suggested here.

1.   Distinguishing Tape Recordings From Transcripts
In terms of validity, academic researchers have long held the view that primary, first hand data are far superior to secondary, self-report data. It is the nature of the human condition that the actual event is stronger evidence than any later reports about that event. Thus, actual toothpaste purchasing practice is stronger evidence of consumer preference than survey reports of which toothpaste the consumers claim to purchase. The irony of this situation is that the field of law has historically relied heavily on such secondary, self-report or observational recall as primary evidence in court cases. Prosecution and defense witnesses thus report their perceptions of what happened, often in contradictory ways. Nor has the evidence of eyewitness testimony been free from controversy (Loftus 1979).

In contrast, video or audio taped representations of the actual event as it is happening can provide more primary evidence of a criminal event. There are several important dangers in such practice, however, particularly for the accurate evaluation and analysis of such evidence. Even though the actual event is captured on tape, there can remain questions about its adequacy, its completeness, its methodology, and its interpretation which may cause the evaluator to reject the evidence, at least at this point.

The fields of intelligence and law are extremely literary in orientation. The written word takes precedence over the spoken, as evidence by the court reporters written transcripts of the oral proceedings of a trial or deposition (Walker 1985). This literary predisposition causes attorneys, courts and intelligence analysts to move, as quickly as possible, to produce a written transcript of all oral presentations, including the surreptitiously taped conversations of suspected criminals.

As an index or guide to such conversations, written transcripts can be useful. But even courts of law claim that transcripts are not the evidence; tape recordings are. Thus, transcripts are usually not permitted during jury deliberation although jurors *are* permitted to follow transcripts while tapes are being played in court. As harmless as such practice may seem, the effect of the written word, accurate or inaccurate, in front of jurors causes them to hear on the tape what they see on the printed page. It is not unusual for the prosecution and the defense to submit competing transcripts in a criminal case, the judge often deciding that it cannot be determined which one is accurate.

The point here is that tape recorded intelligence is unlike other types of intelligence. For one thing, language goes by the listener very quickly and *many* listenings are absolutely necessary.

A common procedure for addressing the odious task of multiple listenings is to produce a written transcript, to slow down the rapid oral process for analytical purposes. Another common procedure is to have a secretary prepare such a transcript, since secretaries often do dictation and are familiar with such practice. Still another common practice is to then have the government representatives (agents, cooperating informants, etc.) go over the tape and transcript draft to correct it from their own perceptions of what occurred. As logical as such procedure may seem, it is fraught with dangers of perceptual bias. People who participate in the taped events are actually less able to determine what is actually on the tape than are well-trained total outsiders to the event. Defendants in criminal cases are no better able to use conversation after the event is over, simply because the average person does not have the metalanguage to describe his/her own language. Likewise, agents or surrogate agents who are wearing the microphone are easily influenced in their listening by their goals in taping a suspected criminal in the first place. That is, they may think they hear the suspect utter a given word or phrase simply because it is their goal to capture such words on tape. In a Nevada case in 1981, the prosecution and the defense were at total odds about one crucial sentence:

| Prosecution transcript: | I would take a bribe, wouldn't you? |
| Defense transcript: | I wouldn't take a bribe, would you? |

A simple machine analysis of this sentence could have made clear to the prosecution that syllable sequence argued for the defense's transcript and against the prosecution's. Representing each syllable as a dash, the actual words on the tape were as follows:

$$\overline{\quad}\ \overline{\quad}\ \overline{\quad}\ \overline{\quad}\ \overline{\quad}\ \overline{\quad},\ \overline{\quad}\ \overline{\quad}?$$

That is, the tape displayed six syllables with a junctural pause (comma) followed by two syllables, not the five-three sequence argued by the prosecution. This clearly indicates that the defense transcript was the accurate one.

The point here is that the evaluator of the intelligence offered by the tape had a schema in which the suspect said he would take a bribe. Therefore, the analyst heard it that way, despite the physical evidence to the contrary. The intelligence analyst must not fall into the trap of over dependence on the written transcript of an oral event. Hours of painstaking effort must be spent on listening to the tape itself before a transcript is used at all. The transcript is *not* the evidence.

Figure 1

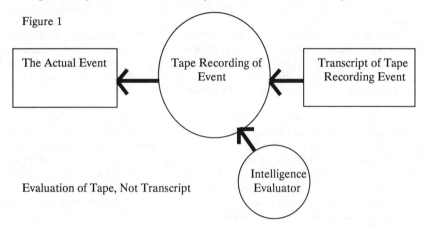

It is, at best, only a weak representation of it or guide to the tape. Accurate intelligence evaluation is made of the tape recording, not of the transcript of it, as Figure 1 indicates.

There is a real danger in relying entirely on the written transcript of a conversation to determine exactly what is going on. Transcripts do not specify to whom a particular speech is intended or who has heard it. Assuming that transcripts are accurate in recording the words that were said (and they are often not accurate), they do not usually provide the important clues to conversation such as: stress (loudness), intonation (question marking vs. statements), pauses (which carry their own form of meaning), interrupting (which can be a significant indication of speaker control and speaker intention), and many other things.

As defense attorneys try more and more tape cases, they are becoming increasingly aware of the principle of tape superiority to transcript both in their analyses of the evidence and in their courtroom presentations (Guiberson 1981). It is therefore crucial that intelligence evaluators examine the tapes rather than the transcripts. Since transcripts are useful as points of reference, and for reporting purposes, it is equally important that they be as accurate as possible in order to avoid being discredited by more accurate defense transcripts at trial and, more importantly, to obtain a fair and accurate indictment.

2.   Distinguishing Ambiguity From Clarity
When evaluating tape recorded intelligence, it is extremely important to predict, in advance, the possible variant interpretations of ambiguous or unclear conversation. This is useful for two reasons. For one thing, ambiguity is a very common occurrence in everyday talk. What may

seem very clear to the agent who utters a sentence may not be as clear to the listener. Undoubtedly this is the principle undergirding the second guideline for undercover FBI operations; "making clear and unambiguous to all concerned the illegal nature of any opportunity used as a decoy" (Heymann 1980, p. 138). It is wasteful of the intelligence agency's time, taxpayer's money, and the defendant's civil rights and emotional stability to misevaluate ambiguous language to suit the purposes of establishing criminality when it is possible that the defendant did not comprehend such statements in the same way.

Over zealous investigators and prosecutors may want to overlook such ambiguity, but it is the duty of the intelligence evaluator to prevent such possibilities from occurring by rejecting such evidence as ambiguous or by, at least, pointing out the possible variant interpretations to a listener. Good police work builds on unambiguous evidence and does not make a case in which defense attorneys can discredit the agency because of their overreaching inferences.

3.   Attending To Contextual Isolation

In cases involving tape recorded evidence, what is *not* said often turns out to be as important as what is said. Particularly when the case involves large numbers of tapes covering a lengthy period of time, and many participants, it is easy for later listeners to lose track of who should know what at any given time. A case in point is the Abscam case involving ex-Senator Harrison A. Williams, Jr., of New Jersey. Of the hundreds of hours of taped evidence in the Abscam operation, Senator Williams appears on a total of seven hours of tape. During the intervening meetings between other participants, a great deal of planning is done and information is shared. Consequently, when Senator Williams attends a meeting, much of the talk goes right by him. In the six meetings in which the Senator is present, 60% of the topics he introduces are requests for information. When a speaker spends 60% of his time trying to find out things that the others already know he is an "outsider" to the conversation.

Of the topics which the Senator *does* introduce in these conversations, not one of them is on the subject for which he was presumably being recorded, including stocks and money. The other meetings, when the Senator is not present, dwell on the topics of money and stocks, but these subjects are strangely lacking when he attends. An analysis of Senator Williams' responses to the topics introduced by others also supports the idea that he is an "outsider" to these conversations. Forty-two percent of all of the Senator's responses are feedback markers, "uh-huh," "yeah." Feedback markers are common in everyday conversation. Linguists assert that their meaning is not "I agree," but rather "I hear you," "Keep talking," or "I'll hear you out." To 24% of all topics introduced to him, Senator Williams does not respond at all. To 15% of the topics introduced by others, the Senator defers the topic to a later time. This leaves only 19% of the Senator's responses as full responses to the topics of others, and when carefully analyzed, none of these topics was supportive of criminality.

How is it then that Senator Williams was associated with criminality in this case? In the tapes when the Senator is not present, a great deal of criminal topics occur and promises are made about the Senator's possible assistance to the scheme by already co-opted participants. When the suspect is an "outsider" to the shared information, the already co-opted "insiders" can help the agents try to convince the suspect to perform the desired act. The peer pressure of friends and acquaintances is great. The desire not to appear ignorant or belligerent to an event which others may have agreed to tends to cause suspects to go along with something about which they may know very little. The danger, of course, is that the suspect, even though unwilling to do or say the act, will be conversationally trapped into agreeing with something he does not fully understand. This may happen even though he is not predisposed to do so or intends to do so, but out of social pressure or from false assumptions that his "insider" friends have done the proper thinking or preparation on an issue about which he is still uninformed.

It would seem only reasonable that it is not the purpose of law enforcement to capture people on tape agreeing to things they would not agree to if they only had the full and proper information, if they were not "outsiders." Isolation from appropriate or complete information runs counter to the FBI's second guideline, as noted above and to all good law enforcement work. Any evaluation of the intelligence collected by means of tape recorded conversations must consider carefully whether or not the target is isolated contextually from information which, if he had, would lead to a different interpretation of the event.

4. Noting Contamination Created By The Agent

Those who wear microphones and tape other people in criminal cases, whether government representatives or free-lancing individuals, can have only one purpose for taping -- to capture illegality, or language crimes, on the tape. The intelligence evaluator of such tapes must be very careful, therefore, to separate the eagerness and behavior of the person doing the taping and any co-opted individuals from the person who is the focus of the taping. In the process of creating a scam operation, government agents or their surrogates (such as Mel Weinberg in Abscam, Joe Hauser in Brilab or James Hoffman in the DeLorean case) necessarily use language to create the impression of illegal behavior. The resultant tape, therefore, may contain clearly illegal language and behavior. It is crucial, however, that the illegal language and behavior of the agents or surrogate agents not contaminate the intelligence evaluator's perception of the suspect's language and behavior. The principle of contamination (Shuy 1984) avers that if an outsider should overhear two people talking and one of them slanders a non-present third party, the person overhearing that conversation will generally recall the event as *both* participants slandering the third party. If one person tells a dirty joke, it is assumed that *both* people are telling dirty jokes. If one persons swears, both are remembered as swearing.

In the Abscam tapes relating to Senator Williams' case, for example, the ratio of swearing was seven times greater in conversations where the Senator was not present than when he was there. A major strategy of defense attorneys in tape case trials is to point out to juries that most, if not all, of the illegality, foul language, dirty jokes, etc., occurs when their defendant is not present. When such charges are true, it is better to assess this fact when the intelligence is being evaluated, before an indictment is made, rather than to see the case crumble embarrassingly because it was the government's own representative who accomplished the illegality or appearance thereof.

Whether or not it is efficient or embarrassing, the government does not want to produce an indictment which is not sound. If it is only the government's own representatives who are creating the crime and not the suspect, we should be able to separate this out at the intelligence evaluation stage. To do so, however, requires a painstaking linguistic analysis of the tapes, as will be seen later.

5. Considering Factors Caused By The Quality Of The Taping

The intelligence evaluator should also be aware of the fact that the quality of the taping, whether audio or video tape, can seriously affect the viewer's perception of innocence or guilt.

Although the FBI and other agencies often use high quality audio recording equipment, such as Nagras, the actual event of recording conversation surreptitiously is never optimal for capturing complete or audible language. Often such events take place in noisy restaurants or on city streets, where external noise sometimes obliterates large portions or even crucial individual words from audibility. Even sophisticated enhancement techniques may not improve audibility sufficiently, especially if the external noise, such as an airplane, covers a wide range of sound frequencies. Generally speaking, speech sound frequencies are at the lower range of the spectrum. The only external noises that can be filtered out of tape recordings are those that occur at the higher frequencies. But if a noise has a broad range of frequencies, filtering it out will, at the same time, filter out the simultaneous speech sounds.

There are, however, some things that an intelligence evaluator can watch for. Since audio tape recordings give no clear indication of who in a group is near the mike, or for that matter, even present in a room, the evaluator must try to determine whether or not a suspect can actually hear an agent's voice by attending to other signals. One such signal is whether or not the suspect is audible at all before and after the key words are uttered. If he *does* say something, is it clear that such speech is uttered to the person saying the key words, or is there a simultaneous conversation going on in another part of the area? There have been tape cases in which the government's charges has crumbled when it became clear that what the suspect said was not to the incriminating question of the agent, but rather, to a different person in another simultaneous conversation. In such circumstances it is highly unlikely that the suspect even heard the agent's statement, much less responded to it.

The intelligence evaluator should also attend to the participant location indicators of language. Such include words as "here," "over there," and references to the target as "he" or Mr. X." When a person is present to a conversation, that person is not usually referred to as "he." Such referencing is rather a clear indication that "he" is somewhere else and that the speaker is talking to somebody else about "him." A non-language indicator of participant location, of course, is the sound of footsteps. As one listens to hundreds of hours of taped conversation, one learns to distinguish certain types of movement sounds such as car-door buzzers, gear-shifting, footsteps or the body movement swishing picked up by a body microphone. Such sounds should be carefully assessed as an indicator of distance, and coupled with reference pronouns, locatives, and the presence of simultaneous conversation, used as indicators of whether or not the suspect is actually responsible for hearing the incriminating language uttered by agents or other participants.

Video taped evidence offers more clues to such relationships, but at the same time, it offers new problems. On the whole, video tape provides better data than audio tape, simply because there is more information available. One crucial utterance by Mel Weinberg in Abscam occurred during a meeting in a hotel room. Senator Williams was present, and if one were to merely read the transcript or listen to the audio tape, one might believe that the Senator heard Weinberg's statement and agreed with it. But the video tape showed Weinberg talking in one corner of the room with two other people while the Senator was on the opposite side of the room making a telephone call, reading an airline schedule and exchanging words occasionally with a man sitting next to him. All of this occurred during a room service meal, and meals are social events in which large group discussion normally breaks down into dyadic or tryadic talk. When the Senator said "yes," therefore, it is clear from the video tape that his response had nothing to do with Weinberg's statement, even though the audio tape picked it up sequentially following that statement.

Video tape equipment was developed to high qualities in recent years, but only under conditions of optimal lighting. Since surreptitious video taping would be obvious if the hotel rooms were brightly illuminated, the government has to do the best it can. Color video tape requires good lighting so most such taping is done in black and white, the lighting requirements for which are considerably less. As a result, elegant, modern hotel rooms, such as the Key Bridge Marriott in Arlington, Virginia (the sight of much of the Abscam video taping), has a dark and somewhat sleazy appearance. Rooms with normal lighting appear to be covertly darkened. Faces have dark shadows and are sometimes not even visible, making facial reactions difficult to determine. Where light comes through windows on speakers' faces (as in the John DeLorean video taping), the image blossoms, obliterating evidences of possible smiles, frowns, confusion and in some cases, even whether or not that person is speaking. These effects create difficulties for the intelligence evaluator, even though, on the whole, video tape evidence is preferable to audio tape because it provides more information.

The evaluator is, like the jury, at the mercy of camera angles and the agent's ability to manage optimal seating arrangements or prevent a person from standing in front of the camera. In such cases, the evaluator must rely on the audio track alone. In one Abscam video tape in the Senator Williams case, a vote was taken to determine whether or not the potential investment group would sell the investment once it was purchased and reinvest in another venture. The transcript shows the five participants saying "aye." The video tape, at that moment, does not show Senator Williams mouth. Careful listening to the audio tape reveals only four "aye" votes. The question, then, was whether or not the Senator's voice was one of the four. Voice quality eliminated three of the "ayes." The Senator's voice is bass, as was Angelo Erichetti's (the mayor of Camden, New Jersey). But Erichetti's face *was* visible and his lips moved at the time the deep voiced "aye" was uttered. The intelligence evaluator should have picked this up, but apparently did not. There were four votes at that point, not five, consistent with the Senator's passive, almost total non-involvement throughout that conversation. From other tape evidence, it is clear that the reinvestment scheme was a new idea to him. That meeting had been declared "an official meeting" earlier in the tape and the Senator was clearly unprepared to be involved.

The work of the intelligence evaluator for both audio and video tape analysis, is highly technical and it is not enough to rely on training in criminology or even on background knowledge in sociology or psychology. It is the task of a trained linguist who has worked with audio and video data, as we will point out in the following sections.

Intelligence Analysis

If the evaluation of tape recorded intelligence requires technical linguistic knowledge and skills, the analysis of such intelligence requires even more. Tape recorded conversation is unlike other kinds of data that intelligence analysts work with. For one thing, it is deceptively complex. A multitude of social, psychological and cultural factors drive a person's use of language. In addition, the inventory of available ways of expressing things is extremely large. Human language can be direct or indirect. Congressman Richard Kelly, in his Abscam case, indirectly rejected the FBI agent's offer of money nine times before overtly putting the money in his pockets (he never did accept the money verbally). This complexity of language use is not often understood by courts of law, some of whom appear to believe that language is habitually explicit and clear.

We begin by taking Harris' definition of intelligence analysis as "that activity whereby meaning, actual or suggested, ... is derived through organizing and systematically examining diverse information" (Harris 1976, p. 30). At the core of the study of language is the examination of meaning. Human conversation is functional, self-generated and interactive. That is, conversationists have something they want to say (their agendas and intentions), they say it themselves (they are not scripted puppets or actors) and they say it in a context involving other people. Meaning is traditionally associated with lexical items, or words. Linguists refer to such meaning as lexical or dictionary meaning. But there is a great deal more to meaning than words alone. This other kind of meaning is referred to as discourse meaning, that type of meaning that can be understood from the entire context, verbal and non-verbal, and which may be quite different from the meaning of individual words in isolation. For example, in the context of a baseball game, it is generally agreed that the words: "Kill the umpire," do not constitute a threat on that person's life. Although *kill* may be defined as "to make dead," in other instances, the American culture does not subscribe to this meaning in the context of a baseball game.

Therefore, the intelligence analyst's need to derive meaning, actual or suggested, requires understanding of the larger context of discourse meaning. The study of language discourse, referred to as discourse analysis, is a relatively recent specialization in the field of linguistics. As with other academic fields, linguistics has many types of analytical routines.

Phonological Analysis

Phonological analysis is the analysis of the sounds used by speakers of a language. Such analysis can be helpful to the intelligence analyst in determining muffled sounds on a tape, as in the example cited earlier -- ("I wouldn't take a bribe, would you?" versus "I would take a bribe, wouldn't you?"). Various high quality tape recorders and headsets can help the analyst immeasurably in such instances, but familiarity with phonological analysis is a key asset for the analyst. In general, however, phonological analysis is reserved for certain places on the tape where questionable sounds occur. It would be wasteful of time to carry out phonological analysis on an entire conversation.

Syntactic Analysis

Syntactic analysis is common in linguistics. It operates on the sentence level and helps to disambiguate grammatical relationships. Perhaps the most useful aspect of syntactic analysis for taped conversations is that of anaphora, or referencing. For example, when a speaker says: "I want *you* to do it," the "you" is potentially ambiguous, since "you" can refer to one person present (the person being addressed), to more than one person present ("you" has the same singular and plural forms), or to some combination of persons present or absent with whom the addressee is associated (his company, his family or his group). The same can be said, of course, for the referencing of "your," "yours," "our," "we" and "ours." Even the pronoun "I" has potential for ambiguity, particularly when a speaker uses "I," "me," "my," or "mine" when he refers to his role as employer or officer in a company rather than to his personal self. There are other anaphoric markers in English as well. Nouns refer to other nouns. Verbs, especially the dummy verb "do" (as in "I'll pay it if you *do*"), serve as anaphora.

Again, it would be wasteful of time and energy to perform a syntactic analysis on all the taped conversation, but such analysis can be extremely useful for specific problem areas, especially where attribution plays a crucial role.

Discourse Analysis
Whereas both phonological and syntactic analysis can help clarify ambiguous micro level sounds and referencing, discourse analysis approaches the taped conversation from a more holistic, macro perspective. There are several types of discourse analysis, or sub-analyses. Those which have proven more useful in analyzing tape conversations used as evidence in presumed criminal activity are: topic analysis, response analysis, topic-flow analysis, language function analysis and contrastive analysis.

1.   Topic Analysis
Probably the most crucial unit of measure in a conversation is topic. At issue is who introduces which topics and whether or not they are recycled or reintroduced at a later time in the conversation. This is important as one of the clues to a speaker's intentions. Earlier we noted that conversation is functional and self-generated. That is, people talk about what they have on their minds, their agendas. If a suspect is thought to be predisposed to solicit the murder of someone, it would be natural to expect that person to introduce such a topic in a conversation with an agent who represents himself as a hired killer. In the case of Texas vs. T. Cullen Davis (1979), for example, Davis was indicted for solicitation to murder on the basis of two taped conversations in which he never introduced the topic of murder.

Such evidence, by itself, may not be enough to exonerate a person, but it offers strong clues to his intentions. The topics which Davis did introduce had to do with the ostensible reason for the meeting (selling a gun) with the other man's employer and with various small talk.

Topic recycling is another clue to a speaker's intentions. It should be clear that no linguistic analysis can determine, beyond doubt, what a person's intentions are. The best that can be done is to find *clues* to such intentions that are situated in the tape recorded speech. Recycling a topic is one such clue. If a topic is brought up over and over again, the analyst can be relatively certain of two things. For one thing, it is clear that such a topic is foremost in the speaker's mind, or else he would not keep introducing it. Secondly, the recycling of a topic is a clear indication that the topic being recycled has not yet been resolved. The cooperative principle in conversation (Grice 1975) specifies four maxims of conversation, the maxims of relevance, quantity, quality and manner. These maxims note that people are cooperative in conversation to the extent that they do not reintroduce resolved topics. Therefore, if the agent's agenda is to get the suspect to incriminate himself on a specific topic, the very fact that the agent recycles this topic may be evidence that he has not yet received what he considers to be a sufficiently incriminating response.

Topic analysis is also a useful measure of conversational dominance. One can expect, in a normal everyday conversation between two equals, that the topics will be more or less evenly distributed in quantity. A conversation in which one person introduces 80 percent of the topics and the other person only 20 percent results in an asymmetrical relationship. If the agent dominates the topic introductions, he is providing little opportunity for the suspect to self-incriminate. Research in classroom interaction as well as police interrogation has shown that there is a truth-value correlation to the type of question asked by a teacher or police interrogator. The more open ended the question, the more the student or suspect self generates his or her own knowledge. Figure 2 illustrates this scale of truth-value.

As Figure 2 indicates, the authenticity of reported knowledge (truth-value) is greatest when the respondent has the freest hand to self-generate his or her knowledge. The more the question

Figure 2

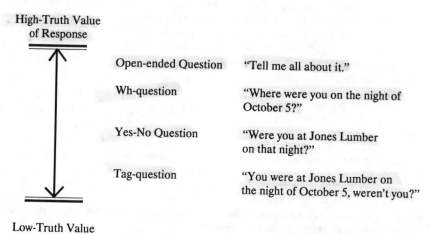

High-Truth Value
of Response

Open-ended Question   "Tell me all about it."

Wh-question   "Where were you on the night of
                        October 5?"

Yes-No Question   "Were you at Jones Lumber
                        on that night?"

Tag-question   "You were at Jones Lumber on
                        the night of October 5, weren't you?"

Low-Truth Value
of Response

Truth-Value of Response to Question Type

in the interrogator's mind is focused and specified (wh-questions, and to a limited extent, yes-no questions), the more the respondent has the opportunity to provide the answer that the questioner wants. The level of tag-question is relatively useless for truth-value since the manner of asking practically guarantees the response.

Police interrogation of suspects is very much like teacher interrogation of students; the more we focus and specify the desired answer, the less we let the respondent self-generate. In the case of intelligence collection, the most convincing evidence is that which is self-generated by the suspect (self-incriminating evidence). Congressman Ozzie Meyers, in his Abscam investigation, required very little question specifying. He self-generated his own guilt without the need of clever probing by the agent. His guilt was clearly evidenced by his unambiguous language and his domination of the conversation. In cases where agents dominate the conversation (as in the case of Senator Williams), there are limited opportunities for self-incrimination. In fact, careful analysis of the Williams tapes reveals no such self-incrimination, leading the analyst to the conclusion that there was either poor intelligence collection or absence of criminality.

Topic dominance is also a clear signal of social or psychological relationship. If a person is suspected of being a king-pin, a leader, an instigator who is trying to get others to do his will, his language will display such power in several ways. He will give directives, he will warn or threaten and he will dominate the topics in the conversation quantitatively, leaving those whom he dominates the role of responding to his topics.

Elsewhere I have described the process of topic analysis in more detail (Shuy 1981), but one last point should be stressed--the visual effectiveness of such analysis for easy comprehension of the conversation. Harris states that the role of summarizing intelligence information "reduces the analyst from being swamped by data that are only marginally relevant" (Harris 1976, p. 30). Although Harris is referring here to written data rather than to oral conversation, the same principle obtains. Some tape cases involve hundreds of hours of taped conversation involving thousands of pages of transcript. It is easy to get lost or swamped in the morass of words. Topic analysis provides an outline of an entire conversation which enables the analyst to read only the topic introductions in order to recall the flow of conversation. The following actual topic analysis (Figure 3) will serve as an illustration. The video tape is from The U.S. vs. John DeLorean. It was made on September 4, 1982. There were 77 topics initiated in this conversation between the government informer, James Hoffman, who was wearing the microphone, and John Z. DeLorean, president of DeLorean Motor Company (DMC) in Ireland.

Figure 3

Topic Analysis in DeLorean Case

	DeLorean	Hoffman
1.		greeting
2.		lunch?
3.		building
4.		alternate Rockville
5.		drink?
6.		Thought we'd be together
7.		Where do you stand with company?
8.		delays
9.	prior to interim financing?	
10.		got group has ability-30 million
11.	They have an interest?	
12.		Colombian folks

	DeLorean	Hoffman
13.		dope program
14.		2nd level, 5 million
15.		tell me how really pressured you are
16.	It'll be dangerous	
17.		800,000 investment returns
		40 million
18.		2 ways: (1) Interim financing, quicker.
19.		or (2) or this, buy 100 Kilos
20.		300 investment, 14 million in 10 days
21.		Biggest concern if you can't follow through
22.		Absolute confirmation would be to invest it again
23.		They want to make sure not wind up short
24.		JB handles money thru my boss-see him
25.		He operates thru more than a bank also
26.		He (JB) understands what's going on
27.		He's not able to write bank guarantee

	DeLorean	Hoffman
28.	I'm getting money thru Irish group	
29.	So its gotta be legitimate	
30.		We don't want you not comfortable
31.		You're not compelled
32.		if you get money somewhere else, do it
33.		either we go ahead or end
34.	I'll get hold of them	
35.	I want to do it, but they confirm it	
36.	What should I do?	
37.		Probably move in 2-3 days
38.		I built other program in because within my control
39.	first part of money has to be by Friday	
40.		How long take to get confirmation of funds available?
41.		I gotta go see wife, see Jim
42.		My part equity, Vicenza next level
43.		Your big deadline 28th or 29th?
44.		Any way you can accelerate funding?
45.	I'll hear from you Tues or Wed?	

	DeLorean	Hoffman
46.	I'd like to do this anyhow	
47.		Not many people could pick up 30 mill in 3-4 days
48.		Their rep. an American guy
49.	Their interest as loan or equity investment?	
50.	We'll be doing 400 mill by end of next yr.	
51.		Their interest megamillion drug, coke
52.		They have to move money every 90 days
53.		So their interest is stock
54.	We're accustomed to no disclosure requirement, off-shore trading CO's.	
55.		desirable part facility to use
56.		This a deal originally we weren't going to do
57.	What's your opinion?	
58.		Jim going over there, we'll sit here
59.		Turn a few cars loose?
60.		What are sales now?
61.		Anybody with any interest is saying wait and see
62.		media blitz
63.		Jim hasn't been able to do anything

DeLorean	Hoffman
64.	You got another place to go for credit now
65.	We are ready to move
66.	He has some other banking people in Ireland.
67.	Know what's going on?
68.	You ought to tell 'em it's craps game
69.	nobody wants you not comfortable
70.	From here on, dealings with Jim through Jim's boss and by boss
71.	*(Telephone interruption JH on phone]*
72.	You got anything Jim doesn't have?
73.	Thatcher
74. We built plant in 2 1/2 yrs	
75. I think Sec. of State made deal... with that English to take it over	
76. Where will I get you?	
77.	*Close*

The first thing to notice about this conversation is that DeLorean introduces only 18 of the 77 topics, some 23 percent of the topics in the conversation (note that the words used to depict the topic initiations are the exact words used on the tape). From this it is clear that the major agenda of this conversation is Hoffman's, yet DeLorean is accused of soliciting an interest in the drug business. The major contextual factor to keep in mind is that for two months, DeLorean had been discussing a loan for his sinking automobile company from a presumed representative, Jim Benedict, (an undercover FBI agent) of California's Eureka National Bank. Hoffman was instrumental in setting up these meetings and telephone calls, and now, toward the end of the investigation, the scenario changes. Hoffman (and later Benedict) claim that the bank loan will not be possible, but that they will personally either finance a loan to DeLorean from their drug business or they will help to get other investors or loan sources for the ailing company.

At issue in the September 4 conversation is whether DeLorean is agreeing to invest in their drug business, as a show of good faith, or whether he is still interested in a legitimate loan. The prosecution claimed that DeLorean was indicating an interest in investing in drugs. There is no question about the fact that Hoffman claims to be in the drug business (explicitly in topics 13, 19, 51 and indirectly elsewhere).

DeLorean's only drug relevant topic is his topic 16, in which he comments that the drug business ("it") is dangerous. The other critical topic is that of investment. That DeLorean believed Hoffman was referring to their interest in investing in DMC is clear in his topic 49. Hoffman's use of the terms *investment*, and *financing*, however, are more ambiguously stated. What is missing is Hoffman's explicit words that *investment* means DeLorean's investment in their drug deal. Since DeLorean never promises this, he has no reason to believe that Hoffman's use of *investment* means DeLorean's investment in their drug deal.

The point which this example is to make is that topic analysis is a very useful guide to the gist of the conversation. It enables the analyst to avoid being swamped by the irrelevant talk and points out the areas which require a more micro analysis, such as the reference to drugs and the references to investment.

2. Response Analysis

Once the macro, overall picture of the intelligence information is described by topic analysis, it is possible to focus on the crucial spots for a more micro, detailed analysis of the responses made by the target.

Obviously, speakers in a conversation not only introduce topics but also respond to the topics of other participants. Again, most people are unaware of the fact that they have strategies, consciously or unconsciously, of responding to the topics of others. Suppose, for example, an agent introduces a topic with which the target is uncomfortable in some way. The target has several strategy options. He can agree with it. He can disagree with it. He can say nothing at all. He can say, "uh-huh," "right," or "okay," none of which are clear indications of agreement, but on the other hand, are what linguists refer to as feedback markers. Or he can change the subject. Figure 4 displays these strategies.

Figure 4   Topic Response Options

   1. Resolve topic
   2. Resolve part of topic
   3. Request clarification or amplification of topic
   4. Provide off-topic response
   5. Change or redirect the topic
   6. Provide vague, ambiguous or no response
   7. Provide clarification which denies or changes the premise of the topic
   8. Deny the premise of the topic

The fact that most people are not conscious of the strategies they have learned to use in rapid-fire conversation since early childhood makes response analysis even more powerful as a clue to the intentions of the suspect. What causes a person to become conscious of response strategies is the realization that his utterance will be examined later, as with a tape recording, or that it is being examined at present (as in a trial). Speakers become very conscious of their response strategies in a courtroom. Likewise, they become very conscious of their response strategies when they know they are being recorded. For this reason, the agent can be assumed to be aware of the significance of his response strategies since he knows he is taping the conversation. But the suspect is unaware of this and does not monitor his response strategies. He speaks naturally, not realizing that he is making a record for later examination.

Thus, if the suspect responds with a feedback marker such as "uh-huh," he is not carefully agreeing. In sharp contrast, he is producing a natural conversation feedback marker, the meaning of which can range from "I hear you," "Keep talking," "I haven't gone to sleep," to "I think I understand what you're saying, but I'm not sure so I'll hear you out." If the suspect changes the subject, again recognizing the fact that he does not even know that he is making a record for later examination, the clue to his intentions is even more apparent. In an unmonitored, unconscious manner, he is indicating lack of interest in or agreement with the agent's proposition and/or considerably more interest in his own agenda than that of the agent.

If the suspect says nothing at all to the agent's proposition, we can also get a clue to his intentions. In conversation, when a person does not respond, it is an indication of negativity. We do not respond when we are uncomfortable or want to disagree, but for some reason, are afraid to. All language use is a social event, not just a cognitive one, and there are many socially structured influences on disagreement. One of the major characteristics of conversation, as noted earlier, is that, it is cooperative in nature. Otherwise there would be no conversation at all. Certain types of people are more affected by open disagreement than others. Elected officials, for examples, can be expected to avoid disagreement as much as possible for obvious political reasons. Employee subordinates tend to avoid disagreement with their superiors for reasons of job security. Those requesting assistance, such as for a loan, avoid disagreeing with those who can offer it, for fear of losing the opportunity. It is often assumed in court that a witness' silence is taken as an indication of agreement or guilt. Whether or not this is true in court, a person in a natural conversation indicates exactly the opposite with silence: disagreement which he is hesitant to offer, for whatever reasons.

Intelligence analysts, then, should perform a response analysis on the parts of the taped conversation in which it is useful to display the clues to the target's intentions.

3.   Topic-flow Analysis

A third useful analytical tool is topic-flow analysis (Shuy 1985). By this I mean that all topics of discussion are first classified into three categories: substantive topics (what the goal of conversation was all about), corollary topics (ways of achieving or arriving at the substantive topics), and transitional topics (formulaic aspects of a conversation such as greetings and closings, but also including the non-substantive and non-corollary small talk that occurs so frequently in conversation, often providing psychological breaks from the heavier conversation). Topic-flow analysis maps the topics sequentially, noting the conversational movement among substantive, corollary and transitional topics, and marking the successes or failures of the speakers in their efforts to achieve their goals. As noted earlier, the speakers who introduce a given topic clearly had those topics on their minds, probably as their agenda or goal in the conversation. Thus, *topic analysis* reveals exactly who brought up which topics. Likewise, the responses of the other speakers to these topics, *response analysis*, reveals clues about those persons' intentions. They may change the subject, defer the subject, not respond at all, or respond only to a minor part of that topic, all giving clear clues to their lack of interest, discomfort or failure to agree with that topic.

Topic-flow analysis traces the topics of the speakers throughout the conversation, while at the same time noting response categories which can give indications of what the next conversational strategy of the agent or surrogate agent will be. If the agents are rejected or deferred in their conversational strategies, they may move toward a safer topic to rebuild rapport and try to get the other person talking again. This is very much like a well-recognized sales approach. The salesperson tries to get the customers to agree to small, less important matters as a kind of training mechanism for getting them to agree and/or respond to more important things, in this case, to purchase the product. Topic-flow analysis is useful for displaying an overall picture of a conversation and the conversational strategies of both parties.

One product of topic-flow analysis is to assist the intelligence analyst to separate, categorize and understand the flood of topics and events that occur in the tape recorded conversation and to map the interaction between the participants.

Theoretically, topic-flow analysis enables the intelligence analyst to develop his or her hypotheses about the presumed criminality of the conversation by attempting to obtain the perspective of the suspect at the time the conversation was taking place. This theory is supported by several research traditions in psychology and linguistics. From psychology the notion of cognitive "schemata," also known as schema theory, says that a subject remembers new events in light of what is known from before (Bartlett 1932, Rummelhart 1980). Although the focus of such research has been primarily on memory, the task of understanding, or making sense out of the taped data, operates in essentially the same way. Schema theory argues that new information which is processed by a subject is understood as it relates to all that is understood before, forming a combined standard, or schema, against which any following new information is measured. Other researchers may identify such schema as *organizing principles, world knowledge* or *frames* (Goffman 1974).

To accomplish the task of separating what was said by the suspect from what was said by the undercover personnel, therefore, the intelligence analyst must be able to assume the role of the suspect at the time and in the context of the actual event being taped. Such separation is difficult. In other fields, such as psychotherapy, it is referred to as perspective taking.

The application of schema, frames, etc., to the intelligence analyst's task of understanding taped evidence should be immediate and clear. Listeners to tape recorded conversations understand what they hear, in light of what they know, or think they know, as they hear it. Thus, if intelligence analysts think they know that the suspect has been doing something illegal as they hear the tapes, they tend to interpret any ambiguities in favor of the prosecution and not in favor of the suspect. In order to avoid unsupportable indictments, however, the intelligence analyst must also try to understand the taped conversation from the perspective of the suspect. Topic-flow analysis contributes to this goal.

In order to accomplish topic-flow analysis, it is first necessary to carry out topic analysis and response analysis. The following example will serve to illustrate. In a solicitation to murder case, the man wearing the microphone had claimed that a Mr. Hazen had asked him to kill his wife. The law enforcement agency wired the informant, Mr. Iggers, and sent him to meet with Hazen and capture on tape the solicitation. There were three tape recorded meetings, the last of which will serve as our illustration. The police apparently felt that the first two meetings did not accomplish their goal since in those meetings, whenever Iggers introduced the topic of murder, Hazen offered only non-committal responses. In the third conversation Iggers introduces all eight topics, as Figure 5 indicates:

Figure 5

Topic Analysis, Hazen Case

Topic	Hazen's Topics	Topic Type	Iggers' Topics
1		Transitional	Greeting
2		Transitional	How you like that truck?
3		Transitional	You going to the station?
4		Corollary	You get my stuff?
5		Substantive	I'll take care of every-thing for you.
6		Corollary	Goin' on vacation?
7		Substantive	That's when we kill your wife.
8		Transitional	Anything else?

Plotting this conversation in topic-flow analysis, the conversation can be represented as Figure 6 on the next page.

This conversation begins at the transitional level, topics one, two, and three. Hazen is cooperative and responsive, so Iggers moves up to the corollary level in topic four ("You get my stuff?"). Hazen provides the response Iggers wants, so he then moves up further to the substantive level in topic five ("I'll take care of everything for you"). Before Hazen can respond, Iggers changes the subject to the time of Hazen's vacation. Even though Hazen offers only feedback marker "uhhuh" responses, Iggers then returns to the substantive level in topic seven ("That's when we kill your wife"). Again, Iggers changes the subject before Hazen can respond, shifting the topic to the gas station. Hazen responds to the topic of the gas station and Iggers concludes with small talk in topic eight.

This analysis of Iggers' topic flow indicates clearly that Hazen is consistently cooperative about small talk topics, occasionally cooperative in corollary topics, but never cooperative about substantive topics. To substantive topics, Hazen's reposnse patterns are completely different in the three conversations. In the first conversation, he consistently defers substantive topics. In the

Figure 6   Topic - Flow Analysis, Hazen Case

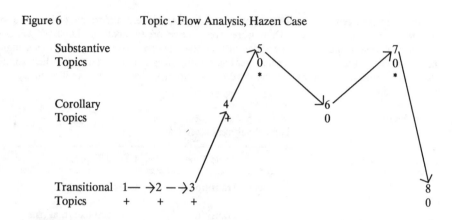

Response Effects	
+	Iggers gets cooperative response from Hazen
0	Iggers gets silence or feedback markers from Hazen
*	Iggers changes the subject before any response by Hazen is possible

second tape, he consistently uses feedback markers or silence. In the third tape, he is never given the opportunity to respond to substantive topics, since Iggers changes his own subject before Hazen can respond.

Iggers management of the topic-flow is also instructive. In the three conversations, he makes a total of seven strong moves to the "homerun" territory of the substantive topic. Three strong moves are made in the first tape, two in the second tape and two in the third conversation. In the first tape, these strong moves are at the beginning, middle and end. In the second tape, the strong moves are at the beginning and middle. In the short, third tape, they are toward the end. Each conversation is shorter than the preceding one. Iggers' positioning of his strong moves is indication of his increased awareness of the problem he faced in eliciting the desired response from Hazen. In the first tape, Iggers got only deferrals from Hazen. Obviously, the police did not get the responses they wanted, or there would have been no need for further tapes. The second tape, if anything, was even less successful. Hazen gave uncooperative responses at the substantive level, and changed the subject at the corollary level at the most crucial points, especially at the end of the conversation, blocking Iggers' possibility to move up to the substantive level once again. By the last tape, Iggers' strategy changed dramatically. In his two strong moves to the substantive level, he gave Hazen no opportunity to defer, or give any response at all (perhaps not taking any chances that Hazen might reject his statements again), and shifted the topic before Hazen could respond to it.

It should be clear from this example that the intelligence analyst should have provided a better road map of these conversations to those who make the decision about whether or not to press for an indictment. There was certainly talk of killing in these tapes, but it was always introduced by the informant and never by the suspect, whose responses were always of the type called deferral, feedback markers, silence or changed subject. None of these responses is clear evidence of intent to commit a crime. By carrying out a topic-flow analysis, it could have been clear to the intelligence analyst that the appearance of criminality in these conversations was a direct result of the conversational strategies employed by the informant. The primary strategy, seen clearly in the third conversation which is presented above, is what is termed the "hit and run" strategy: dropping the illegality on the suspect, then changing the topic before the subject can respond. Whatever incriminating information external to these taped conversations existed, the fact remains that the tapes were not good enough evidence to press for a just indictment. Information analysts should prevent the prosecutor from being embarrassed by such data. Topic-flow analysis can point out the reasons for the weakness in the taping operation.

4. Language Function Analysis

Language functions exist at a level closer to intentionality. Levels of language range from small to large: from the sounds of language, to the affixes and other word parts, to the words, to the sentences, to the functions. Functions are, quite simply, the ways people use language to get things done. Speakers promise, deny, report facts, complain, give opinions, request, advise, thank, etc. Each of these functions has a structure to identify it as what it is. People have many ways of realizing a specific function, many of them indirect. When offered a cigarette, for example, one can reject the offer without being explicit or direct. The rejection can come in the form of a reported personal fact, as for example, "I don't smoke." This utterance then functions both as a reported personal fact and as a denial of the offered cigarette at the same time. Language analysis gets complicated at the functional level but so does language use. It takes a complicated analysis to account for complicated speech.

At this point it may be useful to explain that linguistic analysis of tape recorded conversation is analogous to the different ways a biologist examines a specimen. He puts it under a microscope and then examines it at different magnifications to obtain different patterns of the specimen and its environment. Similarly, a photographer may use different lenses to capture something on film: a close up shot, a long range or a medium shot.

Functional language analysis is like another magnification or a different lens. By analyzing a speaker's language functions, intelligence analysts can see still another pattern of a persons language behavior. For example, Figure 7 displays the language functions employed by Mr. I, a real estate salesman who was indicted for accepting a bribe and for racketeering in a case in which the agent kept telling him that he wanted to buy property to build a club to hold private poker parties. The agent gave Mr. I $300 to give to the sheriff as a campaign contribution. At no time did Mr. I request money of any kind. His language functions in this and other tapes provide a clear picture of the clues to his intentions.

By carrying out language function analysis based on clear definition of the functions (also referred to as speech acts by linquists), the intelligence analyst can determine and chart visually the way a suspect uses language to get things done. The very categorization of these speech acts or functions provides insights to the hypotheses being formed by the analyst about suspected criminality. If the agency is looking for offers, threats or promises, for example, such analysis makes clear that in Mr. I's case, at least, the hypothesis of criminal behavior is not yet supported and that it is unlikely that an indictment could be supported by the taped evidence. The analyst then can do one of two things. He can offer feedback to those who are collecting the intelligence

Figure 7   Language Functions of Mr. I

	Gives	Reports	Gives	Requests	Complains
	Real Estate Advice	Personal Facts	Sales Routine	Clarification	
Mr. I	8 times	1 time	4 times	1 time	1 time

that the language behavior of the suspect is not sufficient for possible indictment, and that they should tape another conversation that would provide better evidence, or the analyst can advise the prosecutor of the weakness of the evidence so that he or she will be able to gear up for the attack of the defense attorney in court.

5.   Contrastive Analysis

All sciences involve comparing things with each other to see how much they are the same or different. As Harris points out, the comparison of data is the critical step in analysis since, through this activity, meaning is derived. The analyst, by referring to a hypothesis, formulates a set of expectations and compares actual observation with those expectations (Harris 1976, p. 30). Tape recorded language is no exception to this principle.

Certain types of conversations contain language routines or genres which are common for specific types of actions. By routines, or genres, linguists refer to structural types of language use which become expected through conversational practice by the participants. The sales event, for example, can be expected to contain certain phases in which the seller and buyer engage. The seller asks if he can help the buyer, the buyer makes his desire known, the seller offers a product, both may negotiate a price and the sale is concluded, rejected or deferred. One such conversational routine commonly found in tape recorded government evidence is the structure of a proposal conversation, often involving in such cases, the offer of a bribe for specific services. Figure 8 displays the structure of such an event.

Figure eight offers a model which accounts for all the conversations of that type in the body of data presented by the intelligence collectors. This model can be used as a comparison with other conversations in which proposals are made and bribes are suspected. The analyst must look beyond specific cases to determine the similarities and differences among many different cases (Harris 1976, p.27). Past tape recorded conversations in which bribes were clearly offered and accepted follow this model completely. The intelligence analyst's task, therefore, is to determine whether or not the suspects in their current cases match the model (see Shuy, in press, for a more detailed analysis model). In one of the Texas Brilab cases involving the Speaker of the House of Representatives and two attorneys, for example, careful application of this model revealed that all of the conversation took place at the problem phase, and that the talk never reached the proposal, completion or extension phases at all. As it turns out, an indictment was recommended and a trial ensured in which all the defendants were acquitted. Such waste of effort and finances could have been averted by a more exhaustive and careful contrastive intelligence analysis. The prosecution simply did not have the taped evidence that they thought they had.

Other types of contrastive analysis are also useful to the intelligence analysts where tape

Figure 8   Structure of a Proposal Conversation

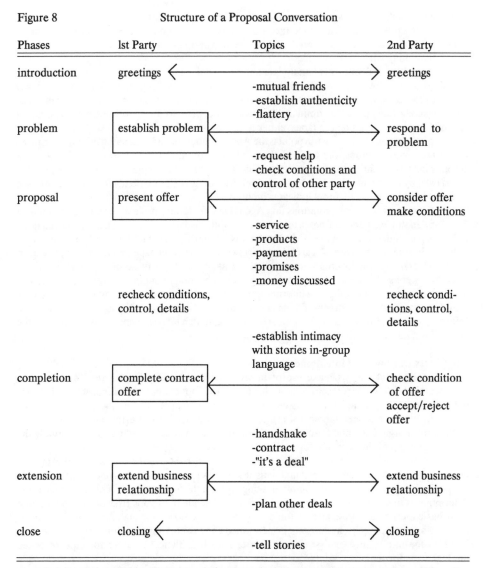

Phases	1st Party	Topics	2nd Party
introduction	greetings		greetings
		-mutual friends -establish authenticity -flattery	
problem	establish problem		respond to problem
		-request help -check conditions and control of other party	
proposal	present offer		consider offer make conditions
		-service -products -payment -promises -money discussed	
	recheck conditions, control, details		recheck conditions, control, details
		-establish intimacy with stories in-group language	
completion	complete contract offer		check condition of offer accept/reject offer
		-handshake -contract -"it's a deal"	
extension	extend business relationship		extend business relationship
		-plan other deals	
close	closing		closing
		-tell stories	

recorded data are available. The more obvious ones include a contrast or comparison of the police reports or FBI investigative reports with the actual words on the tape.

It is not uncommon for an officer or agent to paraphrase the suspect's words in a report to the extent that it appears to imply a quite different message than the actual spoken words indicate.

It is useful to make such comparisons early so that the prosecutor will know what he will be facing when the defense attorney calls such inconsistencies to question in the courtroom. Even more important, however, is the intelligence analyst's need to point out such inconsistencies as evidence of a potential injustice to the suspect.

A final type of contrastive analysis is one which gets at the core problem of separating the illegality suggested by the agents from the actual words used by the suspect. No government agency wishes to convict a person who is not guilty. Yet the paradox of cover + taping is that agents must give the appearance of being criminal. This leads, of course, to the agent's uttering criminal or criminal sounding things on the tapes, either to get the suspect to agree with such criminality or to deny or disagree with it. A case in point is the Abscam tapes involving Senator Williams. In three of the tape conversations, the topic of the Senator's potential future interest in the business corporation being planned was brought up. This is an appropriate topic for conversation, but the terms used by the agents, Tony DeVito and Mel Weinberg, differ markedly from the terms used by Senator Williams, as Figure 9 indicates on page 143.

It is clear from these quotations that Agent DeVito defines protection as a hidden interest whereas Senator Williams defines protection as a public declaration, a blind trust. The Senator's indictment included words to the effect that he was attempting to achieve a hidden interest in the potential business enterprise. A careful intelligence analysis of the taped conversation, however, reveals clearly that such words were those of the agents and not those of the Senator, whose intentions were self-generated as a legal blind trust. The indictment in this case, was erroneous and not justified by the intelligence information. A contrastive analysis of terms used for this topic would have avoided this problem. To use Harris' suggested procedure, the intelligence analyst, in referring to the hypothesis of the Senator's desire for a hidden interest, should have compared the actual observation with that expectation or hypothesis.

The Effects Of Linguistic Intelligence Analysis

Intelligence analysts make use of information provided by investigators and "...make judgmental decisions concerning the short and long term implications of criminal activity in terms of tactical operations and strategic assessment" (Harris 1976, p. 27). Analysis assumes that the basic information has been largely collected, and that the task is to determine meaning which is derived from organizing and examining such information. These procedures are essentially the same, regardless of the type of information that has been collected.

When the information consists of tape recorded conversations, however, the task of determining meaning requires certain linguistic skills, as noted above. It is one thing to be able to speak a language. It is quite another thing to be able to analyze, describe, organize and determine its meaning. Without linguistic expertise, such activity runs risks of overlooking the most basic units of analysis, such as topic, response, topic flow, language functions, anaphoric referencing and syllabicity, among others mentioned above. This paper outlines some of the ways in which the intelligence analyst can make use of such analytical routines for tape recorded intelligence information.

Three products of such intelligence analysis are: useful feedback to those who collect the tape recorded information, hypothesis testing about the presumed criminality of the activity being tape recorded and informing those who make decisions about whether or not to indict the suspect.

Figure 9   Hidden Interest Vs. Blind Trust in the Willams Case

	DeVito	Weinberg	Sen. Williams
Aug. 5	. get your position protected... 100% protection.	. keep it secret.	
Sep. 11			. Right, pay my taxes.
Oct. 7	. Everything was going to be hidden. . Everybody else can declare, you can't.	. Sandy spoke of you going to declare 17 million dollars profit or something.	. No, I'm going to find a way to protect myself with some kind of declaration.
	. declare it in some other way		. I'm going to have to go public.
	. The Senator was trying to protect himself by coming up with some gimmick.		This is where my lawyer comes in. . We can blind trust me, you know. . A blind trust, that's the way for my purposes. . There we have it under the trust...so I've done what I had to do.

1.   Feedback To Intelligence Collectors

An important task for those who analyze the raw data consisting of tape recorded conversations is that the quality of such evidence be communicated to those who are collecting it so that the intelligence collectors can modify their procedures, collect additional taped data or stop the operation altogether. This is, at the same time, a matter of efficiency and justice.

What may appear to be good conversational evidence of criminality to the investigator may turn out to be inadequate from the intelligence analyst's perspective after the evaluations noted earlier are carried out. The examples given in this paper are cases in point.

In recent years, educational evaluation has developed a distinction between two types of program evaluation: summative evaluation and formative evaluation. *Summative* evaluation occurs at the end of the process. Like a final examination in school, it assigns a grade. *Formative* evaluation, on the other hand, occurs from the very onset of the process. Evaluators help the program participants construct the project in such a way that the outcome will be optimal. They consult with the program throughout its duration, offering feedback and suggestions to make it work better. The analogy to the intelligence operation should be obvious. Intelligence analysts and evaluators should feedback their insights to the investigators during the operation and not be limited to a summative role.

2.   Hypothesis Testing About Presumed Criminal Activity
Where explicitness exists, hypotheses are less necessary. But it is the nature of language use to be regularly ambiguous and incomplete. When ambiguity occurs in conversation, there are ways to disambiguate. One can say, "I don't understand. What do you mean?" The problem with this, however, is that in everyday conversation there are social constraints which limit the frequency of requesting clarification.

A person who requests clarification over and over again tends to insult the speaker and is thought to be uncooperative, if not unfriendly. So listeners often try to infer the speaker's meaning

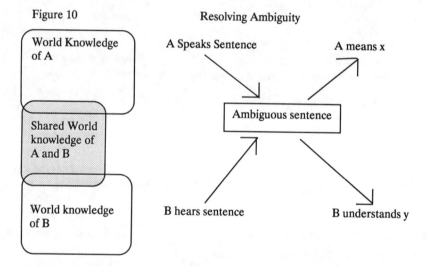

Figure 10   Resolving Ambiguity

even in spite of its ambiguity. When people infer, they call on what they know to try to disambiguate what they do not understand. Figure 10 above illustrates this point. Speaker A and Listener B, like all humans, have different knowledge of the world, but also they have some overlapping shared knowledge. As long as speaker A is explicit and clear, communication to B of his intended meaning can take place. But when he is unclear or ambiguous, listener B must either request clarification or infer A's intended meaning. When inferencing takes place, one cannot always be sure that B actually understood A's intended meaning.

In the DeLorean case noted earlier, both the agent and Mr. DeLorean were talking about investment, but linguistic analysis of the conversation reveals that they were each referring to different types of investment. The investment that would secure an indictment was one in which

DeLorean would agree to invest in the drug business, and this was the investigator's ill-formed impression. Later analysis revealed that the intelligence analyst pursued only one hypothesis. It is imperative, as Harris points out, that the analyst "formulate alternative hypotheses where there is limited information available..." This approach, often used in the early collection of information, keeps the analyst from focusing too soon on a single hypothesis (which may be wrong) (Harris 1976, p. 34). Harris continues, "the business of intelligence is to probe allegations and suggestions of criminal activity rather than to build an evidential case" (Harris 1976, p. 34). In this case, the lack of alternative hypothesis building led to an indictment and trial for which the defendant was acquitted.

It is not without reason that the FBI's second guideline is that the agents must make clear and unambiguous the nature of the criminal activity which they are pursuing. Such clarity is the antithesis of ambiguity and actual language use contains a great deal of ambiguity. By the same token it is clear that when such ambiguity exists, the intelligence analyst must develop and pursue

Figure 11   Models of Hypothesis Testing

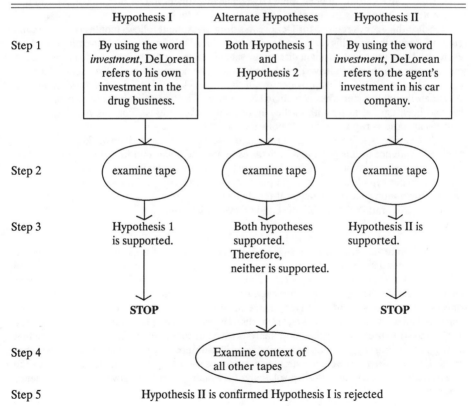

alternative hypotheses. Figure 11 on page 145 is a strategic model for such a procedure, using the DeLorean case as an example.

Figure 11 illustrates the analytical routine as a five step procedure. Step one is the hypothesis stage. The prosecution posits hypothesis one, supposing criminality. The defense posits hypothesis two, supposing innocence. The center position is one of alternate hypotheses. The second step is to examine the tape in question. By positing only one hypothesis, by step three, both the prosecution and the defense can confirm their hypotheses based only on the tape in question. But since two contradictory hypotheses cannot be true, there must be more. Noting this ambiguity, the alternate hypothesis approach goes further, based on ambiguity resolution in linguistics. This principle is that when explicitness or completeness is not evident in a specific conversation, accurate meaning can be found in the context of preceding conversations. Step four, then, is a search for the support or rejection of both hypotheses in the other preceding tape recordings. The DeLorean case contains a series of conversations in which both parties agree to pursue the notion of the agent's possible investment in DeLorean's auto company. The other tapes also reveal one conversation in which the agents ask DeLorean to invest in their drug business. This latter conversation differs from the ones about the agents' investment in DeLorean's company in that there is *no* resolution or agreement by DeLorean to their topic.

Since the agent's request for DeLorean's drug investment follows months of DeLorean's request for investment in his car company, it is logical for DeLorean to defer their topic and not resolve it. To be too negative might discourage them from investing their money in his project. A safer approach for him is to leave them hanging and to be non-committal. The fact is, however, that the clearest context clues provided by all the 65 tapes in this case are that *investment*, to DeLorean, meant the agents' investment in his company. This was the only meaning of *investment* that had been agreed to by both parties in all their conversations. For this reason, step five confirms hypothesis two and rejects hypothesis one.

Such analysis, if fed back to the investigators would have clarified the weakness of the government's evidence at this point and perhaps even aborted a wasteful indictment and trial. By pursuing alternate hypotheses, the intelligence analyst can follow Harris' advice and not focus too soon on a single hypothesis which might prove wrong. Such a procedure also is consistent with Harris' observation that the business of intelligence is to probe allegations and suggestions of criminal activity, rather than to blindly build an evidential case.

3.   Informing Decision Makers About Whether Or Not To Indict The Suspect

This point has already been suggested in the preceding discussion. Good information coupled with good analysis is the optimum product that intelligence can provide. The decision makers, for whatever reasons, may decide to accept or reject such intelligence; they may or may not ask for advice. The point here, however, is that information that is based on tape recorded conversation requires a different type of intelligence analysis than the types discussed in the literature and offered in most training programs. This is because spoken language is so complex, diverse and structured in ways that most analysts have not conceived of. It is indeed strange that many defense attorneys have already recognized the differences that tape recorded evidence offers and have already developed strategies, much the same as those outlined here, to work to their advantage, while little of this type of analysis is evident in police or government intelligence analysis.

References

Bartlett, F. C.
(1932) Remembering. Cambridge: Cambridge University Press.
Goffman, Erving.
(1974) Frame Analysis. Cambridge: Harvard University Press.
Guiberson, S. A.
(1981) "How to Send Prosecutors Reeling with their own Taped Evidence." The
National Law Journal, October 5.
Grice, H. P.
(1975) "Logic and Conversation." In Syntax and Semantics Volume III, Speech Acts, ed.
P. Cole and J. Morgan.
Harris, Don R.
(1976) Basic Elements of Intelligence. Washington, D.C.: Law Enforcement Assistance
Administration.
Heymann, Phillip.
(1980) Testimony before the Subcommittee on Civil and Constitutional Rights of the
House Committee on the Judiciary, 96th Congress, March 4.
Loftus, Elizabeth.
(1979) Eyewitness Testimony. Cambridge: Cambridge University Press.
Rummelhart, David E.
(1980) "Schemata: The Building Blocks of Cognition" in Theoretical Issues in Reading
Comprehension. Hillsdale, N.J.: Lawrence Erlbaum.
Searle, J. R.
(1969) Speech Acts. Cambridge: Cambridge University Press.
Searle, J. R.
(1979) Expression and Meaning. Cambridge: Cambridge University Press.
Searle, J. R.
(1983) Intentionality. Cambridge: Cambridge University Press.
Shuy, Roger W.
(1981) "Topic as the Unit of Analysis in a Criminal Law Case." In Analyzing Discourse:
Text and Talk, ed. D. Tannen. Washington, D.C.: Georgetown University Press.
Shuy, Roger W.
(1984) "Entrapment and the Linguistic Analysis of Tapes" Studies in Language, 8:2.
Shuy, Roger W.
(In Press) "Some Linguistic Contributions to a Criminal Court Case." In Discourse and
Institutional Authority: Medicine, Education and Law, eds. S. Fisher and A. Todd.
Norwood, N.J.: Ablex.
Shuy, Roger W.
(1985) "Evidence of Cooperation in Conversation Topic-Type in a Solicitation to Murder
Case." Paper given at conference on Language in the Judicial Process, Georgetown
University.
Walker, Anne Graffam.
(1985) From Oral to Written: The Verbatim Transcripts of Legal Proceedings, PH.D.
dissertation, Georgetown University.

Chapter Seven

The Development Of Inferences In The Assessment Of Intelligence Data

Robert J. Kelly

Introduction

If it does not lead to action, most knowledge is dead. This pragmatic variation on a theme of Plotinus lies at the heart of the intelligence enterprise. In their comprehensive study of intelligence more than a decade ago, Godfrey and Harris defined it as a process, "made up of a series of interconnected functions or activities: collection, evaluation, collation, analysis, dissemination and re-evaluation" (Godfrey and Harris, 1971: 11).

In more recent work, Dintino and Martens (1983) follow up on the notion of intelligence as a process and point out that the term itself is used often without clear, specific definitions. And this is not without purpose. Like the concept "history" or "science," the term "intelligence" has more than one meaning. As Godfrey and Harris note, the term refers to the organizational methods for collecting and evaluating information, and to the information itself that has been gathered. In the present context, there is no need to go into the complexities of the process nor is any purpose served by an examination of the abuses and uses of intelligence.

The focus of this chapter concerns an aspect of the production of intelligence that can be transformed into useful policy aids and operational tools. Because the processes of intelligence work are as much art as science, they are bound to be less than adequate from time to time. As with any collective activity demanding cooperation and coordination, mistakes, biases and insufficient information are to be expected. But even with the crudest methods practitioners have demonstrated the effectiveness of decisions derived from a fairly reliable data base.

Pitfalls and Structural Problems in Modern Intelligence Work

Intelligence successes are much less heralded than failures; in fact, almost by definition, intelligence cannot "succeed" in the usual sense of the term. If intelligence correctly predicts the initiatives of a criminal organization, and if, as a consequence, proper counter responses are taken and a criminal group fails or refrains from its purported activities, it is possible that the intelligence agency may be blamed for making false predictions. Clearly, little is to be gained from a preoccupation with scorecards.

Many of the problems inherent in the process of reaching valid conclusions from data do not lie in the inferential procedures as such but precede them. One of the most common difficulties confronting the analyst is "mirror imaging." Here, the analyst projects assumptions of intentions onto others whose motives and strategies are alien. The analyst steadfastly resists the challenge of facts or experience and proceeds in accordance, undauntingly perhaps, with his or her biases and conceits. No analyst can of course avoid starting from some assumptions. Too often, however, the models and hypotheses employed to function like a grid on a mass of facts to order and make sense of the data reflect the analyst's prejudices and parochialism (Laqueur, 1985). For example, it was widely believed that the identification and arrests of bookmakers would break up or contain the growth of organized crime. Historically, most law enforcement officials have contended just this - that illegal gambling was the "lifeblood of organized crime" (Task Force Report, 1967:2).

While it is certainly necessary to confront any illegal activity, the interdiction of street dealers and bookmakers permits some other hypotheses to be entertained. One may wish to know the role of loansharking -- a prominent underworld activity -- in illegal gambling. A hypothesis, a question to explore, might be developed that postulates that the control of illegal gambling depends on and is affected by the money lent to bookmakers who are unable to cover their "action" (Goldstock, 1977). The hypothesis says that the more insolvent a bookmaker is, the more likely he will use the services of a loanshark. "Thus," as Martens succinctly puts it, "an enforcement policy that creates financial insolvency among bookmakers may unintentionally organize the gambling market by forcing insolvent bookmakers to patronize loansharks" (Martens, 1987:132). The very opposite of what was expected may result from the inadequacies of the data and from hasty reasoning.

"Routine" thinking represents another hazard in the assessment of intelligence data, that is, the inclination to fall back on past experience in the light of new phenomena. Naturally, there is a tendency to look for confirmation of already held beliefs; after all, without some element of stability, utter confusion would result. But this conditional conservatism can become dangerous if it leads to the rejection of new information, simply because this information contradicts existing beliefs.

For some years law enforcement intelligence agencies have known of the rise of Asian organized crime groups. Still, the concentration of effort has remained on La Cosa Nostra apparently because they had been widely defined as the most important groups in a variety of vice rackets and illicit markets. What seems not to have been anticipated was that as the attention to the Mafia paid off, the vacuum would be quickly filled. "There are thousands of police intelligence divisions in this country . . . and every one of them," according to one New York police official, "is still looking for criminals whose names end in vowels" -- an allusion to Italian names and La Cosa Nostra gangsters (Kerr, 1987: 30).

There are some reasons for the "structural blindness" of intelligence agencies. They may pertain to the phenomenon of the self-fulfilling prophecy that systematically excludes any evidence that fails to meet the requirements of the operational paradigm. And this is not sheer arrogance, clumsiness or ineptitude. Because every assessment is influenced not only by contemporary constellations of events but also by those that preceded them, the more momentous the events , the larger the shadow they cast. The governing model of La Cosa Nostra dominance eventuates in a "selective attention" to data where the model acts as a filter or lens and screens information out of a collection plan or an evaluation process that deem them extraneous.

Closely connected with the driving power of a preponderant paradigm that shapes the approaches to relevant intelligence data is the very vividness of the data itself. There is a considerable body of research showing that the more vivid the information, the more likely it is to be picked up. Social judgment are scarcely ever hard-nosed, they do not always depend upon purely objective criteria:
Research indicates that highly probative data-summary information is ignored

while less probative, case-history information has a substantial impact on infer- ences. Although people's responsiveness to vivid information has a certain justifi- cation and confers occasional advantages, the policy of weighing information in pro- portion to its vividness is risky. At best, vividness is associated imperfectly with probativeness. Consequently, highly probative but pallid information sometimes will be ignored, and conversely, evidentially weak but vivid information sometimes will have an undue impact on inferences (Nisbett and Ross, 1980:62).

Information or data may be described as "vivid" when it is emotionally interesting, proximate in sensory or spatial ways, and image provoking. The Kefauver Hearings in the 1950's, Valachi's sensational testimony on La Cosa Nostra in the 1960's (when he coined the term), the revelations in the 1970's by Jimmy "The Weasel" Fratianno, and the film bombshells, "The God- father" series, have had an enormous impact on public understanding, and misunderstanding, of organized crime. To say further that the public's grasp of the organized crime problem or for that matter any type of major criminal activity has little effect on law enforcement reactions is simply disingenuous. With its appetite whetted on the imagery of blood oaths, codes of secrecy and honor, strict obedience, gratuitous violence and membership restricted exclusively to those of particular ethnic origins capable and willing to do murder, it is not surprising that tangible, anecdotal information communicated dramatically in the mass media is more memorable, more immediate and more salient to those exposed to it. The power of such information compared with more abstract statistical data is obvious, even though much of it may not be reliable. No matter how logically compelling, abstract, aggregated quantitative data may be when constrasted with the case histories and personal accounts, it is the latter that appears to have the lasting, formative influences on how the phenomenon is understood. How the public is to be weaned away from fictionalized accounts is an ongoing concern for criminal justice officials. No practicable solution seems in sight.

In some respects criminal justice agencies are partly to blame for this state of affairs. They have not hesitated to use melodramatic devices to stimulate public interest and the techniques may have backfired. In any case, the irony is that while reports filled with tables, charts and statistics may be thrilling to technologically-oriented eyes, we seem to assign more inferential weight and priority to the evidence of our senses even though we acknowledge that our senses and perceptions may mislead and deceive, and that personal experiences are not necessarily reliable representa- tions of a phenomenon. This is rather odd actually as we do have cautions against depending too much on subjective experience. The vividness of information is correlated only modestly with its evidential value.

Another issue that impinges on the analytical activities of law enforcement agencies has to do with the growth of their bureaucracies and the division of labor that occurs within them. Analysts and investigators, workers who must cooperate with each other, may begin to inhabit positions in a bureaucracy which breed friction and conflict: the intelligence analyst is situated in an information processing and evaluation unit, while the street investigator working with informants, offenders, other police officers, concerned citizens, and others may not be able to see the forest for the trees. "Personal truth technologies" - - being on the scene, may make more of an impression on the investigator than is actually warranted by the information he or she gleans. Add to this the inertia of bureaucracy that infects all large-scale organizations, it is not difficult to see how the efficiency of intelligence operations can be affected. Still, most observers would agree with Ianni that, "organizational intelligence analysis (rather than individual case development) could dramatically improve the ability of the criminal justice system to address the social, cultural and economic factors that allow organized crime to survive and thrive" (Ianni, 1974: 331).

This issue has become the subject of some serious study. In an investigation of rackets bureaus, it was observed that, "if an organized crime control unit is to develop an appreciation of the problem it faces ... it must establish some systematic method of regularizing the now largely unsystematic approach to gathering, indexing, analyzing and disseminating intelligence related to organized crime units" (Blakey et. al. : 33). In an examination of the investigative process in the DEA (Drug Enforcement Agency), Wilson found that, "the dominant ethos of DEA, created and sustained by the central tasks of street-level investigators, does not provide a bureaucratic environment that nurtures, rewards or pays heed ... to intelligence analysts" (1978: 155).

Even though intelligence units where analytical work goes on are generally acknowledged as invaluable tools in police work, there is still resistance to their full-fledged acceptance. Part of the opposition to their proper funding and functioning may have to do with the inherent conflict of the various role-players in an enforcement agency. According to Moore, who studies the operations of the DEA:

> There is a basic hostility toward intelligence functions in enforcement organizations. Although the exact reasons for this hostility remain somewhat obscure, one can point to a few major features of the situation. The functions of an intelligence analyst are almost wholly included in the functions of an investigator. No investigator would be happy to admit that he had not mined the files of his organization for every nugget of relevant information. Consequently, investigators think they should be doing what the intelligence analysts are doing, and also believe that they can perform this function more effectively and less expensively than analysts. A corollary of this contempt is the fear that analysts will discover things the agent did not notice or suggest things that agents would never take seriously, or steal credit for cases that analysts helped to make. The possibility that intelligence analysts could embarrass, propose to guide, or steal credit from agents is particularly galling to agents because the intelligence analysts face no risks. They do not know how hard it is to debrief a defendant or crash a door. They sit secure in their offices to embarrass and guide street agents who risk their necks and work long, irregular hours. These bureaucratic factors may have prevented enforcement organizations from investing in intelligence systems even though their productivity could have been increased by such investments. The problem is not resources: it is a managerial problem of changing the style of an organization (1977: 168-169).

The multitude of tasks confronting modern law enforcement organizations requires a rational division of labor in order to maximize the use of their resources. The milieu in which intelligence work goes on may be filled with strife and fractured by dissension which engenders the parochialism of bigness (Kelly, 1978). But as Moore indicates, investigator jealousies notwithstanding, a determined integration of investigators and analysts can only enhance the capabilities of each.

Investigators may be brilliantly intuitive but they lack the time, energy and omnipresence to put together creditable accounts of the intricacies of complex conspiracies, security frauds, politically radical dissent groups and the activities of illegal firms that only the intelligence operatives including link and network analysis can churn out. The field investigator is doubtlessly presented with numerous opportunities for gathering useful information. At the same time, he or she is vulnerable to deceptions, mistakes and the stresses of time from which the analyst is largely insulated. It is not a question of the investigator being replaced by desk-bound analysts and technicians with their computer printouts. Rather, the relationship is, or should be, interactive and symbiotic: the analyst needs the hard, raw data that only the investigator can provide; and, in turn, the investigator benefits from the evaluations of that information by the analyst. Neither, in short, can function effectively without the other.

The settings in which analysis takes place may be usefully compared with the clinical environments in which physicians conduct their work. Both the medical doctor and the law enforcement intelligence analyst collect and evaluate information about events or entities. Secondly, the physician's diagnostic approaches involve a sort of detective work and inductive reasoning from a cumulative record of complaints, systems and bodily signs of a condition. Much the same approach towards evidence applies to intelligence work as well (Bamford, 1982: 190).

The importance and distinctive difference in the analogy between medical workers and intelligence analysts is that in most cases, a patient willingly cooperates with his or her examiners; the incentives to lie, deceive or manipulate vital information are usually muted by the need to relieve pain or illness. The cooperation of the patient in the medical setting is a given; it is part of the role of "patient" to cooperate fully with medical staff. And should a patient enthusiastically embrace the patient role and be disposed to submit to the regimens of the doctor, much of what is revealed and presented by the patient is uncertain and invaluable. Ideally, the physician equips himself or herself with the state of the art in their specialty. Similarly, with intelligence analysts, decisions are based on bringing to bear the extant body of knowledge available to the analysts and as much information investigations are capable of generating. It is at this point that the resemblances between the two kinds of activity end.

The experienced physician relying on clinical experience and the intimacy of the relationship between a doctor and a patient can and often does resort to the "dramatic insight," a conclusion about a patient reached after many hours of reflection and observation. The process does not diminish the relevance of scientific knowledge as such, but augments the doctor's skill and experience. But even here the physician is liable to error and misjudgment: he or she may miss a pattern of symptoms because of a concentration on details; the doctor may stubbornly adhere to a clinical diagnosis in spite of strong contrary evidence, and so on. For the intelligence analyst and his investigative colleagues who do not have the luxury of cooperative subjects, they must confront many of the same problems. The difference between them -- no face to face ongoing interaction in the case of the analyst with criminals -- makes the relationship to the sources of information a mixed blessing: distance from the criminal behaviors and/or actors permits some degree of objectivity; it reduces the distractions of incidental details that are mere contingencies to the key probes and problems. With these circumstances in mind and the analogical similarities laid out between some kinds of investigation and analysis, certain questions especially relevant to the problems of inference and the assessment of intelligence data may be raised. How does one selectively and accurately attend to relevant data? What typical processes sensitize us to implications hidden in data that have important policy and operational ramifications?

Logic and Reasoning: The Meaning of Inference

The term "inference" refers to the process of reaching conclusions derived from evidence.

It is reasoning from something known or assumed to something else which follows from it. In an inference, one adduces by deductive and inductive methods, or brings forward a conclusion from data or premises.

We make inferences. Because data is often fragmented or not readily available, or not stated in exact terms, we must fill the gaps by supplying our own information from details or ideas only suggested by what we have. We cannot be certain that what we do is absolutely right, but by following hunches based on the evidence in a logical manner, we can gain confidence in our assessments even if they are based on hints. Making inferences includes the processes of drawing conclusion, predicting outcomes, evaluating evidence and generalizing from the body of information at hand. Often, one must go beyond surface details and "read between the lines" in order to grasp the sense of explicit facts.

Inferential reasoning can be illustrated by examining some of the facts available about the drug problems involved in the manufacture and distribution of crack. It is known that the manufacture of crack is relatively simple. Because the conversion process of crack involves small amounts of cocaine, the law enforcement response is complicated by the nature of the marketplace that emerges.

An evaluation of the chemical/manufacturing processes of crack suggests several characteristics of the distribution networks that are likely to appear. First, the simplicity of the cocaine/crack conversion process allows almost anyone with access to small amounts of cocaine to manufacture crack. Secondly, as a result, crack manufacture and distribution is likely to consist of numerous "cottage industry" distributors, instead of several large identifiable organizations controlling significant market areas. Third, because there is no need for manufacturing consolidation and distribution centralization, intelligence gathering on crack trafficking encounters problems. Crack trafficking does not exhibit the more conventional and familiar structure found in the illegal distribution of almost all other controlled substances. Numerous individual entrepreneurs in the crack trade have created a proliferation of small markets. Fourth, law enforcement strategies to deal with crack must, therefore, be organized in significantly different ways compared with other drug control and containment policies such as heroin importation to street distribution. Thus, from a chemical analysis of the substance several street operational factors might be projected, and this, in turn, suggests a number of initiatives and procedures that law enforcement intelligence and enforcement units might pursue. An inference is the result, the end state of an argument. In presenting an argument, reasons are put forward from which a conclusion is teased out. The verbal formulations of the reasons and the data are called the premises of the argument, and the transition from premises to conclusion is expressed by such words and phrases as, "and so," "therefore," "consequently," "it follows that," or, "hence" (Quine, 1981; Ackerman, 1966).

Both psychologists and logicians pay attention to what may be called the principles of logic. We all use them everyday; nobody doubts them as being the rock-bottom of our everyday talk and thinking although until we study logic in a formal manner, we have probably never heard or seen such principles formulated explicitly.[1]

The words and phrases above are commonly found in everyday speech. They are decision-facilitating expressions and their precise uses and implications are the concern of the logician. We are then, intellectual clients of logicians not so much in the sense that we might learn some new thinking techniques - - that may or may not occur; rather, the examination of logical processes, the rules of reasoning, has the advantage of clarifying our patterns of thought in making correct and incorrect arguments.

Do we gain new knowledge from deductive reasoning? The rules of deductive inference do not enable us to know whether the premises from which we reason are true; they only help us decide whether our reasoning is valid or, in other words, whether we have committed a fallacy in drawing conclusions from premises. Strictly speaking, drawing inferences has nothing to do with the truth or reliability of the statements or propositions that are the premises of an argument.

The word, "argument" is often used to refer to the process itself which may be very emotional, but it is used here in a narrower, more technical sense. An "argument" is not a mere collection of propositions (the meaning of a sentence or statement), but has a structure. "Premises" and "Conclusion" are the fundamentals of the structure. The conclusion of an argument is that proposition that is affirmed on the basis of the other propositions, the premises, of the argument.

Arguments are either valid or invalid. In a widely used text in logic the dynamics of logical reasoning are laid out in this way:

An ... argument is *valid* when its premises do provide conclusive evidence for its conclusion, that is, when premises and conclusion are so related that it is absolutely impossible for the premises to be true unless the conclusion is true also. Every deductive argument is either valid or invalid, and the task of deductive logic is to clarify the nature of the relationship which holds between premises and conclusion and thus allow us to discriminate between valid and invalid arguments.

An inductive argument, on the other hand, does not claim that its premise give conclusive evidence for the truth of its conclusion, but only that they provide *some* evidence for it.

Inductive arguments are *neither valid nor invalid* in the sense in which those terms are applied to deductive arguments. Inductive arguments may, of course, be evaluated as better or worse, according to the degree of likelihood or probability which their premises confer upon their conclusion (Copi, 1955: emphasis in the original).

It is important not to confuse the *validity* of a deductive argument with the truth of the sentences that make up its conclusion and premises. It is possible for an argument to be valid when some or all of its premises are false.

A. 1. All waste disposal firms in the State of North Dakota are owned by criminals.
2. The Empire Waste Disposal firm of New Jersey operates in North Dakota.
3 . The Empire Waste Disposal firm is owned by criminals.

This is a valid argument even though the premises (statement #1 and #2) are false. The trap to avoid is in thinking that only arguments with true premises can be valid. Typically, we associate validity and truth in arguments of the form:

B. 1. All government employees are subject to the law.
2. Intelligence analysts are government employees.
Therefore,
3. Intelligence analysts are subject to the law.

In this example, since the premises are true (statements #1 and #2), then the conclusion (statement #3) must be true also because the conclusion in any deductive argument is no more than a restatement of something already in the premises. If a conclusion were false, and the premises are true, the conclusion is *not* just an expression of information already in the premises. It would go beyond the premises and say something not in them.

Two things are important to keep in mind about truth and validity. First, validity is a relationship ("follows from") and the mere presence of false premises does not mean that an argument is invalid. Second, no valid argument can have true premises and a false conclusion. This latter is an example of a "sound argument"- - that is, arguments that are valid and *also* have two premises. The last point to make at this stage of the discussion is that the validity or invalidity of a syllogism (a three-part argument with two premises and a conclusion) depends exclusively upon its form and is completely independent of the specific content or subject matter of the premises.

An Excursus on Sound Arguments and Deductive Proofs

To return momentarily to a question raised earlier as to whether any new knowledge is gained from deductive reasoning, it can be said that sometimes surprising and unsuspected conclusions can be drawn from premises. And scientific theories which are explicitly expressed as groups of premises (theoretical laws or principles), often yield information no one dreamed was there. Again, what is gained through the process of deductive reasoning can often be tedious. In a simple argument like this:

C.   1. All criminals have broken the law.

       2. <u>John Smith is a criminal.</u>

Therefore

       3. John Smith has broken the law.

The conclusion really tells us nothing new. But if an argument is complex, the idea that the conclusion is "contained in" the premises is not at all obvious or apparent. The conclusion is not literally contained in the premises as a cigarette is in a pack; it is rather implicit. The answer to the question it seems is that sometimes we do and sometimes we do not learn anything new. Further, the learning itself may be purely psychological - - meaning that the sense of discovery of something new may vary from person to person. In (C), the conclusion probably does not give anyone any new or unexpected information. This becomes more apparent as the complexity of an argument increases. The conclusion to the following argument would probably constitute new knowledge for most of us:

D.   1. If Jones the bank guard was not paying attention at the time, the armored car was not noticed when it came in.

       2. If the witness's account is correct, the bank guard was not paying attention at the time.

       3. Either the armored car was noticed, or Jones is hiding something.

       4. <u>Jones is not hiding anything.</u>

Therefore, the witness's account is not correct.

For someone with highly perfected reasoning powers, like John Stuart Mill or Aristotle, who could instantly see the implications of every statement or combination of statements uttered, doubtless no conclusion would come as new information; but since most human beings are not so gifted there are many conclusions of valid deductive arguments which do come as new information in spite of the fact that the conclusion is "contained in" the premises.

Take the following argument:

E.   1. If law enforcement concentrates its limited resources on La Cosa Nostra, then its ability to cope with non-traditional organized crime will be weakened and crime in general will rise.
2. If more resources are made available for OC control, then the cost of the law enforcement will increase.
3. If the cost of law enforcement increases or crime in general rises, then the people will lose confidence in government.
4. If the cost of law enforcement increases, then the poor and minorities will suffer.
5. The citizens at large want policies that reduce crime.
6. If citizens at large want policies that reduce crime, then law enforcement will concentrate its resources on LCN.

Therefore, people will lose confidence in government and the poor and minorities will suffer.

In this kind of an argument, it is just not possible to take a look and tell whether its conclusion follows from its premises or not. It is not obvious that the conclusion is already "contained in" the premises. To show that the conclusion of argument (E) does follow from the premises a fairly simple process may be employed. The basic idea is that we can use some of the premises of the original argument to construct other valid arguments that are more modest and shorter. Since the conclusions of these arguments follow from the premises belonging to the original argument, we are free to use these conclusions as if they were extra premises.

The prudent strategy insists that we examine the conclusion we want to establish. Then we look through the set of premises to determine what interim conclusions might be useful in deducing our final conclusion. When we spot interim conclusions, we then construct shortened arguments in order to establish them.

In the example given above, examine premise #4. If it can be established that, "the cost of law enforcement increases (or will increase), then we could assert the rest of the statement in Sentence #4: "the poor and minorities will suffer" (economically and from a reduction in general enforcement activities). Since this is half of our conclusion, it makes sense to try to get a short argument to establish the first sentence as an interim conclusion.

When we look at the other half of the main conclusion to argument (E), that, "people will lose confidence in the government", we see it in premise #3. If we could establish the first component in premise #3 ("If the cost of law enforcement increases or crime in general rises...") as an interim conclusion, then the second component could be asserted. If achievable, then what needs to be done is to place it together with, "the poor and minorities will suffer," and the conclusion that is desired will have been deduced.

By working backwards and attempting to find what short arguments can be constructed out of the premises, plus the new conclusions, that will have the sentences as *their* conclusion, we ought to be able to establish the main conclusion of argument (E). A sequence of short arguments will yield conclusions that will produce still other arguments that reproduce the conclusion of the whole. In the sequence below, the numbered sentences are original premises from argument (E), and those with the small letters are interim conclusions that will serve as premises in other arguments. Thus:

(E')
(1) 6. If citizens at large want policies that reduce crime, then law enforcement will

        concentrate its resources on LCN.

5.   The citizens at large want policies that reduce crime.

a.   Law enforcement will concentrate its resources on LCN.

(2)1.   If law enforcement concentrates its limited resources on La Cosa Nostra, then its ability to cope with non-traditional organized crime will be weakened and crime in general will rise.

a.   Law enforcement will concentrate its resources on LCN.

b.   Its ability to cope with non-traditional organized crime will be weakened and crime in general will rise.

(3)a.   Law enforcement will concentrate its resources on LCN.

b.   Its ability to cope with non-traditional organized crime will be weakened and crime in general will rise.

c.   Law enforcement will concentrate its resources on LCN and its ability to cope with non-traditional organized crime will be weakened and crime in general will rise.

(4)2.   If more resources are made available for organized crime control, then the cost of law enforcement will increase.

c.   Law enforcement will concentrate its resources on LCN (OC control), and its ability to cope with non-traditional organized crime will be weakened and crime in general will rise.

d.   The cost of law enforcement will increase.

(5)3.   If the cost of law enforcement increases or crime in general rises, then the people will lose confidence in government.

d.   The cost of law enforcement will increase.

e.   People will lose confidence in government.

With interim conclusion "e," half of the argument is completed. By continuing the same process of creating mini-syllogisms, we shall get the other half of the general conclusion.

(6) 4.   If the cost of law enforcement increases, then the poor and minorities will suffer.

d.   The cost of law enforcement will increase.

f.   The poor and minorities will suffer.

(7)e.   People will lose confidence in government.

f.   The poor and minorities will suffer.

Therefore, people will lose confidence in government, and the poor and minorities will suffer.

The seven arguments show that the conclusion does follow from the premises. Each connecting link in the chain is itself a valid argument. Thus, the whole chain of arguments constitutes a single valid argument. The chain of arguments leading to the final conclusion is a deductive proof of the validity of the original argument. The purpose of the proof is to answer the questions, How does the conclusion follow from the premises and, How can it be shown that the conclusion is already "contained in" the premises?

Returning to the arguments of (E), certain valid argument forms are evident. Two forms, in particular, are basic to the series of proofs given. They are:

A.   <u>Modus Ponens</u> (MP)   1. If p, then q   e.g. 6. If citizens at large want policies that reduce crime, then law enforcement will concentrate its resources on LCN.

                                        p   5. The citizens at large want policies that reduce crime.

                                        ———   a. Law enforcement
                                          q   will concentrate its resources on LCN.

B.   <u>Conjunctive Syllogism</u> (Conj.)

                                  2.   p   e.g. e. People will lose confidence in government.

                                              f. The poor and minorities
                                    q   will suffer.

                                        ———   People will lose confidence in government
                                p and q   and the poor and minorities will suffer.

The Rules of Inference [2]

The argument forms have been given their traditional names and common abbreviations, and they can be used as rules. Accordingly, each conclusion reached can be justified. Thus, conclusion "a" in argument (E') is established by deducing it from premises #6 and #5 by way of the Modus Ponens (MP) rule. By indicating the appropriate premises and the rule governing the valid argument form, the premises and the conclusions can be listed one after another. For example, using argument (E).

Premises   Name of the Rule and
                                                          Premises Involved

1. If law enforcement concentrates its limited resources on LCN, then its ability to cope with non-traditional organized crime will be weakened

and crime in general will rise.

2. If more resources are made available for OC
control, then the costs of law enforcement will increase.

3. If the costs of law enforcement increases or crime
in general rises, then the people will lose confidence in
government.

4. If the costs of law enforcement increases, then the
poor and minorities will suffer.

5. The citizens at large want policies that reduce crime.

6. If citizens at large want policies that reduce crime, then
<u>law enforcement will concentrate its resources on LCN</u>.

7. Law enforcement will concentrate its limited   (MP) 6, 5
resources on LCN.

8. Its ability to cope with non-traditional OC   (MP) 1, 7
will be weakened and crime in general will rise.

9. Law enforcement will concentrate its limited   (Conj) 7, 8
resources on LCN and its ability to cope with
non-traditional OC will be weakened and crime in
general will rise.

10. The costs of law enforcement will increase.   (MP) 2, 9

11. People will lose confidence in government.   (MP) 3, 10

12. The poor and minorities will suffer.   (MP) 4, 10

13. People will lose confidence in government   (Conj) 11, 12
and the poor and minorities will suffer.

In this presentation of proof and deductive demonstration, each statement in the list is
either a premise or one that follows from the statements above it as the conclusion of a short, valid
argument. Rather than working out each of the short arguments, the same thing has been done
by referring to a valid argument form (Modus Ponens, and Conjunction; vide Note #2) and the
sentences that are used as premises.

Many more rules could be given and there really is no limit to the number of valid argument
forms there are. Any argument form that is valid can be used as a rule of inference.

Fugure 1   Figure 2

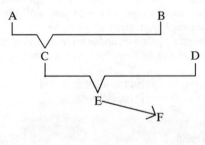

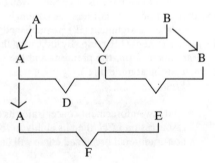

So far, the patterns of arguments have been the focus -- sound arguments, decomposed into shorter, more obvious syllogisms where whatever follows from a conclusion follows from its premises. Schematically, argument (E) above is configured as shown in Figure 1.

If we have a sound argument from A and B to C, and another from C and D to E, and yet another from E to F, then we have a sound argument from A, B and C to F. A physical "chain" may break either because it has a weak link or because it is too long; a logical "chain", however, can break only for the first reason - - if it has a weak link. If, but only if, each link is sound, the whole chain is sound.

The workings of the chain - - known as the "synthetic rule" - - allows that any conclusion drawn from the original stock of premises may be added to those premises to arrive at new conclusions, and the accumulative power to generate new premises and conclusions may be repeated *ad infinitum*. For example, we may get C from A and B, then D from A and C, then E from B, and C, then F from A and E; C, D, E and F all follow from A and B. The pattern appears as shown in Figure 2.

Notice the use of A and B as premises; the arrows from A to A or B to B, are all right, since obviously any proposition follows from itself.

Using the schema, the next line of argument may be reworked in terms of premises and conclusions to see if they fit into either the models in Figures 1 or 2. Then the application of the rules of inference may be used to test the validity of the argument.

1. If the existence of vice laws creates opportunities for high-level criminal syndicates ... then vigorous enforcement may expand their opportunities.
2. Intensive drug enforcement will create competitive advantages for those best able to obstruct the enforcement process.
3. Increasing enforcement at the highest-level of trafficking increases the returns to successful high-level dealing and underscores the value of tight organization and the use of violence as an instrument for doing business.
4. If the strategy of aggressive enforcement against high-level drug dealers is likely to increase the wealth and power of organized crime, then increasing enforcement aimed at the high-level traffickers yields an increase in crime.
5. Top level drug enforcement efforts against importers and distributors affect the price of drugs without much affecting the number and behavior of retailers.
6. Street level enforcement fosters caution among dealers and increases the buyers/purchasers "search time" in acquiring a supply.
7. Under conditions of vigorous street enforcement buyers may spend less money and consume fewer drugs because of the difficulties in "scoring". To the dealers this will appear as an unspecificable decline in demand.
8. While top-level drug enforcement makes drug-users more dangerous and organized criminals richer, effective street enforcement reduces drug use and the pressures for money among users, and, at the same time, hurts high-level dealers in their bank accounts.

Therefore, law enforcement pressure at the street level will make high level dealing less profitable by forcing an increase in retail prices as lower-level dealers will require higher margins to compensate for increased risks, and will thereby reduce the quantity of drugs consumed (Kleiman, 1985).

Clearly there are policy ramifications for the development of law enforcement resources implicit in this argument.

We have been mapping the inference-carrying labors of various concepts -- bloodless ones like "some," "not," "all" and "either." These have to be formed into unnatural idiomatic shapes before logic deigns to employ them. It was seen that valid argument forms pivot on topic-neutral expressions and certain logical constraints. What determines whether a syllogism, an argument, is either valid or invalid is the legitimacy of the work given to "all," "some," and, "not," irrespective of the concrete topics of its premises and conclusion. It bears repeating that inferences are valid or invalid by virtue of their form.

Intelligence analysts are the clients of formal logic, or should be. The relationship of the intelligence analyst to logic is rather like what geometry is to surveying. The surveyor finds no Euclidean straight roads or neatly delineated, mathematically impeccable property boundary lines. Yet, they could not map the twisting roads and the meandering property lines save against the artificial and ideally regular concepts in terms of which alone can they calculate out the relative positions and heights of natural objects recorded in visual observations. Of necessity the surveyor is a student of geometry, a purchaser of its techniques and insights. The possibility of maps and measurements being correct and reliable is the gift of geometry.

A similar relationship exists between the businessman and accounting. His problems are not solely arithmetical, still, he needs the check of the calculator and the balanced debit and credit ledger. The businessman is the patron of the accountant. Of course warfare cannot be reduced to training drills, nor surveying to geometry, nor business to arithmetic. Nor can the handling of intelligence problems be reduced to either the application or derivation of theorems about logical constants. The intelligence analyst is doing what might be called "informal logic" and the suggestion that their problems, results or procedures should or could be formalized is as widely astray as would the suggestions about the soldier, surveyor or businessman's activities being reducible to marching techniques and mathematics.

The logic of inference provides the informal logician/analyst with a "compass" (a set of guidelines) by which to steer through a jungle of facts. It is not, though, a course on which to steer.

Predicting and Inferring: A Distinction With A Difference

To "predict" is to assert that something will happen or is likely to happen. Making a prediction may be just guessing or prophesying. To predict is not to infer. To infer is to be concerned with form -- whether conclusions derived from premises follow logically. Inferring is concerned with whether the propositions (statements, sentences, premises) are true. An individual is concerned with the truth or falsity of the premises yet the major immediate interest is whether the conclusion really follows from them. When the check-out clerk in the supermarket hands you a bill, you may check the figures. There are two kinds of mistake that may have been made. The clerk may have punched in the wrong prices on individual items, or the prices on the items may have been incorrectly added. The logician is only concerned, as a logician, with whether the figures have been added correctly.

The inferences of the intelligence analyst on the other hand are very often inferences like those of the historian or a geologist: they deal with past events and states of affairs. And, like the inferences of a poker player or a physician that are very often inferences about contemporary states of affairs so too with the analyst. Not all inferred conclusions are in the future tense --- that is the role of prediction: asserting something in the future tense. There are dangers here.

Inferences to the unobserved "has-been" and inferences to the unobserved "is-now" may be just as respectable as inferences to the unobserved "is-to-be". The important difference is that the future is inevitably unobserved "now", whereas the, "what-has-been" and "what-is-now" might have been observed or could have been observed instead of having to make predictions.

Some predictions, but not all, are the outcomes of good or bad inferences. One may even speak of a reasoned or reasonable prediction lodged in solid inferential work from known to anticipated outcomes which may form a basis for proactive enforcement strategies.

Assume that: (1) field observations and informant reports indicate that Asian-Americans are moving rapidly into narcotics, mainly heroin, with large-scale distributors. (2) In the locale under surveillance, the known Tongs (Chinese criminal groups) are heavily involved in gambling, extortion rackets and alien smuggling. (3) *The President's Commission on Organized Crime* and other sources point out that Tongs operate unlike other criminal organizations in that they are grouped primarily according to criminal specialty such as gambling, prostitution, and the like (President's Commission, 1986: 26; Kerr, 1987). Several possibilities emerge.

First, if the views of the President's Commission and other sources are reliable, a new criminal organization may be operating. Secondly, field observations and informant reports on Chinese organized criminal groups may have been inadequate and failed to detect the drug dealing among existing organizations. If it can be determined by other methods of data collection and verification that the current means and sources of information are reliable, then it may be concluded that unsatisfactory surveillance and information-gathering are not responsible for the lapse in the data on criminal activity. Thirdly, it may be reasonable to conclude in view of these checks on procedures and after consulting other "non-obtrusive" sources, that a new criminal group is on the scene.

At this point, strategic planners might examine some of the possible consequences of this new development. What impact will the group have on the extant crime picture in the area. What increases and types of crime and violence may be expected? And how might law enforcement gear up to estimate and ultimately neutralize the criminal capacities of the new group?

The Formation of Hypotheses and Theories

The appearance of a new criminal organization is an occasion to generate hypotheses which seek to order the facts into coherent patterns. A hypothesis is no more than a statement put to the facts of a situation; it may entail, and usually does, inferential tasks that are descriptive, meaning that the analyst must be able to characterize and describe the data accurately. We "verify" hypotheses which means that we determine how faithfully they describe the relationships among facts (Stephens, 1968).

Applying order to information requires that variables be assigned to cases that hypotheses are able to discover. A "case" may be events, processes, persons, behaviors or organizations that hypotheses talk about. The "variable" is the characteristic, trait or attribute of the case. In the example given above, a criminal group, a Chinese Tong (the case) may be characterized as a new criminal group, as a specialist criminal organization, and as an ethnic group -- all variables. In hypotheses, variables are "something about" persons, groups, or descriptive of some attributes, or both.

Hypotheses are ordinarily about relationships among several events, persons and/or behaviors or actions. Covariation, a correlation between variables, is an integral part of hypotheses. Correlation may be positive, negative or of zero value. In a positive correlation, variables tend to go together in an "if ... then" form: cases exhibiting one variable also tend to exhibit the other. Conversely, cases which do not have one variable showing a characteristic tend not to have the other; cases exhibiting a low magnitude on one variable tend also to show a low magnitude on the other.

An example: "More crime occurs in slums." Here is a generalization about types of neighborhoods and what goes on in them. Two variables are mentioned as related, or correlated to each other: "slums" and the "crime rate." The hypothesis says that, in terms of magnitude, slummier neighborhoods tend to have higher crime rates than other kinds of neighborhoods. In other words, cases (neighborhoods) high on one variable (slum conditions) tend to be high on the other (the crime rate). Conversely, another hypothesis is implied by this one -- namely, cases low on one variable will be low on the other; non-slums, it is implied, have lower crime rates. Observations on the assessed value of dwelling units in the area, real property value data, is collected and enables us to operationalize, and test, the crime rate. If the crime rate *increases* as the assessed value *decreases*, the hypothesis shows a "goodness of fit" between the evidence and the variables. Likewise, if the crime rate *decreases* as the assessed value *increases*, then the hypothesis is verified but, of course, not proved beyond every doubt.

Theories may be consulted that are capable of causally explaining the covariations formulated and tested. Why, for instance, is the crime rate higher in slums? Are all slums victimized in this way? If the hypothesis is generalizable to other slums other than those specifically studied where the relationship was established, it may be used as a basis for predicting the fluctuation of crime rates in neighborhoods with varying property values. A theory may suggest that "property value" is the concrete indicator, a kind of sociological shorthand, for different lifestyles and social class concentrations among whom crime rates vary with street crimes more common among the poorest. The purpose in putting together a theory is to make causal inferences, judgments as to what factors relate to each other and what factors help explain what is happening. Theories ask about the possible causes of the verified covariations found in the variables. A good theory is one that does at least three things: it makes predictions, it offers useful explanations of the interactions among variables and it makes itself relatively easy to disprove.

Inductive Arguments and Probability Inferences

By its very nature an inductive argument is invalid when compared with a deductive argument. With inductive arguments, their conclusions do not follow from the premises. There is no guarantee that if the premises of an inductive argument happen to be true, then the conclusion will be true as well. The distinguishing feature of an inductive argument is that its conclusion goes beyond the premises, it is typically expansive. At best, the premises may be said to "support" the conclusion; make it "more likely" than sheer guess work; the premises do not irrevocably guarantee it. Inductive arguments do not pretend to demonstrate the truth of their conclusions as following necessarily from the premises. Rather, conclusions are established with a provisional label of "probable."

Most everyday inferences are formed by analogical reasoning which is the most common type of inductive argument form. A spate of burglaries occur in a shopping mall. An analyst infers, given the M.O. of the burglars evident from field investigative reports, that a particular group is involved in terms of their number, methods of stealing and modes of entry into specific retail businesses. Truck hijacking by "crews" of three men and a woman in two cars are being committed around a major port facility. An analyst determines based on the analysis of other descriptions of hijack teams that a particular gang is again operating in the area. Mug files of known hijackers are closely inspected by witnesses and warrants for arrest issued.

Analogy lies at the root of most of our ordinary reasoning from past experience to what the future will hold. Put differently, inductive reasoning is a species of logical "mortgaging" where the conclusions are intuited from the evidence with promises made to search for the confirming premises. It is logically possible, of course, that the shopping mall bandits are an entirely unknown group, and that the hijacking crew was not the one that the evidence led to. Analogy is used in explanations where something unfamiliar is made intelligence through being compared with something else that is known and common. Schematically, analogical inductive arguments have the form as shown in Figure 3.

Though no analogical argument is ever "valid" in the technical sense of the term, some arguments are indeed more compelling and cogent and probable than others. The tentative conclusion that a particular hijack crew is again operating can be established as highly probable on the grounds that: (1) the M.O. in recent robberies closely resembles that of a known group; and (2) victims statements, and the review of mug files have indicated that some of the members of a known group may be in action.

Figure 3:

X, Y, Z all have the properties M and N.
X and Y have the property O.
Therefore, Z has the property O.

Mill's Methods of Inductive Inference

Because of the inherent structural weaknesses in analogical argument, the British philosopher, John Stuart Mill (1879) formulated some techniques for testing causal reasoning. Much of our causal, inductive reasoning occurs in a flash, as in the case of the hijacking's which immediately suggest lines of investigation some of which prove fruitful. The purposes of Mill's methods are to lay out, step by step, what actually goes on when we think about evidence that has many loose ends. Because analogical reasoning is so deeply embedded in inductive processes, a review of Mill's chief techniques is worth exploring.

1) Method of Agreement

Perhaps the best way of examining these rules of reasoning is through example. With the hijackers, suppose that there are four armed robberies of trucks. All of the trucks were tractor-trailers. Of the four vehicles hijacked, two belong to the same trucking firm; three carried home appliances: TV's, microwave ovens, and brand name video cassettes. Each truck loaded at the same depot and each was hijacked in midday along two of the three major arterials in the area.

It is worth reiterating that while this discussion may seem to be laboring the obvious, it is designed to lay out in detail the processes of reasoning in an explicit manner so that it can be applied in more complicated situations where many variables intervene.

Now, making the information more readily accessible to logical analysis and inspection, it might be coded using letters to represent circumstances. The letters "a," "b," "c," and "d" refer to the facts of the robberies, and the letter "r" to the outcome -- the armed robbery. Where the four trucks are the four "instances" examined, the information may be represented as follows:

Figure 4

Robbery Incidents	Circumstances	Outcome
1	a, b, c, d	r
2	a, b, c, d	r
3	b, d	r
4	c, d	r

Key: "a" - trucking firm; "b" - truck load; "c" - trucking loading location; "d" -type of vehicle; "r" - truck hijacking.

From these data we might be led to tentatively conclude that the type of vehicle and the on-load locations were very important in determining the hijacker's M.O. Further, the load on board the trucks and the fact that two of the four trucks are from the same company suggest that these may not be random, hit-or-miss robberies but are planned and dependent on "inside information." This would coincide with our general knowledge about how hijacking's routinely occur. The similarities enable the analyst to match M.O. with previously known hijacking operations. This does not *prove* that a particular group carried out the robberies, but it makes the probability much stronger that a particular group that operates with the M.O., that the analyst is able to uncover, is suspect.

The data used to illustrate the procedure are merely that -- illustrative, constructed for the purposes of demonstration. In real world situations, they may not always be available. Suppose, for instance, it was the case that in the four incidents both the type of vehicle (d) and the on-load locations (c) occurred? The Method of Agreement would eliminate (a) and (b) and leave open the question as to whether it is the type of vehicle (d) or the on-load location (c) or both that is crucial to the investigation.

2)   Method of Difference
If, on further investigation of robberies in the area, it is discovered that other trucks were hijacked which did not contain a load of electrical appliances (b) but that the robberies were similar in every other circumstance, we might still infer that the same group may have been responsible. See Figure 5.

3)   Method of Residues
If in figure 6 on the next page, we eliminate the most common features of the seven

hijacking incidents ("d" - type of vehicle), we are left with "c" (the truck loading location), and "a" (trucking firm) as the secondarily most characteristic features of the incidents. This method has the quality of deductive inference and narrows the parameters of the investigation.

Figure 5

Robbery Incidents	Circumstances	Outcome
5	a, c, d	r
6	a, d	r
7	c, d	r

4)   Method of Concomitant Variation[3]
Using the example of the hijackers once again, this method comes closest to the deductive techniques discussed above. In order to further insure that a particular group with a distinctive method of operation is operating in a specific area, it may be well to examine hijackings elsewhere to see what patterns of activity they exhibit. Assume that information is generated on hijackings in other locales and that they reveal the following patterns:

Figure 6

Robbery Incidents	Circumstances	Outcome
1	a, b, c, d	r
2	a, b, c, d	r
3	b, d	r
4	c, d	r
5	a, c, d	r
6	a, d	r
7	c, d	r

Utilizing the first four incidents (Figure 6) and comparing these with employee attendance patterns, it becomes clear that on days when the four incidents occurred, three employees with pertinent information on the loads, times, and destinations of the vehicles were absent. Deeper probing of incident dates and employee work records indicates the same pattern: incident occurrence and absenteeism of one employee for the last three hijackings.

Figure 7a

Occurrence of Robbery Incident at "a"	Employee Attendance Record at "a"
1	absent
2	absent
5	absent
6	absent

Figure 7b

Occurrence of Robbery Incident Elsewhere	Employee Attendance at "a"
3	present
4	present
7	present

A. In incidents 1 through 7, the frequency of the robberies seems related to two factors, "c" - the location of truck loading, and "a" - the trucking firm.

B. Over six months, robbery incidents occur on weekdays.

C. An analysis of employees at the firms victimized by hijackings reveals that those with access to bills of lading and truck manifests exhibit curious fluctuations in work attendance records.

When hijackings have occurred at firm "a" an employee with vital information was absent on those four dates. However, when hijacking occurred at other firms, the employee at "a" was not absent. The investigation becomes more sharply focused. This method enables the analyst to observe changes in the circumstances and admits a greater amount of data concerning causal linkages between hijackings, their locations, the firm most frequently victimized and the variations in employee behavior when incidents happen.

Together, Mill's methods make for good instruments for the discovery and confirmation of relationships in data. The essential character of the Methods of Agreement is that it helps to eliminate extraneous pieces of information. In the Method of Difference, the exclusion or absence of a circumstance can be extrapolated while leaving the other circumstances the same. The Method of Residues proceeds by systematically eliminating as possible relevant factors those circumstances whose effects have already been established. Concomitant Variation encompasses all of the techniques upon which Mill elaborated.

Causal connections per se can not be decisively determined by Mill's methods nor can they ever be established demonstratively by them. They can, however, aid the process of discovery in critically important ways. What can be said in defense of their use is that they constitute the basic patterns of shifting through evidence in an effort to confirm or refute by observation, hypotheses claiming causal connections.

Inferences based on probability assessments are always estimates characterized by partial knowledge and partial ignorance. What we want to know is "how" from relatively slight stocks of empirical data we can get to reliable assessments. What we want to examine are processes concerning, what may be called, with apologies, "inductive probabilities."

Inductive Probabilities

Descriptions of estimates or assessments as being "probable" or "improbable" ordinarily mean that they are either statistically well-grounded or not. However clear and straight forwarded this may sound, notions of statistical frequencies that underpin the reliability of an estimate are often confused.

Assume that in one year, twenty-six operators out of two hundred auto body repair shops in one jurisdiction dealt in stolen parts. Eighty-seven percent did not. This is a frequency of recorded percentage. We can say that John Smith's auto repair shop in this jurisdiction yields twenty-six chances out of two hundred that he handled stolen auto parts, and 174 that he did not. The odds of his operating illegally are 13/100. In principle, such an actual frequency of recorded percentage is perfectly determinate and certain. Observing recordings, counting and reckoning are the only operations involved. What can be inferred from these facts?

If it is argued that in one year in one jurisdiction 13% of the auto body repair shops were crooked and that, therefore, 13% of auto body repair shops will operate illegally next year or are doing so this year, then we are going beyond our data and making inductive generalizations based on an inferred frequency or an extrapolated percentage. Indeed, we are transcending our data in two ways. First, we are inferring, or, to be more precise, conjecturing that 13% of other auto body repair shops will operate illegally as have 13% of those examined. But the extrapolated percentage is indeterminate in two dimensions. It is not certain that the same percentage will hold among unexamined cases as held among examined cases. Other jurisdictions may have shops operated by more scrupulously honest proprietors, or have ample supplies of legitimate auto suppliers so that demand does not pressure operators to go out to the black markets in stolen parts. Finally, law enforcement in other jurisdictions may have assigned more priority to auto theft and illegally operated shops so that incentives to get into business are not attractive nor potentially profitable in terms of the risks involved.

Worse than this is the flaw in the hypothesis that any determinate percentage will obtain among unexamined cases. For the number of such cases is not determinate: auto body repair shops come and go; auto accidents rise and fall; in short, the factors affecting the number of auto body repair shops - - legal or illegal - - is quite capricious.

For another example, the figures provided recently by a government publication: " (T)hree-fourths of all jail inmates reported using illegal drugs at some time in their lives" (BJS, Annual Report, 1987 : 18). Assume that this proportion will remain constant. What does this assumption mean? It cannot mean that out of any 100 inmates, 75 will be drug users for we might be referring to 100 non-drug-users or to 100 drug-using inmates, perhaps unwittingly. Nor can it mean that out of the next or some otherwise randomly picked 100 or 1,000 inmates 75 or 750 will be drug users. Apart from the fact that if we chose instead the next 101 or 1001 imprisoned offenders, there could not be 75% among them who were drug abusers. There is nothing to prevent the next 100 or 1,000 inmates from containing unusual runs of non-drug-users or all drug-users for that matter. Moreover, nor will it do to interpret the assumption as meaning that out of an infinite number of inmates, 75% will be drug-users. For it makes no sense to say that there will be an infinite number of inmates. Rather, what is meant is something like this: the longer the list of inmates grows, the nearer the proportion of drug-users approaches 75% of the total population. It is unlikely in fact to be exactly 75% at any specified point; at best, we have with the percentage an inductive warrant for relying on an extrapolated percentage.

Returning to the illegal auto body repair shops, these considerations beg the question, What grounds have we to generalize from a finite number of observed cases to strong claims believed to be true of a large number of unobserved cases? In other words, how can an assessment of illegally operated auto body shops apply to purported or expected trends among uninspected auto shops? To infer to the existence of uninspected auto shops is quite different from inferences that certain characteristics are true for any auto shops. We may argue from the distribution of illegal auto shops in certain towns to their prevalence in other locales, but the inference to a certain population of illegal auto shops in other locals is quite different from judgments about the conditions that cause or promote illegal auto shop operations in those other towns. The uncertainty of the former inference would have no tendency to vitiate the latter.

In preparing assessments and estimates, analysts attend to the probabilities of outcomes by calculating patterns of behavior, using Mill's methods, and their possible variations. An assessment that predicts the growth or persistence of illegal auto shops might depend on determining the number of illegal shops in an area and by comparing this estimate with the rate of auto theft in the same area (and with those contiguous to it). Using our hypothetical example of 26 operators out of 200 shops being illegal, we should want to know if this frequency (13/100, or 13%) is tied to such parameters as the rate of auto theft in an area, and/or the economic affluence of the area. We want to develop a hypothesis which pictures the conditions that promote illegal shops. The strength of the assessment and the testing of the hypothesis about conditions conducive to illegal shops depends on the size and representativeness of the data base.

The relevance of the indicators (the auto theft rate, and the economic wealth, the per capita income in the area) requires independent examination to determine whether they may be safely and reliably assumed to affect the actual and projected frequencies of illegal auto shop operation. They may not. That is, the auto theft rate may not fluctuate in either direction while the frequency of illegal auto shops remains the same. Nor might the illegal auto shop rate be affected if the economic affluence index in an area changes - - whether real income goes up or down. To sharpen the analysis, the "auto theft rate" would be specified very carefully by excluding from it joy-riding adolescents (probably the majority of incidents) and to the extent possible, fraudulently reported auto thefts, leaving those committed by professionals.

The prevalence of illegal auto shops compared with the refined auto theft rate may produce a testable hypothesis: if the auto theft rate increases, the number of illegal auto shops will increase. The logical converse, however, may not obtain: the decrease in the number of illegal auto shops may not be a function of the decline in auto theft.[4] A broadened data base with the specification of factors affecting an assessment strengthens the value of the supporting or falsifying evidence. Every step forward in precision improves the efficacy of the Method of Concomitant Variations.

By studying more auto shops and rates of auto thefts, the reliability of the assessment is improved.

The Process and Product of Intelligence Assessments

An intelligence assessment would be incomplete if in its design it failed to go beyond the initial analytical phase and did not offer suggestions about alternative policy and operations. Its chief tasks may be to spell out the interrelationships between auto thefts and the prevalence of illegal auto shops. Then it may venture into speculations about the variables it thinks may be related to each other. If, say, there are solid reasons to believe that there is a causal relationship between the auto theft rate and the number of illegal auto shops, a series of sub-questions may be generated to explore the dimensions of the data and their interrelationships still further. [5] For example:

1. To what extent, if any, are illegal auto shops "organized"? Are there interlocking ownership? Are organized criminal elements involved?
2. Among the owners of record of auto body shops, how many have organized crime connections? How many have previous criminal records involving auto theft?
3. Are there indications that auto theft specialists are tied up with specific auto body shops? (Here a network analysis of previous criminal association patterns might prove profitable).
4. How knowledgeable is the local community about illegal auto shops? What is the community attitude? Does it tolerate the shops?
5. Are the illegal auto shops vulnerable to law enforcement efforts? If so, what techniques should be employed, and what is the probability of success?

Subsequent to the information collection phase surrounding these questions, the following points may emerge:

(a) The majority of the illegal shops are associated with organized crime figures.

(b) The latter are silent partners who function surreptitiously to arrange "auto thefts to order". Illegal shops are not, however, under the control of a few individuals; control and influence in their operations are diffuse.

(c) Most of the owners of record are actively involved in repair work. Some have criminal records in auto theft and the possession of stolen auto parts but these were youthful offenses. Other owners have clean records.

(d) The evidence indicates that auto thieves deal with specific shops and do not "free lance" stolen vehicles or parts to the highest bidders. There is no free-market competition among illegal shop operators.

(e) An analysis of commercial records shows that illegal shops also do a thriving legitimate business. The community of consumers appears to tolerate the shops even with widespread tacit knowledge that they may be "mob places."

(f) Some types of undercover work coupled with a sting operation may succeed in breaking up the more loosely organized illegal shops and theft rings.

With this information in hand, a knowledgeable judgment concerning the allocation and commitment of resources to the problem may be evaluated. Even before an effort is mounted, data collection would still proceed because more information means more flexibility in strategic and tactical operational options. The collection of information also assists the intelligence function which does not stop at the point of operational activities; data collection provides a critically indispensable check on the reliability of the data that made up the initial assessment. Further, the quality of the data may be improved through the filtering out of rumor, hearsay and speculation from fact. And, the continuing collection of information - - especially from independent sources - - helps to corroborate what is in hand.

Individual pieces of data on "organized crime affiliations" or "auto theft professionals" suggest that the preparation of an operational plan requires the inputs of specialists and experts in these types of criminal behavior. The collation of such expert information on organized crime figures and auto theft professionals may suggest other lines of investigation and action.

The preparation of an intelligence assessment plan may be tedious and also delicate work susceptible to errors and misjudgments. Its key task is to transform raw information into a body of fairly reliable knowledge upon which enforcement activity can be launched. There are a number of procedural cautions in the evaluation process of data that may be taken to protect against false information and faulty judgments.

Some Fallacies in Inferential Work

There are a number of ways in which analysis can go wrong. Some fallacies (which need not be treated here) are deductive mistakes in argument that are traceable to the argument's logical form. Deductive fallacies are invalid arguments which were discussed earlier. We are concentrating on inductive or informal fallacies, and they may be divided into two basic types: *fallacies of irrelevance*, and *fallacies of evidence*.

Fallacies of irrelevance pertain to arguments where the premises do not provide reasons or evidence for the conclusion. Premises may not support a conclusion because they are not relevant to it. They neither count for nor against it. They are, in short, beside the point. An example would be a claim which assumes because no evidence shows it to be false that it must therefore be true. It other words, no evidence against a claim is construed - - wrongly - - as evidence for it. Because a claim is not disproved does not make it true. We want always to know the reasons for a claim why we should accept it. The fallacy has this structure:

    1. It is true that no Colombian cocaine traffickers

are active in other vices, because there is no

        (a) evidence to show otherwise.

Or,

        (b) It is false that Colombian cocaine traffickers are

active in other vices because it has not been shown to be true.

The second claim involves the assumption that a lack of evidence is the same as evidence against it. Obviously, this is absurd. "Pornography on the eastern coast of the United States is controlled by two La Cosa Nostra crime families in New York City and Cuban underworld figures in New York and New Jersey." The claim has no hard evidence to support it. Is it false? Who knows? There is no persuasive evidence one way or the other. It is certainly not false because we do not have any evidence that it is true. The claim is subject to empirical investigation to determine its validity.

An argument may fail for these and other reasons. Premises should provide at least adequate support for a conclusion and they ought to represent relevant information fairly. Occasionally, it is easy to mislead by the emotional power of an association that overrides more relevant considerations. This is the fallacy of false cause. In our example of the data collection phase for an intelligence assessment of illegally operated auto body repair shops, some evidence of organized crime appears. It would be foolish to abandon other bodies of evidence and concentrate efforts exclusively against the organized criminal elements identified. Their participation may be peripheral or incidental. Because some evidence of organized crime surfaces should not prompt a leap to the conclusion that the illegal activity is dominated by organized crime.

One of the most common fallacies is that of begging the question where what is supposed to be proven or demonstrated is assumed at the outset. It can occur in several ways. For example, "Large-scale cocaine traffickers are violent because they kill very often in their conduct of business." Here, the conclusion is a paraphrase of the premise. The reason given for the assertion is no more than a restatement of the assertion.

Circular arguments are typical examples of begging the question. Using the illegal auto shops example:

1. Auto thefts are on the increase because of the demand by illegal auto shops for parts.

2. Illegal auto shops demand stolen parts because the public demands bargain priced parts.

3. The public demands bargain prices for auto parts because auto thefts are on the increase.

Such arguments can easily deceive and seem valid and reasonable if they are sufficiently intricate.

Perhaps the most difficult fallacy to confront and uncover is one whose appeal masquerades as practical wisdom, the appeal to "common sense." When we say of someone that they show a lot of common sense it is meant to suggest that they are perceptive, intelligent and judicious in their way of coping with a problem. Conversely, to say that someone lacks common sense does not mean that they are retarded or that they are hopeless bunglers but that they behave or think foolishly or ineffectively. Common sense is supposedly an intellectual authority of ultimate resort in everyday life. It is what the mind and its workings cleared of cant spontaneously apprehends. It is what the wide-awake individual employs in problem-solving.

The "cultural" assumptions behind common sense as the central and most dependable mechanism in our mental apparatus are worth brief examination if only to alert us to the presumptions it cloaks to which we may fall prey. Common sense attributes a "thinness" to reality (Geertz, 1984). Reality is basically "simple" and "literal." The tendency of common sense is to suppose that the central facts of life "lie scattered openly along its surface, not cunningly secreted in its depth," as Geertz puts it (Geertz, op. cit. : 89). Common sense is a facile doctrine that proposes that the world is obvious and accessible. Its key notion is widely appealing: any person with faculties reasonably intact can grasp common sense conclusions. There are really no special skills or recondite knowledge one need cultivate. If something can be understood there is no need for specialized training; and if something can not be expressed plainly, then it must be muddled. Not to see "common sense" as part of our cultural system and assumptions, to think it represents a fundamental mode of thought existing everywhere among all reasonable people, is to attribute to it qualities it does not have. To resort to it as an alternative to scientifically oriented modes of information gathering and assessment may be disastrous to an effective intelligence operation.

Antecedents of Inferential Work

The mechanics of inference may be skillfully mastered and conclusions drawn with logical impeccability. But the effectiveness of any kind of judgmental work is still dependent upon the premises and their content. All of us are prone to inferential errors that precede the decision-making processes. Specifically the analyst, like the scientist, is typically confronted with numerous tasks in the conduct of his or her work. And at each step the process can be jeopardized by mistakes and errors. The analyst's characterization of events may be unduly influenced by prior beliefs. The differential "availability" of data, that which is easier to come by, may distort one's understanding of the data; ignorance of statistical considerations, chiefly of biases in the data, may weaken an analysis. And causal analysis may suffer because an analyst may substitute simple similarities or analogies for more reliable, though ponderous, statistical procedures. In addition, the analyst with little appreciation of the strategies for testing the validity of theories may persist in adhering to a point of view despite a number of exceptions and objections to it.

Judgmental strategies - - heuristic - - on which we rely, and by which we are often misled, are basic to inferential tasks. They are the cognitive tools everyone uses and often abuses.[7]

The initial stages and chores preceding inferential work concern the accuracy and reliability of the data bases. The sheer availability of information, its accessibility, may create a bias that is hardly mysterious but nonetheless difficult to uncover. It is often the case that available information is well-correlated with other data.

Next, coupled with the dangers associated with the mere availability of data are problems concerning the representativeness of information. Sometimes, the "goodness of fit" with preferred categories of classification presumed to be characteristic of events or behavior can pervert or slant a data base. Numerous inferential tasks depend on deciding what class or category of event or individual one is observing, and such judgments often hinge on no more than an intuitive assessment of resemblances or representativeness. When, for instance, criminal events show characteristics attributable to "styles" of specific criminal groups, we may be easily led astray by assuming that the resemblances are indicative of some palpable evidence implicating those whom we've suspected from the first.

Third, sociologist Erving Goffman introduced the term, "primary frameworks of knowledge" (1974), and the social philosopher Alfred Schultz coined the term, "common stocks of knowledge" (1967). Theses concepts equip us with ways of making sense of the factors which influence our social judgments. The bodies of fact, opinion and belief these terms refer to are structured to provide us with handy schemas or "scripts" that help us to relate to the world around us. Social scripts are models which allow us to categorize and fit events into classification schemes that order reality and set in motion expectations and outcomes. Over time, these elementary models of social reality get modified as experience accumulates. New schemes and scripts develop in conjunction with our growing body of experience. Often the term, "stereotype" is used to talk about these cognitive processes. But this term is too pejorative for our purposes. Schemes and scripts speed up and streamline the work of ordering reality. They can, however, lead us down blind alleys if the conceptual grids are not sufficiently attuned to the complexities of experience we encounter. The "La Cosa Nostra" script is a case in point.

The LCN paradigm (another term referring to schemes) may exert undue influence on the thinking of intelligence analysts when they approach criminal activities that have traditionally bore the signature of organized crime. The LCN script possesses a cast of characters, model scenarios that structure the search for evidence and which may predispose the analyst to handle information that confirms his or her hunches and intuitions. The ingredients of the LCN model - - the hierarchial structure of a crime "crew;" the ethnic homogeneity of the members; the styles and kinds of criminal activity LCN engages in - - may lead the analyst to unduly attend to those data that confirm his or her LCN suspicions while ignoring other salient information that does not fit the preferred model.

Fourthly, as noted above, "vivid" information impacts more forcibly on thinking than information that is less dramatic and engaging. This is so for several reasons. The graphic quality of the information is likely to be remembered more than abstract and less glamorous data. Anecdotal information in particular is more easily remembered and retrievable and therefore more likely to be incorporated into our thinking. In contrast, statistically aggregated information is, by comparison, dull and less likely to arouse emotions, interests, though it may be more probative. Presentations of crime communicated with tables, charts and complex statistics are no match against the testimony of a former "hit man" or distressed victim. Thus, there is a tendency to assign weight to information in proportion to its vividness, and can produce serious inferential costs because it is often unrepresentative and misleading.

Fifthly, assessments and estimates involve predictions sometimes and concern two major goals: trends in criminal activity and the capabilities of law enforcement agencies to deal with them. Analysts are involved in projects and operations that require judgments that seek to accurately measure criminal activity and offer estimates about the effectiveness of control and containment policies. In the course of their work, the analyst must decide how much weight to assign to specific information about the target objective. As noted earlier, the very vividness and availability of some information may produce a "base-line blindness" that adversely affects a judgment. Most of us have tendencies towards non-regressive prediction strategies. A "hunch" may be acted on - - and not necessarily impulsively - - when there is some persuasive evidence that is tangible and that "fits" expectations about a connection between, say, auto thefts and the proliferation of illegal auto body shops buying and selling auto parts. Our "clinical" judgments in such matters do not ordinarily utilize prior probabilities, or information about central tendencies. In short, with statistical data, unless evidence is especially strong and overwhelmingly, illustrates a causal connection between variables, the prudent course is to "regress" estimates to the mean in making predictions. One ought to do so for the reason that the mean (the average) is the point in the distribution of the data closest to the largest number of instances and events. The mean is the base line from which deviations should occur in reaching judgments only to the extent that the risks and costs of such deviations are compensated for by the reliability of other evidence that varies from or contravenes the mean.[8]

Sixthly, almost four hundred years ago, Francis Bacon observed, that, "the human understanding when it has once adopted an opinion draws all things to support and agree with it" (1620/ 1960: 50). Psychological research on the perseverance of beliefs tends to confirm Bacon's insight. Moreover, impressions formed from exposure to premature evidence will often cling for survival even when confronted with conflicting subsequent evidence that may discredit the initial evidential base (Lord, et. al., 1979). The work of Robert Merton on the "Self-Fulfilling Prophecy" (1948) shows that individuals will alter reality in the direction of their favored hypotheses and theories: information is filtered and selectively attended to which confirms prejudices and supports biases. Lastly in view of the problems individual analysts must confront in approaching data with objectivity and as neutrally as possible, solo work is fraught with shortcomings and inefficiencies. Group work versus individual problem-solving has the advantage that in group settings open discussions may substantially reduce judgmental errors and uncover deeply-felt but hardly conscious prejudices. As a defense against error, more heads, even non-expert heads, are generally better than one. If this is so, collective problem-solving where tasks can be allocated in a division of labor and freely discussed, may produce inferences superior to those that emerge from analysts working in virtual isolation.

Conclusions

Both deductive and inductive methods of evaluating data are relevant to the production of assessments that form the bases for enforcement activities. The techniques enable the intelligence analyst to assume a more active role in law enforcement work. Armed with these techniques, the analyst is not confined or limited by the data and evaluations supplied by operational units. The analyst is able to generate questions that may lead to the development of new, raw data. Thus a reciprocally vigorous link between analytical and operational units may be forged with these tools.

The rules of inference, like the rules of chess or grammar, are performance-rules. Logical and analytical performances in accordance with them are either legitimate or illegitimate, correct or incorrect, suitable or unsuitable. What is it like to operate with the rules of inference? The rules create a dynamic, a back and forth movement between the "if/then" -- a coherence-making process, and the "as/therefore" decision-making level. The rules of inference tie together precepts of thinking with concrete cases.

Notes

1. Technical treatments of syllogistic reasoning - - reasoning from premises to conclusions - - may be found in numerous texts for those who feel comfortable on the firm pavement of mathematics. Formal logic which examines inference patterns attempts to codify, to "Euclidean-ize" the rules of reasoning. Formal or symbolic logic came to be not only mathematical in style and subject-matter, it is nowadays a science and discipline of such scope and rigor in computer sciences that it is out of danger of surviving only as the nursemaid and governess of philosophy.

2. In canonical form (symbolic language) , the basic inference rules, or elementary valid argument forms, are used to construct "chains" of arguments. To prove that a conclusion follows from a set of premises by the rules is to show the conclusion as the last link in such a chain. The major and most common argument forms are:

A) Modus Ponens : $p \supset q$, $p \therefore q$.
B) Modus Tollens: $p \supset g$, $\sim q \therefore \sim p$.
C) Hypothetical Syllogism: $p \supset q$, $q \supset r \therefore p \supset r$.
D) Disjunctive Syllogism: $p \vee q$, $\sim p \therefore q$.
E) Constructive Dilemma: $(p \supset q)$. $(r \supset s)$, $p \vee r \therefore q \vee s$.
F) Simplification: $p.q \therefore p$.
G) Conjunction : p, $q \therefore p. q$.
H) Addition: $p \therefore p \vee q$.

The logical symbols in the eight argument forms have these English meanings as described in Figure 8 on the following page:

Figure 8

Symbol	Name	English
v	Disjunction	either...or, or
.	Conjunction	and, but, yet
⊃	Implication	if. ..then
~	Negation	not
⅋	Conclusion	therefore, for that reason, consequently

P v q reads, "p or q;" ~ p reads, "not p;" p ⊃ q reads, "if p then q," and so on. For an excellent discussion on the valid argument forms and their operational mechanics, see Irving Copi, op. cit.; and Patrick Suppes Introduction to Logic (1964) 8th printing, New York: D. Van Nostrand & Co.

3) The Method of Concomitant Variations is considered among the more important and early expressions of quantitative methods of inductive inference. Its use presupposes the existence of some methods of measuring or estimating -- if only roughly -- the extent to which phenomena vary.

In his famous monograph, The Rules of Sociological Method, published in 1895, the French sociologist, Emile Durkheim described his use of Mill's method in his researches on suicide which were published in 1897 and became an instant classic. For Durkheim, concomitant variations enabled him to work out the apparent contradictions in his data, where, for instance, high education appeared to lead to higher rates of suicide. Eventually Durkehim was able to show that it was the weakening of religious traditionalism that lay behind this anomaly; as religious commitment and fervor declined two things appeared to happen: the need for knowledge (higher education) was reinforced, and the bonds of social group solidarity were loosened. Together, these tendencies led to increased rates of suicide among specific groups in a population. Higher education, Durkheim was relieved to report, was not then one of the leading causes of suicide.

4) Illegal auto shops may in such circumstances experience a reduction in the percentage of illegal business they do. This may require them to go increasingly legitimate if they wish to survive -- a not uncommon phenomenon. Still, their very existence and willingness to function legally or illegally may act as a stimulus to auto theft since they can function as outlets for stolen parts.

5) For a good treatment of the intelligence process, see Dintino and Martens, (1983: op. cit. 58-134), two well known national experts. Their work offers a comprehensive survey of all phases of intelligence work and the inherent dilemmas involved in it.

6) Fallacies invariably crop up in deductive arguments. Logicians have identified the most frequent and common. A basic fallacy is that of *equivocation* where a term in an argument is used in different senses and fails to meet the criterion of consistency. For example,

A. 1. All law enforcement attempts to control drug trafficking are efforts which should be approved by all criminal justice agencies.
2. All of Turkey's activities on its borders are attempts to control drug trafficking.
Therefore,

    3. All of Turkey's activities on its borders should be approved by all criminal justice agencies.

This argument seems valid because it appears to have only three terms, but there are really four. The middle term, "Turkey's activities on its borders," is used in different senses in the two premises. Only if this term is interpreted as designating such activities as legal searches and seizures and typical anti-drug crime control methods that operate within the confines of the law, can the first premise be accepted as true. But for the second premise to be true, the phrase, " . . . activities on its borders" must have its meaning shifted to include illegal searches, detention and intimidation of travelers, and in some cases, summary executions. When the phrase in question is interpreted in the same sense through the argument, one or the other of the premises becomes patently false. The fallacy of the *Undistributed Middle* entails a mistake that can yield quite bizarre results:

      B.   1. All mafiosi break the law.
              2. <u>All drug traffickers break the law.</u>
    Therefore, 3. All drug traffickers are mafiosi.

    The middle term, "break the law," is not distributed in either premise and this violates the rule that in a valid syllogistic argument, the middle term must be distributed in at least one premise. "Mafiosi" are included *in part* of the class of law breakers, and "drug traffickers" are also included *in part* of the class of law breakers. But different *parts* of that class may be (and are in our example) involved so that the middle term does not connect the syllogism's major and minor premises. To connect them, all of the class designated by it must be referred to in at least one premise.

    A variation on this fallacy is the <u>Illicit Process of the Major Term</u>. In such a case, a conclusion may illegitimately go beyond what is asserted in the premise. For example:

      C.   1. All mafiosi are law breakers.
              2. <u>No drug traffickers are mafiosi.</u>
    Therefore, 3. No drug traffickers are law breakers.

    This argument is invalid at a glance. But why? As an exercise, using the rules of inference it should be possible to unravel the mistake in logic in (C).

    7) This draws heavily on the pathbreaking work of Nisbett and Ross (1980).

    8) Regression analysis is a statistical technique that permits the estimation of the effects of one or more independent variables (auto thefts) on a continuous, dependent variable (illegal auto shops). A regression equation describes how the data represented by the variables and their relationships interact.

References

Ackermann, Robert.
(1966) Nondeductive Inference. NY: Dover Books.
Bacon, Francis.
(1960) The New Organon and Related Writings. NY: Liberal Arts Press. Originally published in 1620.
Barmford, James.
(1982) The Puzzle Palace. Boston: Houghton-Mifflin.
Blakey, G. Robert, Ronald Goldstock and Charles Rogovin.
(1978) Rackets Bureau: Investigation and Prosecution of Organized Crime. Washington, DC: National Institute of Law Enforcement and Criminal Justice. U.S. Gov Printing Off.
Bureau of Justice Statistics.
(1987) Annual Report, Fiscal 1986. U.S. Department of Justice, Washington, D.C. : U.S. Government Printing Office.
Copi, Irving.
(1955) Introduction to Logic, 3rd printing. NY: Macmillan Co.
Dintino, Justin and Frederick T. Martens.
(1983) Police Intelligence Systems in Crime Control. Springfield, IL: Charles C. Thomas, Publisher.Geertz, Clifford.
(1984) Local Knowledge: Essays in Interpretive Anthropology. NY: Basic Books.
Godfrey, E. Drexel and Don R. Harris.
(1971) Basic Elements of Intelligence: A Manual of Theory, Structure and Procedures for Use by Law Enforcement Agencies Against Organized Crime. (November) Technical Assistance Division, Office of Criminal Justice Assistance, LEAA. U.S. Gov Printing Off.
Goffman, Erving.
(1974) Frame Analysis: An Essay on the Organization Experience. NY: Harper & Row. Harper Colophon Books.
Goldstock, Ronald.
(1977) "Letting the Loanshark Off the Hook" NEWSDAY (September 9th).
Ianni, Francis, A.J.
(1974) Black Mafia. NY: Random House.
Kelly, Robert J.
(1978) Organized Crime: A Study in the Production of Knowledge by Law Enforcement Specialists. Ann Arbor, Michigan: University of Michigan Microfilms.
Kerr, Peter.
(1987) "Chinese Dominate New York Heroin Trade," NEW YORK TIMES, Three-part series, August 9th, 10th and 11th.
Kleiman, Mark.
(1985) "Drug Enforcement and Organized Crime" in H. Alexander and G. Caiden, eds. The Politics and Economics of Organized Crime. Lexington, MA: Lexington Books, D.C. Heath & Co. pp. 67-88.

Laqueur, Walter.
    (1987) The Age of Terrorism. Boston: Little Brown & Co.
    (1985) A World of Secrets: The Uses and Limits of Intelligence. NY: Basic Books, A
    Twentieth Century Fund Book.
Lord, C. , L. Ross and R. Lepper.
    (1979) "Biased Assimilation and Attitude Polarization: The Effects of Prior Theories on
    Subsequently Considered Evidence," Journal of Personality and Social Psychology. Vol.
    39.
Martens, Frederick, T.
    (1987) "The Intelligence Function" in H. Edelhertz, ed. Major Issues in Organized Crime
    Control: Symposium Proceedings. The National Institute of Justice (September 24-25)
    U.S. Department of Justice. Washington, DC: U.S. Gov Printing Off.
Merton, Robert K.
    (1948) "The Self-Fulfilling Prophecy" Antioch Review.
Mill, John Stuart.
    (1879) A System of Logic. 8th ed. NY: Harper & Brothers.
Moore, Mark.
    (1977) Buy or Bust. Lexington, MA: D.C. Health & Co.
Nisbett, Richard and Lee Ross.
    (1980) Human Inference: Strategies and Shortcomings of Social Judgment. Englewood
    Cliffs, NJ: Prentice-Hall.
President's Commission on Organized Crime.
    (1986) The Impact: Organized Crime Today. Report to the President and the Attorney
    General (April) Washington, DC: U.S. Gov Printing Off.
Quine, W.V.
    (1981) Theories and Things. Cambridge: The Belknap Press of Harvard University Press.
Rubenstein, Richard E.
    (1987) Alchemists of Revolution: Terrorism in the Modern World. NY: Basic Books.
Schutz, Alfred.
    (1967) The Phenomenology of the Social World. Chicago: Northwestern University Press.
    Translated by G. Walsh & F. Lehnert.
Stephens, William, N.
    (1968) Hypotheses and Evidence. NY: Thomas Y. Crowell & Co.
    (1967) Task Force Report, Organized Crime. Washington, DC: U.S. Gov Printing Off.
Wilson, James Q.
    (1978) The Investigators. NY: Basic Books.

Chapter Eight

Intelligence Report Writing

Charles C. Frost

Introduction
The Vital Reporting Role
Reports are the very lifeblood of the intelligence process. They disseminate the usable product of intelligence collection. They are the medium for analytical support for case investigations and prosecutions. And, perforce, they are the very essence of intelligence publications.

Intelligence reporting is the basis most often used for judging the value of a police intelligence unit. When asked to rate the effectiveness of an intelligence unit, its consumers -- the users of its reports -- will almost invariably refer to some particularly useful report or to the reliability and timeliness of its reports in general. Organizations specializing in enforcement intelligence are especially dependent on the reports medium to serve their member agencies. Visible product must be emphasized whether the mission of the intelligence unit is publications or case building. And, since maintaining a reputation for quality in its reports is a matter of keen concern, it behooves the organization to see to it the analysts are suitably trained in the techniques of reports writing.

Reports and Reporting Skills
The intelligence analyst plays different roles in providing intelligence support to law enforcement, and these roles in turn require distinctive report formats. The most common roles are support to investigations and strategic analysis. (In agencies specializing in security, the support analysis will be related to effective protective security rather than to criminal prosecutions.) Since each agency will organize its analytical effort to serve its particular needs, it may emphasize some types of analysis more than others. Therefore, the agency will not necessarily require development of all reporting skills in the same depth.

Within each analytical role there exists a gradation of skills in reporting. Some types of case analysis reports involve essentially data retrieval and formatting rather than actual analysis; others are best performed by those who have enough familiarity with the rules of evidence to make evaluations and recommendations on the sufficiency of evidence. Similarly in strategic intelligence, some types of reports are brief reference documents that call mainly for the assembly of information, while others require a high order of ability to make trend comparisons into the future.[1] It should, therefore, be clear that the differentiation of skills in intelligence report writing is based on the degree of difficulty of the analysis, not on the type of report. There is no natural superiority of analytical skill that applies more to one category of reports than another so that one could justifiably argue that strategic reports in general need more skillful analysts than case analysis reports or collection reports. A Central Intelligence Agency station chief with years of management experience, for example, may write his own situation assessment reports during a coup or other crisis. Similarly, a top-notch case support analyst may be sought out by the prosecutor and the investigative manager for assessments of the prosecution potential of the available intelligence information. Each category of reports makes its own demands for excellence.

Analyst Interaction with Intelligence Information

Analysts read and file incoming intelligence information that is not immediately needed for writing reports. When analysts must produce reports they retrieve information that was stored for future reference. One should not, however, regard analysts as passive processors of law enforcement intelligence information. The best analysts, like the best journalists, react creatively to information that may have operational significance. They formulate tentative hypotheses and then gather collateral data to confirm, disprove or modify their hypotheses. The analysts' aggressiveness does not end when the information search has been pursued to a logical conclusion; they do not rest until the new development, properly assembled with related information and assessed in a package that is called "finished intelligence," has been brought to the attention of those who can act on it. In the following sections of this chapter the reader will find a number of examples of such creative analyst interaction.

Field Intelligence Reporting

Format

The intelligence unit mounts collection operations in response to approved guidelines and prioritized statements of the department's information needs, called intelligence requirements. Analysts are often involved in the actual gathering of information and, even when they have not participated directly, are routinely tasked to process debriefing notes into intelligence reports. The raw intelligence report is the vehicle for disseminating significant information, collected in such operations, to elements within the department that have a legitimate need for the information, or need-to-know.

For maximum usefulness to the chief and other important consumers, the information "take" from the intelligence unit's sources must be disseminated in a form that can be quickly digested and acted upon. The report should be able to stand on its own feet; i.e., it should be essentially complete within itself. The raw intelligence report usually addresses only one subject. If a source provides information on more than one subject, additional reports are issued. Intelligence reports, unlike investigative reports, have a place for amplifying data and opinion, provided that all information is properly attributed as to source. This can be conveniently accomplished by the use of comments to distinguish amplifying information from that provided by a covert source. Intelligence reporting is not intended to meet the exacting standards of investigative reporting and would be inhibited if required to do so. It is strongly recommended, therefore, that raw intelligence reports have a distinctive format.

A typical format for a raw intelligence report is illustrated in Example #1 located at the end of the chapter. Each element in the heading serves a particular purpose and is necessary for the full understanding of the report.

The <u>area line</u> indicates the localities for which the information in the report is relevant. The subject matter of the report is succinctly categorized on the subject line. The known or presumed latest date of information is reflected in the date of information line; a date span may also be indicated, as would often be the case with a prisoner. The source line describes the nature of the source and indicate how (in a general way) the source obtained the information. Great care must be taken in describing sensitive sources to strike a balance between providing enough detail to show that the source had plausible access to the information and too much detail that would compromise the source's identity. [2] The place and date acquired (PADA) line indicates the time and place the information became available for intelligence dissemination. (In this example the gap in time between the date of arrest and the date of acquisition might reflect a restriction on the use of the information imposed during the judicial process, such as by subpoena of evidence.) A serial number and distribution date are included to provide a convenient accounting and referencing system for reports and to show when the intelligence information was disseminated.

As previously stated, any information not provided by the principal source is set apart in comments. The last paragraph of Example #1 uses such a comment to distinguish the information actually contained in the document from analytical judgments about that information. A properly sourced intelligence report will even delineate judgments by a covert source about information he himself is providing. Example #2 illustrates this latter point. Suppose, for example, that the vice president of a bank in Philadelphia is the source of this report. The information shown in the first paragraph may have been obtained from an unwitting subsource, such as an officer of a local branch bank, in the normal course of business. The second paragraph represents the vice president's unverified evaluation of the presumably accurate information received from the local bank official. Careful sourcing thus cautions the reader that the information in the report is not necessarily of the same accuracy.

Aggressive Information Development

There may be some truth in the saying that success comes to those who seek it. This applies to acquiring intelligence in the sense that one often finds information by aggressively exploiting what one already has. The information is not actually new; it was there all the time only waiting to be discovered. Many diligent analysts have experienced this serendipity in intelligence work by thoughtfully reacting to a piece of information instead of just filing it away, playing a hunch that what they now see may not be an isolated incident but part of a pattern not yet evident. The following scenario illustrates such an occurrence.

Mary Williams is a crime intelligence analyst for the County Police Department, Arlington, Virginia. She receives a routine investigative report prepared by Patrolman Jasper Jacobs on the theft of an expensive radial spare tire from the trunk of a late model Buick owned by a resident of a local apartment complex. Jacobs observed that the trunk lock had been sprung and noted a small hole that had been drilled into the lock. The theft took place on November 20th. Mary checks the Department's auto theft files and finds no reports indicating a similar M.O. She reports her findings to the intelligence unit supervisor.

The supervisor concurs with Mary's recommendation to check other jurisdictions on the chance the tire thieves are picking their victims at random. "We may be dealing with professionals," he observes. "It would appear they got through that lock rather quickly." Mary calls the intelligence bureau of the Virginia State Police, but they have no relevant information. Likewise, the Montgomery County, MD, Police Department and the Washington, D.C., Metropolitan Police have no reports. She then queries jurisdictions in a northerly direction for reports of similar tire thefts, with the following results:

Maryland State Police	Theft reported Nov. 17th by Baltimore County PD at large shopping center (Whitemarsh)
Delaware State Police	No reports
Pennsylvania State Police	Theft on Nov. 13th at apartment complex in middle-income Philadelphia neighborhood
New Jersey State Police	Theft on Nov. 9th at a New Jersey Turnpike service area
New York State Police	Theft on Nov. 4th at Westchester County airport
Connecticut State Police	Theft on Nov. 1st at mall off I-84 west of Hartford (Corbins Corner)

In only one case was Mary able to obtain information on the possible perpetrators of these thefts. The owner of the vehicle at the New Jersey Turnpike service area reported to the State Police that a cream-colored utility van pulled away as he was returning to his car from the restaurant. Another motorist who was eating a snack in his car nearby said the truck stopped behind the owner's car and appeared briefly to have engine trouble. The other motorist reported that the truck had Rhode Island license plates containing the letters "LT." The motorist said the truck was occupied by two men but because of darkness could give no descriptions.

"Perhaps they intend to hit here and there all the way down to Miami" was the way Mary summed up these results for her supervisor. "The information you've collected would certainly warrant that conclusion," he said approvingly. "Even though we cannot positively connect all of these thefts to the same gang, the timing seems more than coincidental. We can be sure of one thing: the roving thief counts on the unwillingness or inability of decentralized police departments to share information with each other. Let's get out an intelligence report to ROCIC."

Mary's intelligence report, shown in Example #3, was teletyped to ROCIC's headquarters in Memphis later that day. ROCIC is the acronym for Regional Organized Crime Information Center, which serves law enforcement organizations in the southeastern states.

Content Considerations

In the foregoing example Mary and her supervisor could easily imagine how the consumers of their intelligence report could use it in a proactive way. The information package was as complete as the local department could justifiably make it. (ROCIC, as the intelligence network serving the most likely area for future impacts, would be responsible in turn for querying the Rhode Island State Police for whatever additional information could be gained from the partial vehicle registration.) Proactive usefulness and completeness, then, are important objectives in field intelligence reports. These characteristics must be borne in mind especially when an immediate tactical use for the information is not apparent, as was the case with Example #2. Here, intelligence gathering was not self-guided but, instead, proceeded against organized crime activities pursuant to general information collection directives. The results are reported as soon as concrete developments occur. If the collection effort has been oriented toward valid targets, the potential for proactive use of the intelligence will become apparent when the accumulation of numerous bits and pieces of information is analyzed. It is to the presentation of intelligence data and analysis in case building that we turn our attention next.

Case Analysis Reports
Overview of Case Building
The operational intelligence analyst plays an important role in the development and presentation of complex and high-priority cases. When the case is initiated the analyst compiles available intelligence documentation, extracting and reassembling holdings from different case files on target individuals. This integration of case-related materials provides a common reference point for organizing intelligence case support and becomes the benchmark for further intelligence research. The analyst then assists the case manager to expand the scope of the investigation by assessing the strength of association among violators in a criminal conspiracy and by identifying other related cases and suspects previously unknown. The analyst also assists the case manager to obtain needed evidence as quickly as possible by reviewing seized material for evidentiary value, listing information gaps and recommending approaches for filling them. In the final stages of the case the analyst often assists the prosecuting attorney by providing data compilations and charts derived from intelligence analysis as aids in presenting the case. Far from merely extracting and collating data, the analyst points out the information needs that are critical to the prosecution's case. The analyst thus exercises a high degree of initiative in determining the most promising lines of research and in focusing information collection on the center of the criminal activity.[3]

Event Chronology
The first step in response to a request for intelligence case support is to prepare an event chronology. This basic reference document is usually focused on the subject individual of the case. The analyst performs data base queries and/or researches central criminal files to retrieve references to case files related to the subject individual. These files are pulled and all relevant documents copied. The event chronology that is produced from the intelligence file review provides a documented and cross-indexed list of criminal events relating to a particular suspect. Each event in the chronology is annotated so that the investigators can have ready access to all materials. Example #4 illustrates such a chronology. Note that the investigative report for each event is cited, along with the names of witnesses that can be called to testify to the reported facts.

Violator File Summary
A file summary may be prepared in conjunction with the event chronology. This refinement is particularly useful when the subject has had a long criminal history and the file has become voluminous. The summary is intended to characterize the subject and his/her criminal activity in the context of the law violations for which prosecution will now be sought. In a drug distributor's case, for example, the summary might indicate the length of time the person has been a drug dealer and how he/she first became involved in drug peddling, what position the person occupies in the organization, and the scope of the organization's activities. Example #5 illustrates such a summary.

Case Organization Analysis
Information retrieval is only the beginning of case support. The analyst must also collate

the information into meaningful categories, tell what information is available against each suspect and what it tends to prove, and how the different pieces of information interrelate. Using the event chronologies as the point of departure the analyst identifies prosecutable acts, both substantive and overt (i.e., as related to criminal conspiracies). The analyst provides lists of such acts, associates, addresses, telephone numbers (including numbers from personal telephone books or lists), vehicles and financial assets that may be seized, and evidence exhibits. Each list entry should be cross-indexed to the event chronology.

With this advanced collation of information the analyst is in a position to provide the key judgments as to whether there is enough information to prosecute the organization or conspiracy as a whole and how the accuracy of the information can be improved. The analysis links possible criminal allegations to the evidence that can sustain such allegations, points out critical gaps in intelligence and investigative information, and shows where there is a potential for filling those gaps. Example #6 provides a sample outline of a case organization analysis. Correctly designed and diligently executed, this type of analysis can assist the case manager to allocate his investigative resources more productively and the prosecutor to understand the information problems that must be addressed in the investigation. The study provides a better focus on the case that helps both prosecutor and case manager to unify their strategy, thus enhancing the prospects for a successful prosecution. The analyst also benefits by getting clearer directions through an agreed approach on the part of the other two key players. It should be obvious that the analyst cannot play this catalytic role in the investigation without some knowledge of the elements of proof for the principal offenses and rules of evidence.

Security Support Analysis
Deterring Terrorism and Violent Confrontations

Terrorism dominates today's security scene to such an extent that nearly every large police department and private security organization must be concerned with it. Terrorists can move fairly easily across international borders. They detonate a bomb, disappear and let the media carry their message around the world within minutes. Kidnappings and bank robberies are some of their favorite forms of fund raising. Government officials, diplomats, judges, senior law enforcement officers, and even religious leaders are key targets for the terrorists' purposes. Terrorism is commonly defined as the use of violence and the threat of violence as a political weapon to achieve control, to influence government policy and/or to destabilize and even overthrow governments. But terrorist acts by organizations that have no political agenda are not encompassed by this legal definition. The latter include organizations that wreak vengeance for past wrongs and criminal organizations that use terrorism to undermine national and international law enforcement efforts.

Security Alert Bulletin
The purpose of a security alert bulletin is simply to convey information of a security nature to those organizations that need it in order to carry out their proper functions. Frequently, a government agency will obtain useful security information and pass it along to interested private organizations. Suppose, for example, that the consul of a Latin American country returning to Miami from a weekend visit to his country's embassy in Washington discovers that his office has been broken into and requests investigative assistance from the Metro-Dade Police Department. Officers of the burglary unit respond, gather evidence and take a statement from the consul. The

consul shows the officers where the burglars attempted to get into the safe where he keeps his authenticating stamps and seals. Looking through his ransacked desk he notes that three blank passports are missing from the drawer. The investigating officers determine the passport numbers from records shown to them by the consul. The essentials of this information, especially the numbers of the stolen passports, will be reported to the Federal Aviation Administration. The FAA's Office of Security will pass the information in turn to the Air Transport Association and other U.S. air carrier organizations in Washington, D.C., to assist them in spotting potential hijackers.

Weekly Security Intelligence Report

The police department intelligence unit plays a central role in ensuring that intelligence information and assessments are provided to the tactical force and to senior commanders on situations with a potential for violent confrontation. The major city departments that must cope with visits of foreign leaders, parades, demonstrations, etc. require a summary of information on upcoming events that may present security problems. Example #7 illustrates, the format for such a report, showing how the input from the intelligence unit is built in.

Intelligence Profile on Terrorist Organization

To have the necessary background information for this weekly summary the intelligence unit should be building and updating its data base on various organizations that have a proclivity for public violence. Besides terrorist organizations these may also include domestic groups that have demonstrated a potential for civil disturbance or violent clashes with other groups (e.g., Ku Klux Klan, American Nazi groups, and outlaw motorcycle gangs). Example #8 illustrates a convenient format for compiling such information. Note the particularly useful chronology of events included in this format.

Security Threat Assessments

A profile on an international terrorist organization that has been kept current can be used to good advantage when alerting security personnel, detectives and tactical commanders to upcoming security threats. The profile, however, does not constitute a threat assessment as such. A proper threat assessment would be a formal estimate in which the intelligence unit analyzes information pertinent to a new or continuing security threat and makes judgments on important issues relating to that threat. The same background information serves as the basis for assessing different kinds of threats for different areas. Armenians, for example, regard April 24 as the anniversary of the Armenian massacre. As that date approaches, metropolitan police departments would be most concerned with the possibility that Armenian terrorist organizations would carry out bombings or assassinations against Turkish consuls or diplomats, while the Federal Aviation Administration and airline associations would, of course, focus on the possibility of airport bombings. Example #9 presents such an assessment as the FAA might disseminate it to U.S. airline associations.

The assessment shown in Example #9 is fairly straightforward, simply alerting U.S. air carriers to the possibility of terrorist action somewhere in the world air transport system on or about a particular date. Although past experience indicates that the Armenian terrorists carry out their threats with some regularity, it would be difficult to predict just where they would strike next.

The threat, in other words, is a general one that is not readily measurable for any particular place. Quite a different assessment is needed when the threat is localized, such as a well publicized event. Here the degree of risk should be rated for the benefit of intelligence consumers. Such an assessment was prepared by the American Embassy in Paris for distribution to American firms exhibiting at the Paris Air Show and is illustrated in Example #10.

Private security organizations responsible for executive protection function much like the Secret Service when one of their clients travels overseas. The organization, like the Secret Service, is concerned with the exposure of a prominent person or a small group of persons to risks. Likewise, the analytical process of assessing risk is very much the same. Example #11 illustrates a typical situation wherein the private security organization would need to prepare a threat assessment. Note the effort to identify the risk that is within the organization's capability to manage.

Recurring Publications

The Responsibilities of Visibility

Recurring reports are principal vehicles for disseminating finished (or processed) intelligence to law enforcement consumers. The increased visibility that an intelligence publication gives a police agency is naturally appealing. Before undertaking such a project, however, the agency should be aware of the resource requirements for producing a weekly, biweekly or monthly publication. A certain investment in analyst talent, training and reference material must be made to the intelligence unit if its publication is to maintain a reputation for quality. Inadequate analytical support will soon be reflected in superficially researched articles and items of little intelligence value. It is not enough to simply assign an analyst to edit the publication; there must be other analysts available who can be tasked to contribute the results of their research and analysis to the publication. The editor's role should be primarily the planning and processing of published material. Given a reasonable commitment to the publication effort, the main limits on what a publication can attempt stem from the charter of the organization and the breadth of knowledge and writing ability of its analysts. An organization that was set up for exchange of narcotics information cannot suddenly start writing on juvenile gangs or home repair frauds, however immediate a threat may be posed to the local community by criminal activity in these areas. (Specialized intelligence units tend to have this disadvantage.)

Criteria for Selection of Topics

Before an intelligence publication is seriously contemplated the agency should develop a clear concept of what the analysts will eventually write about. The publication has a two-pronged mission: to alert readers to new crime developments that may have significance for police operations and to give readers a better understanding of existing crime problems. Both current items and in-depth analysis will be needed to fulfill this mission. Weekly intelligence publications will, of course, provide more scope than monthly ones for purveying analysis of very recent developments. Nevertheless, weekly issuances must maintain a judicious balance between reportorial and analytical offerings for, as the highly competitive national news magazines have shown, readers want not just reporting of the latest facts but timely analysis on the burning issues of the day as well. (Even the daily newspapers present background features on ongoing stories.)

An intelligence publication presents strategic intelligence, which may be defined as a comprehensive and current picture of the scope and direction of a criminal activity. As such, it may be used to highlight particularly significant raw intelligence information that has been collected and to present analysis of trends and developments. Each piece of analysis should, therefore, represent a high degree of generalization about a development or trend, with little if any concern for how the analysis might be used operationally. Although some space may be devoted as a convenience to readers to capturing factual items reported elsewhere, the main fare should be original analytical products.

Each article contributed for publication must be carefully reviewed by the editor, chief analyst or an editorial board to determine that it serves a useful purpose. Reviewers can use the following broad criteria: Is the subject matter of the article suitable considering the mission of the publication or the law enforcement objectives of the sponsoring agency? Does the analysis contribute new knowledge or new interpretations of existing knowledge? Is the analysis based on up-to-date information? Is the analysis complete (i.e., have analytical judgments been clearly made or left fuzzy)?[4] Setting high editorial standards and enforcing them impartially not only protects the reputation of the publication itself but also gives analysts invaluable professional writing techniques for presenting intelligence in such publications.

Spot Item

The spot item, though not strictly speaking a technique in analytical writing, is such a simple and convenient device that it is often used in intelligence publications. "Spots" are usually presented in the compressed reportorial style of a news brief, without additional explanation or analysis. This technique is very appropriate for presenting short information capsules to an informed audience that can recognize their significance at once. Example #12 illustrates a story that could be treated in this fashion. The story might be written up as a spot item for a law enforcement or security information publication like this:

Stolen Passports

Three blank passports were stolen from the Venezuelan Consulate in Miami, FL, during the July 4th weekend. These were Venezuelan tourist passports numbered 156702 through 156704, as determined from records shown by the Consul to officers of the Metro-Dade Police Department. The burglars were unable to steal his authenticating stamps and seals which, unlike the passports, had been secured in a wall safe.

Some publications provide only the "bare bones" facts, sometimes in incomplete sentences, when space is extremely limited. The brief would then look like this:

STOLEN PASSPORTS
Venezuelan tourist P/P #156702, #156703, #156704,
Miami, FL, o/a July 4

This practice is NOT RECOMMENDED. Readability is sacrificed for information storage, with a very high risk of losing the readers' interest completely. Human readers cannot be treated like computers; they quickly fatigue when fed long strings of data, stubbornly demanding a little interest in their reading diet.

Gist-And-Comment Technique
This is probably the writing method most frequently used in intelligence publications. It consists of two parts: a gist, or summary, of the report that triggers the article; and a comment that analyzes the report's significance. The comment section supplies background facts researched from collation files or collected information that rounds out the instant development summarized in the gist and puts it into a meaningful perspective. Every analyst who writes articles for publication should work to master this highly useful technique. Success comes only with diligent practice but can be hastened by following a few simple rules: (1) Use a recent case, incident, or announcement as the springboard for the article [Even a retrospective study imparts a "late-news" flavor to an article if the release of the study is treated as a newsworthy event, such the the issuance of the World Bank's annual report on the international economy; (2) Capture and briskly summarize the salient facts in the instant report; (3) Do as much background research as the pressure of time allows to analyze the significance of the instant development; (4) Keep the gist and commentary separate [jumping back and forth between what the report says and the supplementary information will confuse the reader]; (5) Note any important omissions in the instant report; and (6) Foreshadow events the reader should be watching for in the near future.

Note the payoff in Example #13 -- probably not the first -- from the intelligence unit's investment over a long period in collating background materials. Having extensive files at one's fingertips saves valuable time that can be used for developing additional information. Also note that Example #13 has been composed with some care for accurate sourcing; not only have the gist and comment been kept separate, but the gist has also been phrased to distinguish clearly what the Australian officer knows from the cable in front of him and what he himself is supplying as background information. The officer's obvious lack of enthusiasm for the new organization might, of course, color his comments.

Strategic Estimates
    The Nature of Estimates
We have already seen the need to make predictive judgments in connection with threat assessments. Let us now study "futures" somewhat more systematically. The strategic estimate is a formal intelligence exercise that requires considered judgments on an array of key intelligence problems or issues in order to provide a backdrop against which to make projections into the near-term future. As such, the exercise may involve a team of experienced analysts drawn from several agencies or departments. Estimates may be produced as annual reviews, such as the <u>Narcotics Intelligence Estimate</u> of the U.S. National Narcotics Intelligence Consumers Committee and the <u>National Drug Intelligence Estimate</u> of the Royal Canadian Mounted Police.[5]   With scheduled estimates it is, of course, easier to program supporting research. But estimates may also have to be undertaken under circumstances that are far from ideal, as in a crisis situation.

Dealing With Uncertainty
In modern societies we must constantly make decisions in the face of limited certainty. We gamble on the future when planning a career, getting married and raising a family, buying a home, or making business investments. But we are willing to risk failure because we can observe that most people are better off acting than being intimidated by uncertainty. Implicit in such behavior is confidence that the degree of uncertainty is not so great as to preclude our ability to make

intelligent speculations about the future. The decision maker relies on the analyst to narrow the area of uncertainty to manageable proportions.

Near-term projections are the easiest and most natural because we speculate that the near future will be basically similar to the recent past. More exactly, we postulate that the trends that are operative now will continue into the future either not greatly modified or not modified beyond recognition. Even if a rather cataclysmic event has occurred, it may change how factors operate as much as, and possibly more than, what factors will operate. Consider the following estimate which the U.S. narcotics intelligence community produced within 72 hours of the fall of Saigon in 1975, for example.

The Implications of the Fall of Saigon
For International Narcotics Control

(Summary) The fall of Saigon and the withdrawal of the U.S. presence in South Vietnam will have a significant favorable effect on the international narcotics traffic. That country will no longer be used as a staging base for heroin smuggling into the United States by American and other traffickers. This positive change will be partially counterbalanced by the likelihood that some Vietnamese traffickers succeeded in infiltrating the refugee stream coming to the United States in the hastily-organized evacuation.

To no one's regret, the prediction on the Vietnamese refugees failed to materialize. This was due in part to the fact that the names of applicants for admission were checked against criminal indices because the estimate's warning was heeded!

Using "Futures" Formulas

Although the relationship between the present and the future mentioned above is a useful generalization, analysts should guard against a tendency to rely on it uncritically. It can all too easily become a crutch for the timid or lazy analyst. Those inclined to take the path of least resistance will content themselves with pat statements like "the future won't change significantly" instead of examining how operative factors will impact and be modified over time.

Assumptions are sometimes unavoidable in estimates. They should be used sparingly but acknowledged without hesitation. It is often necessary to resort to assumptions: (a) When stating the methodology will lend more credence to the result [this may be the only way to cope with a complete lack of data, as by the "if . . . then" formula that will be discussed below]; (b) When there are too many variables to determine cause and effect relationships; and (c) When because there are rival methodologies or data systems the reader must be told which one has been employed [as by noting that such-and-such a result was arrived at "on the basis of ..."]. (See heading #ll. of Example #14.)

It is also good practice for analysts to warn their consumers what areas of the estimate are the most tenuous. What areas are estimated with the least confidence, for example? Or, what areas are the most vulnerable to events that cannot be anticipated? Illustrations of such warnings are provided under heading #10 of Example #14. Note that these formulations have been phrased with some specifics, specifics that can facilitate reappraisal at a later date if more information is collected. Estimators ill serve their consumers if they over-use familiar dodges like "it's too early to say..."

It should now be apparent from a careful study of the formulations given in Example #14 that the analyst must not take cavalier "take it or leave it" attitude in presenting an estimate. On the contrary, the analyst has an obligation to explain the reasoning for his/her estimative judgments. The careful analyst also makes an effort to keep his/her judgments from being open-ended.

Footnotes

1. See author's article, "Choosing Good Intelligence Analysts: What's Measurable," Law Enforcement Intelligence Analysis Digest, Volume 1 (Summer/Fall 1985) published by the International Association of Law Enforcement Intelligence Analysts.

2. See Charles C. Frost and Jack Morris, Police Intelligence Reports (Orangevale, CA: Palmer Enterprises, 1983), Part IV.

3. Professor Charles Rogovin has also noted the role of strategic intelligence in stimulating investigative activity. "One of the most powerful investigative weapons against organized crime is the investigative grand jury. In most jurisdictions, however, it can be impaneled only with a strong showing that organized crime is a problem in that jurisdiction. Strategic intelligence is critical in documenting the nature and extent of organized crime in such a situation." Bernard L. Garmire, ed., Local Government Police Management (Washington, D.C.: International City Management Association).

4. Review criteria of usefulness, pointedness and timeliness are discussed in E. Drexel Godfrey and Don R. Harris, Basic Elements of Intelligence (Washington, D.C.: Government Printing Office, 1971), p. 7.

5. The U.S. Coast Guard, U.S. Customs, Department of Defense, Drug Enforcement Administration, Federal Bureau of Investigation, Immigration and Naturalization Service, Internal Revenue Service, National Institute on Drug Abuse, Department of State, Department of the Treasury and the White House Drug Abuse Policy Office are full members of the NNICC. Representatives of the Central Intelligence Agency and the National Security Agency attend NNICC meetings as observers. The Narcotics Intelligence Estimate was first produced for the year 1977. The RCMP National Drug Intelligence Estimate has been produced annually since 1980.

Example 1
Raw Intelligence Report Illustrating Heading

BALTIMORE COUNTY POLICE DEPARTMENT
Intelligence Report

Number: 2272-90
Distributed: July 17, 1990

Area: CA,CT,FL,MO,TX

Subject: Possible Criminal Associates of Person Convicted
of Peddling Child Pornography Materials

Date of Information: April 25, 1990

Source: BCPD records

Place and Date Acquired: Towson, Maryland (June 27)

1. William B. Tick, a resident of Ellicott City, MD, was arrested during the evening of April 25, 1990, near an all-night drug store in Towson, MD, and booked on a charge of peddling child pornography. An address book was found in Tick's possession at the time of arrest and was seized in evidence along with the pornographic materials. Tick entered a guilty plea at his trial on June 24, 1990, and was given a six-month suspended sentence.

2. The following recoverable addresses were contained in the address book, a photocopy of which has been retained in BCPD files:

Alvin Borkum, 457 Corvallis Road, Winter Park, FL 32789

Charles Duggan, 125 Greenhaven Drive, Norwalk, CT 06855

Edward Fosdick, 5523 Baddon Street, St. Louis, MO 63126

Gregory Harris, 81 Telegraph Road, Sugar Land, TX 77478

Irma Joplin, 629 Gresham Way, Sacramento, CA 95833

3. BCPD Comment: No further information is available on these individuals or on the nature of their association with Tick. The case is now closed in this Department.

Example 2
Raw Intelligence Report Illustrating Comments

PENNSYLVANIA ORGANIZED CRIME TASK FORCE
Intelligence Report

Number: 4027-90
Distributed: July 23, 1990

Area: Northeast

Subject: Prospective Purchase of Large Estates in Susquehanna County by Associate of Organized
Crime Family

Date of Information: July 15, 1990

Source: Professional person with access to information on real estate transactions in the area

Place and Date Acquired: Philadelphia, PA (July 18)

1. Watson Caffrey, a prominent Scranton, PA, real estate dealer, has been quietly negotiating with
the heirs of several large estates in Susquehanna County since early June. He has now narrowed
his search to two properties in different parts of the County, both of which are in secluded
woodlands off Interstate Highway 81. One property has a large manor house and a private lake.
The other property has a sizable farmhouse in restorable condition and a small, overgrown hilltop
airfield abandoned after World War II.

2. Source Comment: Judging from the manner in which the deals are being negotiated, it can be
surmised that Caffrey's principals have no interest in subdividing the properties for residential or
resort development.

3. POCTF Headquarters Comment: Caffrey has handled real estate transactions for organized
crime figures in the Scranton and Wilkes-Barre areas in the past. He himself has no criminal
record.

Example 3
Raw Intelligence Report Illustrating Information Development

ARLINGTON COUNTY POLICE DEPARTMENT

<u>Intelligence Report</u>

<u>Number</u>: 3347-90
<u>Distributed</u>: November 22, 1990

<u>Area</u>: VA,NC,SC,GA,FL

<u>Subject</u>: Possibly Related Thefts of Radial Spare Tires from Late-Model Buicks

<u>Date of Information</u>: November 20, 1990

<u>Source</u>: ACPD patrol officer report and records checks with other police departments, as indicated

<u>Place and Date Acquired</u>: Arlington, Virginia (November 20); also VA,MD,DC,DE,PA,NJ,NY,CT police headquarters listed below (November 21-22)

1. On November 20, 1990, a resident of an apartment complex in Arlington, Virginia, reported the theft of a spare tire from the trunk of her 1989 Buick. The investigating officer (ACPD Patrolman Jasper Jacobs) examined the car and observed that the trunk lock had been sprung. He noted that a small hole had been drilled into the lock. The auto theft files of the ACPD show no reports with a similar M.O.

2. The Washington, D.C. Metropolitan Police and suburban Montgomery County, MD, Police Department, as well as the Virginia State Police were queried for reports of similar thefts with negative results.

3. Police jurisdictions north of the Greater Washington area were similarly queried, with the following results:

Maryland State Police	Theft reported Nov. 17th by Baltimore County PD at large shopping center (Whitemarsh)
Delaware State Police	No reports
Pennsylvania State Police	Theft on Nov. 13th at apartment complex in middle-income Philadelphia neighborhood
New Jersey State Police	Theft on Nov. 9th at a New Jersey Turnpike service area
New York State Police	Theft on Nov. 4th at Westchester County airport
Connecticut State Police	Theft on Nov. 1st at mall off I-84 west of Hartford (Corbins Corner)

Example 3 - Continued

The owner of the vehicle at the New Jersey Turnpike service area reported to the State Police that a cream-colored utility van pulled away as he was returning to his car from the restaurant. Another motorist who was eating a snack in his car nearby said the van stopped behind the owner's car and appeared briefly to have engine trouble. This other motorist reported that the van had Rhode Island license plates containing the letters "LT." The motorist said the van was occupied by two men but because of darkness could give no descriptions. (Source Comment: This is the only identifying information provided by any of the police departments queried.)

4. ACPD Headquarters Comment: There is no firm evidence to connect the two males in the Rhode Island-registered van with the New Jersey theft, let alone the other thefts listed. However, the relationships of time and location in the sequence of events exhibiting similar M.O.s suggest that the thefts may be the work of a single criminal gang. On that assumption the gang is most likely to strike next in the Atlantic Coast states south of Washington, D.C.

Example 4
Event Chronology

FCIS INVESTIGATIVE CHRONOLOGY
CENTRAL COMPUTER DATA BASE
CRIMINAL INDEX REMARKS BY DATE

Subject:	John Joseph Holdsworth a/k/a J. J. Holly
	(Index #2794)

09/20/75

Holdsworth was arrested by Chicago Police Department for carrying a concealed weapon within a motor vehicle.

- - -

Document: FCIS-42, serial CHI-81-9227, dated July 27, 1981
See page: 172

File: Holdsworth, et al.

Law Enforcement Witnesses:	J.E. Borman, Chicago P.D. (arresting)
	T.L. Szagas, Chicago P.D. (arresting)

05/07/77

C/I 14 telephonically informed G/S Bender that he/she had arranged for Holdsworth's nephew, known to the C/I only as "Mike," to meet G/S Bender at the Holiday Inn on Michigan Boulevard in Chicago, IL, to discuss multi-pound purchases of quinine for Holdsworth. (On April 24, 1977, the C/I had stated that he/she had made arrangements for G/S Bender to meet Parry [Index #5077], who was interested in trading unspecified quantities of heroin for five- and ten-pound lots of quinine on a regular basis.) On May 7, 1977, G/S Bender met "Mike," who was driving a Pontiac TransAm, Illinois license KKY-423, registered to Michael Holdsworth at 512 Liberty Avenue, Chicago, IL. "Mike" stated that wanted to obtain quinine in one-barrel quantities. "Mike" was informed quinine would be $400 per pound and mannitol $75 per pound. G/S Bender gave "Mike" a 10 gram sample of quinine and a 15 gram sample of mannitol. "Mike" inquired if "his people" could get a better price with a trade. When asked what "his people" had to trade, "Mike" replied "good boy or girl." C/S Bender stated that he was interested but only if the stuff was good and that he was not in the market for any "cut heroin or cocaine." "Mike" and G/S Bender exchanged phone numbers, and "Mike" handed G/S Bender a business card and said he would be calling.

- - -

Document: FCIS-42, serial CHI-77-1246, dated May 8, 1977, by G/S Humphrey Bender.
See pages: 1,2 and 3.

Files: Holdsworth et al.; Major Chicago Heroin Violators; Heroin Diluents Investigations/ Chicago (Table 14)

Example 4 - Continued

Law Enforcement Witnesses: G/S Humphrey Bender (undercover)
                              S/A Bill Murdock (surveillance)
                              S/A Wayne Harris (surveillance)

Potential witness: C/I #14

05/07/77
After the meeting between "Mike" and G/S Bender surveillance agents followed "Mike," who was driving a TransAm, Illinois license KKY-423, registered to Michael Holdsworth to the Favored One Variety Store, 2720 Ferry Park, Chicago, IL. Mike" was observed to speak with several unidentified patrons in the store for about ten minutes and then to walk South on 16th Street until he entered the house at number 221. Utilities at this residence had been listed to Alouisius Holdsworth since 1955. A 1972 Cadillac Eldorado, Illinois license PRF-502, registered to Becky Holdsworth, was observed to park near the 16th Street residence.
- - -
Document: FCIS-42, serial CHI-77-1267, dated May 14, 1977 by S/A Bill Murdock
See pages: 5 and 6.

File: Holdsworth et al.

Law Enforcement Witness: S/A Bill Murdock (surveillance)

03/13/79
"J.J. Holly" arrived at O'Hare Metropolitan Airport and flew to Newark on an American Airlines flight at 8:00 p.m. "Holly" had no luggage and paid cash for his ticket in $20 bills. "Holly" returned the following day at 5:00 p.m. "Holly" is an alias used by John Joseph Holdsworth.
- - -
Document: FCIS-57, serial CHI-80-0045, dated January 15, 1980, by I/A Darlene Woodward (debriefing of C/I #12B) See page: 49.

Law Enforcement Witness: I/A Darlene Woodward (resigned from FCIS and believed to be employed with NYOCTF)

Potential witness: C/I #12B

Example 5
Violator File Summary

FCIS VIOLATOR FILE SUMMARY

Subject: Willie Kingpin a/k/a "King William"
(Index #4405)

Willie KINGPIN is the subject of an investigation by FCIS for violation of Federal narcotics laws and a Title 26 grand jury investigation for possible income tax evasion regarding his 1980 and 1981 tax returns. KINGPIN was convicted on Federal narcotics charges in 1970 and 1978 and has a case pending in the Michigan state courts. Now 35, KINGPIN was introduced to drug distribution as a drug runner for a juvenile gang.

KINGPIN heads a heroin distribution network based in Detroit, Michigan, dealing in Southeast and Southwest Asian heroin. The 10-12 subordinates in his organization deal approximately 30 to 40 ounces of heroin for him per month. Intelligence indicates that KINGPIN also distributes kilogram quantities of high quality cocaine for selected customers.

In the Detroit area, KINGPIN is closely associated with Alice BARNUM, a known heroin source of supply. He has been identified as both a source and financial backer of heroin dealers Charlie DOLFUSS and Eddie FOX. Pen register activity reveals calls by principals in this investigation to documented heroin traffickers George HOLLY and Irma JEBSON. Intelligence further indicates KINGPIN is closely associated with upper echelon members of a retail heroin distribution network called THE MADMEN and is suspected to be one of the network's primary heroin sources. THE MADMEN is believed to be a offshoot of KINGPIN's former juvenile gang.

Outside the Detroit area, KINGPIN has been associated since at least 1975 with Class I Southeast Asia heroin violator Victor WANG in New York. Preliminary analysis of KINGPIN's toll calls also reveals recent contacts with Xavier YOLANDA, a suspected cocaine middleman in Miami.

Information provided by an unwitting informant indicates that KINGPIN receives approximately $7,000 per day from heroin sales. Surveillance has identified three houses and four late-model cars that have been used in KINGPIN's distribution operations.

Example 6
Sample Outline for Case Organization Analysis

WILLIAM EASTMAN ORGANIZATION

I. Organization Profile
   A. Key personalities and roles
   B. Associates and their functions
   C. Criminal capabilities

II. Organization's Measures to Reduce Risk of Prosecution

III. Organization's Vulnerability to Intelligence Penetration
   A. Personal weaknesses, interests permitting approach
      Vices (gambling, drugs, etc.)
      Character traits (vanity, desire for respect through display
         of wealth and being seen with theatrical personalities)
      Hobbies (regular attendance at yachting events)
   B. Operational weaknesses
      Short on couriers (arrests, gunfights, etc.)
      Only one money laundering channel
   C. Vulnerability to technical penetration
      Takes visiting crime bosses to East Side club
      Cars not well guarded while under repair
   D. Money troubles
      Some investments have turned sour
   E. Potential cooperating non-criminal associates
      Accountant country club associates
      Local politicians

IV. Possible Sources of Additional Information
   A. Established informants
      Current status
      Availability
      Access
   B. Potential informants
      Current status
      Availability
      Access

V. Information Required to Sustain Criminal Allegations
   A. Possible substantive allegations
      Evidence and information against major subjects
      Evidence and information against associates

Eample 6 - Continued

      B. Possible conspiracy allegations
          Identification of discrete conspiracies
          Persons and overt acts showing involvement
      C. Continuing criminal enterprise (CCE) allegations
          Persons vulnerable to CCE allegations
          Supporting evidence
      D. Possibilities for financial asset condemnations
          Evidence of ownership by prospective defendant
          Evidence regarding proceeds used to purchase asset
          Evidence of asset use in illegal enterprise

    VI. Conclusions (Assessments regarding)
      A. Lines of investigation most likely to be productive
          Degree of security exhibited in use of telephone
          Prospects for elicitation in conversation
          Tendency to leave a paper trail
      B. Gaps in information critical to prosecution goals
      C. Suggested means for obtaining critical information

Example 7
Illustration of Weekly Report on Events of Security Interest

WASHINGTON METROPOLITAN POLICE DEPARTMENT

<u>Weekly Security Intelligence Report</u>
(Upcoming Events During the Period_____)

PART I.   <u>PARADES AND DEMONSTRATIONS</u>
1.   DATE(S) OF EVENT(S)
2.   ORGANIZATION
3.   TIMES OF ASSEMBLY/DISBANDMENT
4.   PURPOSE OF EVENT (e.g., To protest the visit of the President of Pakistan)
5.   ASSEMBLY AREA AND PARADE ROUTE
6.   TRANSPORTATION TO ASSEMBLY AREA (e.g., special trains, buses, rental of Metro subway, etc. Indicate sponsor)
7.   GROUP ACTIVITY (if applicable)
8.   ANTICIPATED NUMBER OF PARTICIPANTS
9.   PARADE/DEMONSTRATION LEADERS
10.   OTHER INTELLIGENCE

PART II.   <u>STATE OR OTHER VISITS OF DIGNITARIES</u>
1.   DATES/TIMES OF ARRIVAL AND DEPARTURE
2.   NAME AND TITLE OF DIGNITARY
3.   TYPE OF VISIT (state, official, unofficial)
4.   LOCAL RESIDENCE DURING VISIT
5.   ORGANIZATION RESPONSIBLE FOR SECURITY
6.   CONTACT FOR SECURITY MATTERS
7.   ITINERARY (if relevant to a security problem)
8.   GROUPS/INDIVIDUALS WHO MAY DEMONSTRATE AGAINST OR ATTEMPT TO CONFRONT VISITOR (include any intelligence information)

Example 8
Sample Format for Intelligence Profile on Terrorist Organization

SUMMARY

[A brief characterization of the activities of the organization and general assessment of its capabilities and intentions.]

Identification

Name and abbreviation by which the group is commonly known (e.g., Basque Separatist Movement -- ETA)

Formal name of the organization in English (e.g., Basque Nation and Freedom)

Name of the organization in native language (e.g., Euzkadi Ta Azkatasuna)

Origins

Roots: Cultural, ethnic, political, socio-economic

Historical development: (including splinters)

Groups that influenced organization and training during formative stages

Terrorist Mission and Strategy

Mission: Definition of the organization's overall mission (e.g., "to maintain pressure on Israel with a view to eventual return of displaced Palestinians to their homeland").

Strategy: Succinct statement of organization's current objective(s) for carrying out its mission (e.g., "to prevent any accommodation by Moslem countries with Israel and to disrupt Israeli administration and settlement of the West Bank").

Current Targets and Tactics

Political activities: What terrorist acts are being carried out? Who are the targets? To achieve what influence on what audience (e.g., assassinate moderate leader to intimidate others and enforce a "no-compromise-with-the-enemy" policy)? Does the organization carry out terrorist missions to gain the release of its imprisoned members?

Example 8 - Continued

      Funding Activities: Is terrorism a main source of obtaining funds for the
      organization? What acts of violence have been carried out for this purpose
      (e.g., bank robberies, hijackings, kidnaping of business executives, holding
      hostages for ransom)?

      Tactics: How do action teams move to the objective? [e.g., together? separately?
      use false passports (if so, what nationality, birthplaces indicated, etc.)] How
      do they "case" the objective area? What advance information do they
      appear to have? Do they conduct their own surveillance of target
      individuals? How do they gain access to a target installation? Do they take
      hostages? If so, how do they treat hostages? What are their usual demands
      for release of hostages?

Organization and Membership

      Headquarters
      Major concentrations of members and activities
      Estimated number of members
      Pattern of organization (e.g., country or regional branches, cells, etc.)
      Size, nature and location of target constituency (e.g., Armenian communities
           in the United States)
      Principal leaders (brief biographic sketches)

Outside Support

      Ideologically related organizations (fronts)
      Propaganda support
      Logistical support (especially from terrorist organizations not related
           by ideological affinity)
      Funding support

Current Status of Members Imprisoned in Various Countries

Analysis of Behavior Under Stress

Example 8 - Continued   Chronology of Major Events

Date	Location	Target	Method	Group/Aim[1]
			- 1982 -	
1/13	Nyon Switzerland	Match Factory	Bomb	9-J [2,3]
1/14	Toronto	Turkish Consulate	Bomb	ASALA
1/21	Orly France	Luggage Locker	Bomb	Orly [3]
1/28	Los Angeles	Turkish Consul Gen.	Assassination	JCAG/T [4]
4/8	Ottawa	Turkish Com. Attache	Assassin attempt	ASALA
5/4	Boston	Turkish Consul Gen.	Assassination	JCAG [5]
6/7	Lisbon	Turkish Attache	Assassination	JCAG [5]
		(Israel Invades Lebanon)		
7/21	Paris	Cafe	Bomb	Orly [6]
7/21	Rotterdam	Turkish Consul	Assassination	ARA [7]
7/25	Paris	Cafe	Bomb	Orly [6]
8/7	Istanbul	Esenboga Airport	Suicide Squad	ASALA
8/27	Ottawa	Turkish Mil Attache	Assassination	JCAG [5]
9/9	Burgas Bulgaria	Turkish Consul	Assassination	JCAG [5]
12/8	Athens	Kuwaiti Airways	Bomb	? [8]
		- 1983 -		
1/22	Paris	Turkish Airways	Bomb	ASALA
1/22	Orly France	Turkish Airways	Bomb Defused	ASALA
2/28	Paris	Turkish Travel Agency	Bomb	ASALA

Example 8 - Continued

3/9	Belgrade	Turkish Ambassador	Assassin- ation	JCAG [5]
5/24	Brussels	Turkish Tourist Office	Bomb	ASALA
6/16	Istanbul	Bazaar	Suicide Squad	ASALA
7/14	Brussels	Turkish Diplomat	Assassin- ation	ARA/T [9]
7/15	Orly France	Turkish Airways	Bomb	ASALA
7/21	Tehran	French Embassy	Bomb	ASALA [10]
7/27	Lisbon	Turkish Embassy	Suicide Squad	ARA/T [9]
7/31	Tehran	Italian Diplomat	Attempted kidnaping	Orly [10]

- Notes -

1. Unless otherwise indicated, the aim of the terrorist operation was injuring Turkish interests in general.

2. 9-J = Ninth of June, a group affiliated with ASALA (ASALA = Armenian Secret Army for the Liberation of Armenia).

3. Aim of terrorist operation was release of prisoners.

4. JCAG/T = Justice Command for the Armenian Genocide (Tashnag).

5. JCAG = Justice Command for the Armenian Genocide.

6. Aim of terrorist operation was pressure on France for concessions.

7. ARA = Armenian Red Army.

8. Organization perpetrating terrorist operation and its aims are unknown.

9. ARA/T = Armenian Revolutionary Army (Tashnag).

10. Aim of terrorist operation is unknown.

[This Chronology is based on The Middle East, No. 107, September 1983, page 20 (published in London)]

Example 9
Illustration of Security Threat Assessment

FEDERAL AVIATION ADMINISTRATION

Security Threat Assessment

April 13, 1983

TO: Air Transport Association, Washington, D.C. National Air Carrier
                   Association, Washington, D.C. Regional Airline Association,
                   Washington, D.C.

ATTENTION: Security Directors

SUBJECT: Possible Increase in Armenian Terrorist Activity During April

1. According to a Turkish daily newspaper, the month of April has been declared a "month of vengeance" against Turkey by the Justice Command for the Armenian Genocide (JCAG) and the Armenian Secret Army for the Liberation of Armenia (ASALA). Reportedly, two member teams have been sent to several countries on assassination missions. Apparently, the Armenian terrorists intend to take revenge by April 24.

2. FAA Comment: April 24 is regarded by Armenians as the date of the Armenian massacre. Terrorist organizations are known as a general rule to carry out their threats and operations on anniversary dates of past significant events. In this particular case, however, the Armenian terrorists may take action prior to or after the April 24 date since their plans to take revenge have been well publicized by distribution of thousands of posters and leaflets in a number of countries. No specific plans or targets have been indicated, but Armenian terrorists have threatened and/or have taken action against countries holding Armenian terrorists; i.e., assassinations, bombings at airline offices, and suicide attacks on an airport (Ankara, August 7, 1982, by ASALA members). Armenian terrorists are currently held in the U.S., Canada, France, Switzerland, Netherlands, United Kingdom, and Yugoslavia.

Example 10
Security Threat Assessment for 1985 Paris Air Show

The following excerpts are from American Embassy Paris telegram 15555 (unclassified), transmitted inter alia to the Department of Commerce on April 16, 1985, for American firms exhibiting at the Paris Air Show. The text has been slightly edited.

Subject: Threat Alert for Paris Air Show (May 30-June 9, 1985)

Every two years the Paris Air Show is staged just outside the Paris city limits at Le Bourget Airport.... This year it is expected that there will be in excess of 700,000 visitors, 1,000 exhibitors from 33 countries, and 90 exhibitors at the U.S. Pavilion. Included among the visitors will be a great number of high-level U.S. Government and civilian personalities.

Four American firms were recently listed on a Red Army Faction (RAF, German terrorist group) hit list that surfaced during a police raid. The firms are Boeing, Hughes, Lockheed and Northrop, and it should be noted that all firms are involved with aerospace activities. Certain terrorist groups, Red Army Faction (RAF), Action Directe (AD), Cellules Communistes Combattantes (CCC) and the Portuguese FP-25, are outspokenly opposed to "Western imperialism", aerospace, and NATO....

The threat level at the Air Show is rated as high, due in part to the ease with which a terrorist group may gain entry and accomplish its mission. On September 30, 1983, at the Marseille International Trade Fair, an explosion ripped through the U.S. exhibit, killing one man and injuring 26 persons. The bomb was apparently placed during the previous evening behind a curtain that was near the exhibit. Significant destruction was caused by the bomb, which contained 1.5 kilos of dynamite. Credit for the bombing was claimed by four terrorist groups, including the Lebanese Armed Revolutionary Faction. On March 23, 1985, at a Lisbon trade fair, ten terrorists entered the pavilion, incapacitated an armed policeman and two unarmed security guards. One terrorist entered a display area and murdered an exhibitor while his henchmen kept onlookers at bay with their weapons. The reasons for the attacks are not the issue; what should be observed is how easy it was to accomplish the mission. Bombs and gunmen (or gunwomen) are the primary methods used in terrorist attacks.

You may help protect yourself and visitors to your display area by the following measures:

1. Hire security guards to inspect packages and personnel, maintain a security presence at night and to open and search exhibit areas.

2. Whenever possible, access to exhibit areas should be limited to invited guests. Invitations should be numbered, and invitees requested to bring their invitations....

3. Use metal detectors as available.

4. Brief guards as to specific instructions.

5. Design display areas to reduce spaces wherein bombs could be concealed. Unupholstered tables and chairs may be used. Eliminate desks and cabinets with drawers.

6. Toilets and closets should be key-controlled and routinely inspected.

7. When possible, stress the civilian as opposed to the military application of products to be exhibited.

8. The lower portion of challet exhibit areas should be enclosed with metal or wood to prevent the possibility of suspicious objects being placed under exhibit areas.

Example 10 - Continued

    9. Hold corporate meetings and social events in hotels and maintain a low profile by keeping the date, time and place of the meeting on a need-to-know basis and not listed on the hotel schedule...

    10. Vary routes of travel, avoid routines and be alert to surveillance.

    11. Obtain maps of the area and become familiar with the city to be visited. If in large groups utilize bus for transport. Maintain buddy system with an itinerary for a high target individual maintained by his office.

Example 11
Threat Assessment

SECURITY THREAT AT CANNES FILM FESTIVAL

You are the European representative for a private security firm, Worldwide Security Associates, Inc. (WSA). Your Los Angeles office advises that several Hollywood film producers will be attending the International Film Festival at Cannes, France, and requests your assistance. You prepare a threat assessment and send it to WSA Los Angeles for their guidance in making arrangements for the security of the clients during the visit.

Your assessment is drawn up to make key judgments about the security threat at Cannes. The following outline might logically serve this purpose:

Synopsis of main events of the Festival.

The Festival's attractiveness to terrorists.
     What terrorist organizations?
     For what objectives?

Why might American executives be targeted?

What is the posture of the French security services?
     Their awareness of the terrorist threat.
     Their plans to have extra forces on hand.
     Their state of readiness and training (noting the likely possibility that reserve
          units will not be as well trained or as effective as the regulars).
     Existing responsibilities (Will crack units be concentrated and deployed
          principally for protection of the French president? To what extent
          will the French be in a position to provide security for American and
          other foreign guests?)

Plans for securing the area.
     The Festival site (badging procedures, etc.).
     Access control to the Cannes area generally (airport, roads, etc.).

Overall threat assessment.
     Times and places of maximum vulnerability.
     Adequacy of security arrangements.
     Residual risk to be provided for by WSA.

[NOTE: Example #8-type profiles should be included in the package sent to WSA Los Angeles.]

Example 12

Situation Requiring Spot Item

Returning from a weekend visit to his country's embassy in Washington the Venezuelan consul discovers that his office in downtown Miami, Florida, has been broken into and requests investigative assistance from the Metro-Dade Police Department. Officers from the Burglary Unit respond, gather evidence and take a statement from the consul. The consul shows the officers where the burglars attempted to get into a wall safe where he kept his authenticating stamps and seals. Looking through his ransacked desk the consul notes that three blank passports are missing from a drawer. The investigating officers determine the passport numbers from records shown to them by the consul.

The Intelligence Unit Supervisor receives a copy of the investigators' report with a note from the Chief: "Disseminate the stolen passport information to appropriate Washington agencies."

Example #13
Gist-And-Comment Article

NEW CRIMES AUTHORITY FOR AUSTRALIA

A possible crime superagency is being set up in Australia on an urgent basis before Parliament is dissolved next month for the general elections. The new organization is to be known as the Commonwealth Criminal Investigative Authority. The Authority's functions and powers have not been spelled out in information the Australian Embassy's Police Liaison Officer has received from Canberra to date. He has, however, been specifically directed to request that all crime intelligence from overseas agencies be transmitted directly to the Authority rather than through existing liaison arrangements. He also commented that the Authority will apparently implement recommendations made by the Australian Senate earlier this year. A formal announcement on the Authority is expected within a few days.

Comment: The idea of a national crimes authority to strengthen government investigative powers in dealing with organized crime, especially drug trafficking, has been under active discussion in Australia for several years. The Government published a "Green Paper" in June 1983 in an effort to develop a national consensus at the various levels of government and among political parties, professional and community groups. This official discussion paper addressed such policy issues as the need for a standing crimes commission, its functions and powers. In May a Senate committee released a report recommending that a national crimes authority be given wider powers than previously contemplated. In particular, the committee had taken the position that state authorities should not have the right of veto over matters the federal government wants investigated through the authority. It also recommended that the authority investigate a wider range of criminal activities.

December 1 has been set as the date for the next general election. In calling an early election, Australian Prime Minister Bob Hawke is reportedly aiming to subordinate a debate on crime to economic issues which he expects will be of more concern to voters. The opposition has accused the Labor Party of being soft on organized crime and drug trafficking, charges which reduced Hawke to tears at a press conference last month. His wife explained later that one of their daughters is addicted to heroin. Establishing the Authority now could be viewed as a move by Hawke to dispose of a troublesome issue for the time being.

Example #14

Sample Formulations of the Operation of Causative Factors
in Near-Term Projections

1. Show whether the expected future trend is a new or continuing development.

2. Indicate the degree of anticipated change.
   (Example : "major," "minor," "significant")

3. Differentiate a near-term change from a change expected in the more distant future.
   (Example : "Supplies of Asian heroin in Europe and North America are likely to be restored to pre-drought levels from the upcoming harvest. For the longer term, the Middle East-South Asia region has the potential for displacing or replacing other sources of heroin.")

4 . Show the weight assigned to the causative factor.
   (Example: "Prospects for stability in Iran depend heavily/ primarily/ etc. ...")

5. Explain any parallelism in reasoning.
   (Example: "Because the reduction in heroin availability has been an important factor in the upsurge in abuse of dangerous drugs since 1975, the anticipated increase in heroin availability could retard the rate of increase in diversion and abuse of dangerous drugs.")

6. Indicate conditional possibilities (if . . . then).
   (Example: "If the governments of_____carry out effective crop control programs, the flow of marijuana to the United States can be substantially reduced during the next four years.")

7. Point out balancing, or limiting, factors.
   (Example: "Projected population for the key age groups that account for the largest number of marijuana users has begun to decline. This decline could, however, be offset by increased frequency of use.")

8. Show important linkages in predictive judgments.
   (Example: "The gradually rising trend in hashish imports is likely to continue. The tendency of U.S. users to prefer more potent cannabis products stimulates demand for hashish as well as for domestic marijuana.")

Example 14 Continued

9.   Identify important contingencies or raise doubts, where appropriate.
      (Example: "It remains to be seen whether_____'s new narcotics
      law can be enforced in time to prevent the harvesting and export of
      the opium crop now halfway to maturity.")
      (Example: "The capabilities of the_____Police Department Tactical
      Unit have not yet been tested against a crowd as large as the one expected
      this weekend.")

10.   Acknowledge areas of major or complete uncertainty.
      (Example : "The future of opium supplies in Afghanistan is difficult
      to predict because it remains closely linked with the actions of
      Soviet occupation forces against the rural villages supporting the resistance
      of the Afghan freedom fighters.")
      (Example: "The major uncertainties in predicting the trend in opium poppy
      production in_____are lack of verifiable information on the size
      of the stockpile carried over from the recent bumper crop and low
      confidence in our ability to estimate reliably the tonnage of opium required
      for local consumption within the producing region.")

11.   Acknowledge assumptions that are critical to the predictive judgment.
      (Example: "Assuming a return to normal weather, a substantial recovery
      is in prospect for next year's opium poppy crop.")

PALMER ENTERPRISES
P.O. Box 1714, Loomis, California, 95650   (916) 652-3225

More Fine Books By Palmer

POLICE INTELLIGENCE FILES   (1983) $13.95   ISBN   0-912479-00-0

In its second reprint. 100 pages, Illustrated. Composed by a working administrator 20 years with a major state law enforcement intelligence operation. The author offers tips and directions for maintaining quality standards while recognizing right to privacy. A 'must' reading for the intelligence officer who wants to upgrade the vintage file.

POLICE INTELLIGENCE REPORTS   (1985) $12.95   ISBN   0-912479-03-5

In its second reprint. 135 pages, Illustrated. Written by two working law enforcement administrators whose book gives 'how to' directions and explanations complete with easy-to-implement writing formats. This book solves the common problem of poor reporting. It introduces 'event' report writing and displays many 'real' writing examples and problems.

THE DEADLY ROUTINE   (1986) $16.95   ISBN   0-912479-04-3

In its fourth reprint. 154 pages, Illustrated. An officer survival book composed around real case histories. Sufficient details and facts to provide insight into the actions of the murdered officers as well as the motives of the killer criminals. The emphasis is upon the near-habit methods of officers, repetitiveness of their work - combining to make a deadly routine.

CRIME ANALYSIS CHARTING   (1988) $11.95   ISBN   0-912479-01-9

In its fourth reprint and with two entirely new subject areas. 116 pages, Illustrated. This book is the primer used by many law enforcement agencies, academies, and colleges around the world. It covers the three primary charting subjects of 1) events, 2) link, and 3) telephone toll. The book serves as a full training tool for investigators and intelligence officers who are unable to attend classes on the subjects of charting and analysis.

DRAGONS AND TIGERS   (1988) $15.95   ISBN   0-912479-05-1

Totally **NEW**. 178 pages, Illustrated. The latest inside information on Asian crime and Asian criminals from a street-wise law enforcement officer. The book is timely, factual, and helpful. It provides tips and tested procedures for bridging the cultural gaps between western justice systems and the refugees from Vietnam, Laos, China, Japan, Korea, Cambodia and other Asian countries.

POLICE INFORMANT MANAGEMENT   (1988) $13.95   ISBN   0-912479-02-7

In its second reprint. 95 pages of text and illustrations. A truly international book directed entirely upon improving law enforcement handling of contributors of information. The author describes recruitment techniques, contributor motives, the importance of sharing, contributor ownership, management control forms, cash accounting, and many contemporary ideas.